GENESIS

Making use of both literary and social theory, this book argues that Genesis can be read as resistance literature.

Mark G. Brett sheds light on the complex construction of the text of Genesis, and shows that it was designed to undermine covertly the ethnocentrism of the imperial governors of the Persian period. The editors used the traditions, whether ancient and reliable or not, to engage in current socio-political issues, and in particular with the debate over what constituted an authentic community. This is clear in the details of the marriages of Abraham, Isaac and Jacob, which call in question the holy ideal of marriage within the covenanted community, and in the narratives of Hagar, Dinah and Tamar, which subtly subvert traditional notions of genealogical exclusivity or moral superiority.

This coherent approach to the disparate traditions of Genesis will be essential reading for students and scholars of theology, and will be of interest also to those engaged in postcolonial studies.

Mark G. Brett is Professor of Old Testament at Whitley College, Melbourne. He is the editor of *Ethnicity and the Bible* (1996) and the author of *Biblical Criticism in Crisis* (1991).

OLD TESTAMENT READINGS
Series Editor: Keith Whitelam
University of Stirling, UK

EZRA-NEHEMIAH
Lester Grabbe

GENESIS
Mark G. Brett

PSALMS
Alistair G. Hunter

Forthcoming books in this series:

BOOK OF JUDGES
Marc Brettler

GENESIS

Procreation and the politics of identity

Mark G. Brett

London and New York

First published 2000
by Routledge
11 New Fetter Lane, London EC4P 4EE

Simultaneously published in the USA and Canada
by Routledge
29 West 35th Street, New York, NY 10001

Routledge is an imprint of the Taylor & Francis Group

© 2000 Mark G. Brett

Typeset in Garamond by
Keystroke, Jacaranda Lodge, Wolverhampton
Printed and bound in Great Britain by
Clays Ltd, St Ives plc

All rights reserved. No part of this book may be reprinted or
reproduced or utilised in any form or by any electronic, mechanical,
or other means, now known or hereafter invented, including
photocopying and recording, or in any information storage or retrieval
system, without permission in writing from the publishers.

British Library Cataloguing in Publication Data
A catalogue record for this book is available from the British Library

Library of Congress Cataloging in Publication Data
Brett, Mark, G.
Genesis : procreation and the politics of identity / Mark G. Brett.
p. cm. — (Old Testament readings)
Includes bibliographical references and index.
1. Bible. O.T. Genesis—Socio-rhetorical criticism. I. Title. II. Series.
BS1235.2 B72 2000
222′.11067—dc21   99–087410

ISBN 0–415–14149–4 (hbk)
ISBN 0–415–14150–8 (pbk)

FOR LYNLEE

CONTENTS

	Acknowledgements	ix
	Introduction: the contest of methods	1
1	Genesis 1–11: creation and dominance	24
2	Genesis 12–25: the making of nations	49
3	Genesis 26–36: on tricksters	86
4	Genesis 37–50: reasons of state	109
5	Whose Genesis? Which orthodoxy?	137
	Notes	147
	Bibliography	155
	General index	163
	Scripture index	166

ACKNOWLEDGEMENTS

This book is the product of innumerable conversations which I have instigated over the past few years. The basic thesis was first presented at the invitation of Professor Judith Lieu in a research seminar at Macquarie University, Sydney, in the School of History, Philosophy and Politics, October 1997. Other aspects of the argument were presented the following year in Melbourne at meetings of the Bible and Critical Theory Seminar and at the Fellowship for Biblical Studies. I would like to thank all those who took part in those seminars, as well as my students at Whitley College, whose spontaneous questions and observations have ensured that my lectures on Genesis are always being revised. Thanks are also due to a number of colleagues who have helped to clarify ideas along the way, especially, Merryl Blair, Keith Dyer, Terry Falla, Ross Langmead, Ilana Pardes, Frank Rees, Paul Tonson, Howard Wallace, Pothin Wete and Keith Whitelam.

I am particularly grateful to Jim Barr, David Brett, Ron Ham, Graham Paulson and John U'Ren, friends who have had a less direct influence on the making of this book, but whose contributions have, in different ways, been no less significant. Anusha and Mattheus have never been far from my mind over the last two years, and they have been wonderfully accepting of all the time I spend writing.

INTRODUCTION
The contest of methods

Overtures

In the context of protracted violence between the European churches of the seventeenth century, there were good reasons for a flight from religious claims to authority (Stout 1981). The religion of the day had demonstrated itself incompetent to deal with the complexities of politics, and the Enlightenment's drive to secularise philosophy and public discourse was a reasonable outcome. Questioning the authority of religion has been a constitutive feature of modern Western culture ever since.

With the emergence of what has come to be known as postmodernism, however, there has been not only a resurgence of interest in indigenous spiritualities, but a sociological re-evaluation of religion in general (see e.g. Turner 1994; Löwy 1996). As the West becomes progressively multicultural, it becomes increasingly evident that we need to come to terms with the disparate religious traditions influenced by the Bible. The biblical traditions have been refracted through the many innovations of cultural hybridity both among the global networks of Catholics, Anglicans and Muslims, and also among groups with smaller memberships like the Christian Ethiopian Orthodox or the Jewish Falashas. The intertwined features of culture and religion are not so easily expunged from public discourse, even if religious groups within democratic systems of government can no longer lay special claims to authority.

The pluralist condition of contemporary Western culture is reflected in microcosm in professional research on the Bible. The Enlightenment's optimism, which suggested that there were universal standards of reason that could be applied also to biblical research, now appears implausible. While there are diverse powerful institutions that underwrite biblical experts, there is no centralised scholarly authority,

INTRODUCTION

only a variety of interpretative communities embedded in complex ways in the larger frameworks of the academy and of society. The contemporary discipline of biblical studies, insofar as it is still a single discipline, is nevertheless shaped by the Enlighteners' injunction to question authority, whether the authority is located in the primary text or its interpreters. No one writing on the Bible, especially in the last two decades, can claim mastery of all the disciplines that are potentially relevant, for example, to reading the book of Genesis. And no one school of interpretation can claim mastery of biblical studies as a field.

There is a sense in which all reading takes place within interpretative communities (Fish 1980), but such 'communities' are often so complex in their inter-relationships that the term would need to be stretched beyond all normal connotations. The approach to Genesis in this book is perhaps an extreme example: it combines older styles of historical scholarship with a pastiche of narratology, reader-orientated criticism, anthropology, the so-called New Historicism and postcolonial studies. The pluralism proposed here is not a new method but rather a dialogical style of engagement with the text which begins by confessing the variety of readers' questions, contextual concerns and interpretative frameworks and then enters into a reading process, expecting to be enriched by the conversation, and perhaps even 'enraptured' by it (Rorty 1992: 106–7).

Being enraptured by a conversation need not imply the total eclipse of a reader's subjectivity, and for this reason, I do not indulge the formalist fantasy of interpretation that constructs an ideal reader, entirely fabricated by the dictates of a text. How a text engages us, and perhaps even changes us, is shaped, at least in part, by our 'horizon of expectation', which includes both the focused questions of an explicit interpretative tradition and the customarily unacknowledged backgrounds of culture, gender, class, and institutional matrixes that are inevitably part of a reader's subjectivity.[1] Thus, in recent years, there has been a shift in reader-orientated studies towards flesh-and-blood audiences, the analysis of scholarly discourses, and even towards so-called 'autobiographical criticism' (e.g. Veeser 1996; Kitzberger 1998).

While it would be impossible to articulate all the features of my 'horizon of expectation', it is worth registering at this point some of the connections between my biography and the traditions of criticism represented in this book. As is commonly the case in an age of globalisation, my own subjectivity is constituted by an heterogeneous collection of identity markers. To highlight Australian citizenship, for example, would be important but complex: although born in Australia, I was brought up in Papua New Guinea, and when, for a few years, I went to boarding school in Australia, I perceived the country of my birth not just as foreign but as hostile. My undergraduate degree, in philosophy and history, was taken in an Australian university (Queensland), but subsequently I have absorbed a range of educational sub-cultures, studying the Hebrew Bible within an American seminary (Princeton), a German faculty of theology (Tübingen), and an English faculty of arts (Sheffield). Each of these institutional matrixes is highly distinctive in its history and ethos, each with its own story of ideological contestation. Each institution has made its own mark, layering its influence on a biography which begins with expatriate identity and has taken shape within the larger postcolonial politics of both Papua New Guinea and Australia. All of this forms a background to my civic commitments – to the recovery of the 'common good' as a political value, reconciliation with Aboriginal communities, and the affirmation of multiculturalism in public discourse. My biography does have some affinity with the tone of this book, but I doubt whether the identity pastiche determines, in any strong sense, the details of interpretation. Nor is it necessary that anyone with a similar biography would arrive at the same commitments.

I belong also to a non-conformist denomination of Protestantism, which has been constituted, in part at least, by an assertion of religious freedom over against the established Church (Hill 1988), and one might suggest that this would help to explain the overall argument. Jewish scholars have certainly identified Protestant prejudices at work in some of the supposedly historical research on Genesis (Levenson 1993a: 25–32, 56–61). In the final chapter I will discuss this issue more fully, but for the present it is simply worth noting that very few of my scholarly mentors have been non-conformist Protestants. Some of those who might agree to religious self-descriptions at all would call themselves Anglican, Roman Catholic or Jewish. For those mentors who resist religious self-descriptions it would be necessary to revert to professional role descriptions (like literary critic or anthropologist) or inter-disciplinary schools of thought (like poststructuralist, feminist or postcolonial theorist).

Reading Genesis as a Protestant, one might find it ironic that the book should so resolutely resist the Reformation's presumption of textual perspicuity: the idea of the 'clarity' of scripture was forged in contest with Catholic hierarchy, making priestly interpreters redundant, and the doctrine is best understood in that historical context (Thiselton 1992: 178–85). The laconic style of Genesis, and

INTRODUCTION

its opacities and ambiguities, suggest that we can engage with it only partially: we can never exhaust the peregrinations of its meaning. This precludes the pretensions of scholarly objectivity that have too often marred the historical biblical scholarship of the last two centuries, pretensions shaped by the confident epistemological tones of both Protestantism and the Enlightenment.

But the epistemological modesty that has slowly been gaining ground in recent years need not collapse into total scepticism or failures of rigour (cf. Miller 1987). Whatever one's religious or non-religious commitments, a genuine conversation with the primary text requires neither full understanding nor full agreement. Disciplined understandings and agreements, however partial or unstable, are more valuable than either sweeping dismissals of canonical texts or prefabricated religious readings that are all-too-credulous. There is no reason why a reader cannot play the role of an anthropologist, feeling his or her way into the weave of a foreign culture, or the role of literary critic, illuminating the nuances of the language. Indeed, the recent contributions of anthropologists and narratologists have greatly enriched professional biblical scholarship. Neither the holiness of the text nor the religious convictions of the reader need determine interpretative outcomes in advance: genuine conversations are more unpredictable than that. The arguments in this book do not depend on holiness, whether of the text or of the reader.

This preliminary discussion of my horizon of expectation has highlighted heterogeneity and contestation. To focus now on the particular text at issue, my over-arching argument will be that the book of Genesis is *itself shaped by contestation* – in the diversity of its cultural influences, in its representation of ethnic relations, and in its numerous narratives that explicitly and implicitly question the political authorities of the day. In his recent *History of Israelite Religion in the Old Testament Period*, Rainer Albertz argues that Genesis should be understood 'not as a preliminary stage but as a substratum of Yahweh religion' (1994: 29). The surface of the narrative suggests that the religion of Abraham comes prior to the religion of Moses (Yahwism), but the process of editing introduced a complex mixture of the two – indeed, the final editing of the book took place only in the fifth century BCE, during the period of Persian imperial rule (1994: 24).[2] Instead of assuming that the sources of Genesis survive relatively intact, and that biblical interpretation should focus on their reconstruction, my approach will be more synchronic: this book advocates the view that the received Hebrew version of Genesis can be quite directly related to the politics of the Persian period.

THE CONTEST OF METHODS

The overall proposal is that the final editors of Genesis have set out to undermine the theologically legitimised ethnocentrism found in the books of Ezra and Nehemiah, expressed in particular by the notion of the 'holy seed' (Ezra 9.1–2). It is not important to my case that the historical careers of these two Persian emissaries be reconstructed in detail; I will simply assume that the polemics against foreign marriage in the books of Ezra and Nehemiah are in some sense representative of the dominant ideology of the fifth century, emanating from the native administrators of Persian rule. The resistance of Genesis can, I suggest, be read both in theological and in economic terms. Theologically, the final editors are proposing a less ethnocentric understanding of Israelite identity through a re-telling of Israelite origins. But this theological purpose may well be related to economic issues insofar as the discourse of the 'holy seed' was part of a strategy to control land tenure within this administrative district of the Persian empire.

The details of this argument will be unfolded in the subsequent chapters, but some preliminary matters, both methodological and historical, need to be clarified at this point. First, some historical studies that provide a framework for my reading of the text need to be noted. The assumption here is not that history can be grasped in some naive objectivist sense, but only that critical historical discourses can provide interpretative frameworks for articulating the social energies not explicit in the biblical text (cf. Greenblatt and Gunn 1992). Second, we need to clarify the kind of reading strategy – inspired especially by postcolonial theory – which legitimises my interpretation, even though there is no explicit polemic in Genesis against Ezra and Nehemiah.

For my present purposes, a key work on the period is Kenneth Hoglund's *Achaemenid Imperial Administration in Syria–Palestine and the Missions of Ezra and Nehemiah* (1992). Perhaps the most significant aspect of Hoglund's work is the argument that the fortification of Jerusalem under Nehemiah (see Neh. 2.8 and 7.2) was part of a wider imperial response to an Egyptian revolt against the Persian empire, which was fomented in the mid-fifth century by a certain Inaros and supported by a Greek coalition, the Delian League. The rebuilding of the walls of Jerusalem was comparatively unusual within the widest context of Persian policy, since such walls could be turned to advantage in the case of indigenous revolt. However, after reviewing the archaeological evidence, Hoglund suggests that the threat presented in this period by the Egyptians and the Greeks apparently resulted in a proliferation of imperial fortresses throughout the Levant, and Nehemiah's citadel can best be understood as part of this defensive strategy (1992: 209–10).

INTRODUCTION

Hoglund suggests that the prohibition of foreign marriage in Ezra and Nehemiah served related interests of imperial social control. The focus on genealogical purity is seen as a way of establishing the legitimacy of land tenure, thereby asserting control of land and property. The biblical evidence for this comes particularly from Ezra 10.8 where the text suggests that anyone failing to attend the prescribed convocation would face severe penalties: 'by the instruction of the officials and the elders, all his property is forfeited, and he is excluded from the assembly of the exiles'. Furthermore, the letter from Artaxerxes in Ezra 7 concludes by saying that anyone who does not obey the law of Ezra's God would suffer severe consequences, including the confiscation of property (7.26). Ezra's ethnic version of holiness was contested by a number of theologies of the second temple period, notably in the latter parts of Isaiah and in the book of Ruth, but Hoglund's work has made clear the connections between the administrators' theology and the economics of the Judean restoration. Along with other scholars, he has shown that the rhetoric of the holy seed may well have been a distortion of Israelite tradition which served the imperial interests.[3]

Hoglund's work converges, in some respects, with a view expressed recently by the anthropologist Mary Douglas (1993). She argues that the ostensibly Priestly concern with ethnic purity that underpins the prohibition on foreign marriage cannot be derived directly from the Pentateuch. In particular, the book of Numbers stands *against* the idea that the 'holy seed' was a clearly defined group, established by legitimate birth. Drawing attention to Numbers 15.22–31 and 19.10, for example, she points out that the purity system is there specifically designed to include the non-native *gerim* ('aliens' or 'sojourners'), and unlike the tendency of Deuteronomy (e.g. 23.3), there are no blanket rulings against strangers simply by virtue of their ethnicity.[4] Douglas concludes that Numbers opposes the separatism of Ezra and Nehemiah: 'the concern of the priestly editor is to constrain a populist xenophobia' (1993: 39). Recent biblical scholarship is perhaps less willing to speak of Priestly theology as a unified system, but certainly by the time of the Persian period many would agree that the so-called Priestly texts in Numbers and Leviticus have declared aliens to be on the same legal footing as native-born Israelites.[5] Rolf Rendtorff similarly has raised the possibility that the Priestly laws concerning the *gerim* were shaped and edited in opposition to the marriage policies of Ezra (1996: 86–7). Thus, the work of Mary Douglas converges with a number of recent studies on the Pentateuch in a way which lends an initial plausibility to my reading of Genesis.

In view of the work of Douglas and Rendtorff, it seems that the older scholarly tendency to associate Ezra's idea of the 'holy seed' with Priestly tradition is misguided. Assuming for the moment that a Priestly tradition can be reconstructed from the text of Genesis – an assumption which is, in fact, not necessary to my thesis – it is worth drawing attention to one key text that has consistently been identified as part of this tradition. The promises to Abraham in Genesis 17 are associated with a body marking that has often been thought to be a definitive indicator of identity: the practice of male circumcision. *All* of Abraham's household are to be circumcised (17.12), and thus Abraham circumcises Ishmael in v. 23, even though this son of an Egyptian concubine is expressly excluded from the covenant in vv. 20–1. The so-called Priestly text explicitly includes persons bought from foreigners: 'For the generations to come every male among you who is eight days old must be circumcised, including those born in your household or bought with money from a foreigner – he who is not of your seed' (17.12).[6] A reader from the Persian period, I suggest, might well have heard a resonance here with the language of the 'holy seed' in Ezra 9.1–2. Those who are 'not of your seed' are explicitly included in the covenantal rite, and this inclusivism is found precisely in a Priestly text. Moreover, as the narrative of Genesis unfolds, it can hardly be accidental that several of the key figures contract foreign marriages and that accounts of ethnic relations often depict the covenantal insiders as narrow-minded.

I also suggest the possibility that the final editors of Genesis saw an analogy between two 'native' administrators of imperial rule – Ezra and Joseph – and that the concluding chapters of Genesis make good sense if we see the representation of Joseph as ambivalent. The analogy suggests that the Persian audience of the Joseph story would have been suspicious of any representative of the Persian monarchy who made extravagant claims to divine wisdom (Gen. 41.39, cf. 41.8) and providence (50.20) while expropriating property (Genesis 47). Ezra 7.25–6 has Artaxerxes praising Ezra's divine wisdom, legitimising the imperial desire that those who disobey the law should be banished or have their goods confiscated. A covert polemic against Persia would be all the more subtle since it appropriates a story set in Egypt, i.e. the immediate enemy of the Persian administration. Any criticism of Egypt would ostensibly have served Persian interests, but the cunning of Genesis may be that Egypt in the Joseph story can be read as a cipher for Persia.

This summary of my argument brings together a number of different hypotheses about the interpretation of Genesis, and they are not all of

INTRODUCTION

the same kind. Each interpretative hypothesis requires further specification in terms of its goals, the limits of its claim and the framing of the relevant evidence. For example, my approach does not logically preclude the reconstruction of literary sources and editing; it is just that these activities are largely irrelevant to the purposes of this particular interpretation. Nor do I claim that the editors of Genesis invented all their narratives; it is more likely that their work is a subtly hybrid construction. My argument could include even the possibility that earlier layers of these traditions were in some sense xenophobic, but that the final editors have organised their materials so as to exclude this possibility. Since, however, the editors were thereby calling into question the official ideology of the imperial governors, opposition had to be formulated with extreme subtlety. James Scott's *Domination and the Arts of Resistance: Hidden Transcripts* (1990) and Homi Bhabha's *The Location of Culture* (1994) would lead us to expect that resistance is often exercised behind the back of powerful ideologies. These works by Scott and Bhabha, an anthropologist and a literary critic, converge to provide a model of agency exercised at the margins, at times paradoxically absorbing much of the dominant discourse (cf. Brett 1997). It is this kind of resistance that I have in mind.

In order to be clear about this kind of editorial agency, I turn now to an account of the methods appropriate in interpreting it. For most readers the discussion of methodology that follows will be unnecessary: having identified the Persian period as the historical context of the final editing, one could move straight to the discussion of the primary text in the next chapter. And, in the final analysis, the persuasiveness of the argument depends on the details of how each chapter of Genesis relates to the overall hypothesis. For some readers, however, it will be necessary to provide a theoretical defence of my methodological pluralism before any particular interpretation of the biblical text can be considered coherent.

Methodology

One contemporary mode of biblical interpretation is best described by the term 'narrative poetics'. This mode is concerned primarily with the communicative devices which constitute the most explicit layers of the text; the focus is on the details of dialogue, the development of character, the flow of the plot, the nuances of repetition, and on the variety of 'points of view' represented by the respective characters and by the narrator. This mode of reading, pioneered in particular by the literary critics Robert Alter (1981) and Meir Sternberg (1985), was at first perceived to be thoroughly antagonistic towards the older styles of historical criticism that dissected the text of Genesis into successive layers of oral and literary composition. And, indeed, some practitioners of narrative poetics were scathing in their condemnation of historicist scholars whose only tool for dealing with literary complexity, it seemed, was a scalpel.

Alter and Sternberg have provoked much self-examination among biblical specialists; and the influence of historicism has waned significantly in the last decade. However, in their reaction against the atomistic reconstructions of historical critics, Alter and Sternberg promoted a style of formalism that excluded questions not only about the history of a text's composition but also about the location of a text within sites of ideological contestation. Alter, in particular, has resisted interpretative practices which move beyond the aesthetic limits of a text to engage with ideological matrixes within which the Bible was produced and read (e.g. Alter 1990; cf. Alter and Kermode 1987). Sternberg (1992) has become embroiled in a similar kind of debate about the possibility of ideologically neutral poetics, defending his impartiality against the idea that readers' identities are an ineluctable part of all interpretation (Fewell and Gunn 1991).

A pluralist approach to methodology would suggest that some of this conflict – but not all of it – is misplaced. If, as I will seek to show, there are diverse interpretative goals, then it follows that there will be a corresponding diversity of method proper to those goals. My study of Genesis will illustrate that biblical critics now have a wide range of interpretative interests, from the aesthetic to the socio-scientific, and many of these interests are compatible even where they have often been perceived to be in conflict. There are cases where, for example, fresh observations at the level of narrative poetics have placed older hypotheses in doubt. In other words, I am not arguing for a genial pluralism which overlooks any genuine cases of disagreement. I am suggesting, however, that the dream of an all-inclusive method is to remain unfulfilled. We need to arbitrate between competing perspectives on a case-by-case basis, and a prior goal of any such arbitration is to sort out genuine disagreements from spurious ones.

At this point it may be helpful to provide an example of what appears to be a genuine interpretative disagreement and then show how it could represent simply a difference of focus, rather than an irrevocable disagreement. The example provides also a sounding of some of the key issues that are discussed in the following chapters. In Genesis 27.46, Rebekah complains to her husband about the possibility that her son will marry a Hittite woman: 'If Jacob takes a wife from among the

INTRODUCTION

women of the land, from the Hittite women like these, what will life mean to me?' Historicist critics have long been in the habit of dissecting the surrounding narrative into a 'doublet' – two literary sources which offer competing reasons for Jacob's trip to his uncle Laban (e.g. Gunkel 1910: 386; Emerton 1988: 398). In Genesis 27.1–45, Jacob's life is threatened: having stolen his brother's blessing, he needs to find refuge from Esau's anger, and Rebekah suggests that her brother Laban's house would be a good place to hide (27.43). In 26.34–5 and 27.46–28.5, on the other hand, Jacob needs to contract an endogamous marriage, i.e. a marriage within the kinship group. The second text has been consistently identified with the so-called P tradition, which is usually dated late in Israel's history and associated by many scholars with a theologically legitimised ethnocentrism, such as can be found in Ezra 9.1–2. In summary, such an argument would suggest that Rebekah's (implied) plea for an endogamous marriage in Genesis 27.46 betrays the supposed ethnocentrism of the P tradition.

There is, however, another way of construing this conflict of interpretations, one which makes the history of composition irrelevant. A narratological analysis might suggest that this conclusion has been reached too quickly and with far too many assumptions. Genesis 27.1–45 depicts Jacob's theft of the blessing that (according to an implied principle of primogeniture[7]) properly belongs to his older brother Esau. Esau's rage is entirely justified, but so is a mother's concern for the well-being of her younger son, and she counsels Jacob to run for his life. In a patriarchal society, however, it is natural that a father's permission should be sought. The narrator has chosen not to tell the reader of Isaac's reaction to Jacob's deceit, so the possibility is left open that he disagreed with Rebekah's reasoning in 27.42–4. After all, 25.28 indicates that Esau was Jacob's favourite son. The received text of Genesis moves naturally from Rebekah's manipulation of Isaac for Jacob's sake in 27.1–45 to her manipulation of Isaac in 27.46. Her expression of concern for endogamous marriage could be simply a ruse designed to obtain paternal permission for Jacob's flight, exploiting the tension with her Hittite daughters-in-law (rather than expressing a general xenophobia) mentioned in 26.34–5.

We have here, then, what appears to be a genuine disagreement between the historicist perspective on the one hand (that fuses Rebekah's speech in 27.46 with Priestly ethnocentrism) and a narratological analysis on the other (that sees 27.46 as simply a ruse on a par with 27.5–13). In the first case, Rebekah's speech is taken to be a transparent window on Priestly ideology, and ethnocentricity is attributed both to her character as well as to a reconstructed P writer. In the second case, Rebekah's character is marked by tricksterism rather than by ethnocentrism: there is no necessary connection between Rebekah's speech and the narrator's ideology. The division of the story into two separate sources is not required.

My proposal to read Rebekah consistently as a trickster does not depend for its force on the historical unity of these chapters (cf. Carr 1996: 321–2). On the contrary, it may well be that there is a history of composition behind the received text of Genesis; the heterogeneous elements of the text speak strongly for this view, even if there is no one reconstruction of that history that has secured a scholarly consensus. Practitioners of narrative poetics characteristically tend to read the text *as if* it were a unity, whether or not this was historically always the case. They have been charged with historical naivety for doing so, but it is quite possible to understand their work as a contribution to the question of what the received or 'final' Hebrew text might mean – ironically a somewhat neglected topic in the last two centuries of professional biblical criticism. Sometimes this quest for the meaning of the received text has been expressly opposed by literary critics to the historical question of what the final editor may have 'intended', but I argue below that authorial intention is a legitimate interpretative goal as long as we are clear on what we mean by *intention*. The standard historicist hypothesis for understanding Rebekah's motivation in 27.46 does not actually deal with the question of what the final editor may have intended to communicate in preserving chapters 26–8 of Genesis in just this way. In short, the standard historicist approach has neglected at least one legitimate *historical* question – the purpose of the final editor – which might be answered by considering the contributions of narrative poetics. The standard assumption has been that the final editor merely collects up the traditions with no apparent purpose other than antiquarianism; but to say that this assumption unjustifiably reduces the interpretative options would be something of an understatement.

I have here begun to deconstruct the opposition between narratological analyses and the old historicism: on the one hand, narratology does not require unified texts; and, on the other hand, the old source-critical dissections of the biblical text have habitually excluded a legitimate historical question – the communicative purpose of the final Hebrew text. Yet it is precisely the final text which has been the focus of narratologists.[8] Is it plausible, then, to construe narrative poetics as a contribution to this particular historical question?

INTRODUCTION

The present study advocates a model of pluralism that suggests that narratology *can* make a contribution, but that a range of factors beyond the aesthetic limits of the text would have to be considered also. The purposes of the final editor of Genesis can also be illuminated, for example, by comparative anthropological studies of kinship (which range far and wide beyond the limits of the biblical text), but before we consider these anthropological perspectives we need to look more philosophically at the notion of *intention*.

If we are to be concerned with the communicative purpose of the final form of Genesis, we have to be clear about the nature of this interpretative goal. The notion of intention is highly complex, and a methodological pluralism that wants to defend intentionalist criticism will need to be aware of the conceptual problems involved; many of the attacks on authorial intention have exploited these conceptual ambiguities. Scholars have meant at least three, quite different, things by authorial *intention* or *purpose*. The distinctions between the three facets of intention are discussed more fully in the course of the book, but for the present we may distinguish between:

1 an explicit communicative intention
2 an implied or indirect communicative intention
3 a motive.

Initially, we may take the first two together, and distinguish a communicative intention (*what* an author or editor is trying to say) from a motive (*why* it is being said). The motives behind a communicative act may be complex, contradictory and even unconscious, never coming to expression in language at all. This domain is the focus of psychoanalytical criticism. At the level of language, on the other hand, an author's intention may be relatively explicit in the text or it may be only implied – something which must be inferred from the often unstated circumstances of utterance. These unstated circumstances may include literary allusions and the like, but also non-linguistic features of the communicative context.

Thus, one can distinguish between *explicit* communicative intentions and *indirect* communicative intentions, although in practice the distinction may be more of a continuum (cf. Brett 1991b).[9] Analyses of indirect communication have been provided especially in the linguistics literature on pragmatics (e.g. Leach 1983; Levenson 1983), but also in anthropological studies of communication (e.g. Gumperz 1977; Sperber and Wilson 1986). The important point here is that an interpretation of communicative intention need not restrict itself to the explicit communicative features embedded in a text but may need to encompass the unspoken features of a reconstructed historical situation, or at least those features of the situation which may be relevant to an author's purpose. An interest in indirect communication inevitably leads into the domain of hypothesis; interpretation in this area will require finely balanced judgements of probability.

As already suggested, the three senses of *intention* blend into each other to such an extent that it is sometimes practically impossible to distinguish between them. But a conceptual distinction is always possible, and the lack of conceptual awareness on this issue has led to a great deal of confusion, both in biblical studies and in literature studies generally. As Annabel Patterson has rightly observed (1990: 146), much of the controversy about literary intention in the last four decades could have been avoided if the participants had been clearer in their uses of the term 'intention'. Further, if the various schools of interpretation that have conspired against authorial intention had been more modest in the formulation of their goals, some of the antagonism could have been ameliorated. The case for critical pluralism requires that we distinguish the immodest claims of these anti-intentionalist schools (e.g. New Criticism, structuralism, and poststructuralism) from claims that might be, at certain points, complementary.

My argument about intentionality is, for example, quite compatible with some aspects of the theory of reading made famous by Stanley Fish. While some critics have read Fish to be recommending only methods of interpretation that focus on readers rather than authors, this view of his work is misleading. Apart from one early essay, Fish's theoretical arguments have been focused on the *epistemology* of interpretation, not the *goals* of interpretation (see Brett 1993). He is concerned with general philosophical reflections on the nature of reading, no matter what school of criticism. The idea that interpretation takes places within communities is meant to encompass all forms of interpretation, not just the enlightened few who gather under the banner of 'the reader'. With regard to authorial intention, his point is simply that an author's mind cannot be known directly, as if it were a bit of evidence independent of the process of interpretation. If he makes the point that 'interpretation *creates* intention' (1980: 163), it is not that interpreters need to give up all quests for intention. Indeed, in *Doing What Comes Naturally*, Fish even suggests that we cannot do without some notion of intentionality: 'One cannot understand an utterance without at the same time hearing or reading it as the utterance of someone with more or less specific concerns . . . someone with an intention' (1989: 15). This statement does not depart from his original position, since he clarifies the point by saying: 'Intentions are not self-declaring, but must be constructed from evidence that is itself controversial' (ibid.: 98–100).

My case for pluralism necessarily rejects any naive intentionalist interpretation that would regard a reader's intuition about authorial psychology as a relevant source of evidence. The author's mind is clearly not accessible. It does not follow, however, that interpretation of a biblical text needs to be restricted to the evidence available in a single text. On the contrary, if we are interested in indirect communicative intention (examples of which would be irony, parody, allusion and other forms of covert communication) it is necessary to consider evidence from the situation of authorship, insofar as this can be reconstructed. To be sure, in the case of the Hebrew Bible the historical situation of the author or editor must always be reconstructed from evidence that is itself controversial. We can have only better and worse hypotheses, arguments which are more and less coherent, interpretations which are based on more and less evidence.

In addition to this epistemological self-consciousness, the case for critical pluralism would also need to refute any theories of interpretation which made immodest claims for the unique contributions of particular interpretative interests. Thus, although the present study of Genesis reflects an interest in communicative intention, it does not subscribe to the kind of arguments advanced by E. D. Hirsch which suggest that quests for intention can claim some kind of moral high ground (e.g. 1967: 24–5; 1976: 7).[10] I argue that good ethical grounds can be adduced for a variety of interpretative interests, and therefore we should not pre-empt the ethical debate by endorsing a generalized claim that the author's intention is always to be respected.

Similarly, in order to be coherent, a critical pluralism needs to reject some of the more extreme claims of literary formalism. While accepting that there is a mode of poetics that focuses on the conventional communicative devices evident in the surface of the text, I would reject the New Critical idea that the interpreter of a successful poem should not make reference to non-linguistic evidence; as already indicated above, there are other potentially appropriate sources of evidence beyond the sources imagined in Wimmsatt and Beardsley's classic statement of New Criticism, i.e. beyond 'grammars, dictionaries, and all the literature which is the source of dictionaries' (1972: 339). The unspoken features of a reconstructed historical situation may well turn out to be relevant to an author's purpose. Even Sternberg's poetics can be seen, ironically, as a revised version of formalism, in the tradition of the erstwhile New Criticism; although he has elegantly demolished some of the anti-historicism among his fellow literary critics, the contribution of historical research turns out to be largely irrelevant to the details of his exegesis. While he has illuminated the dynamic tensions between what is said and what is *not* said in a narrative, the tension carried by the not-said is conceived entirely in literary terms – as a 'gap' which will be filled out by the unfolding of the narrative. All the questions left over, not specifically answered by the text, are relegated to the non-literary rank of 'blanks'. But it is precisely the domain of the blank that must be considered relevant to any examination of ideological contestation. The domain of the not-said is potentially rich with indirect communication. (A great deal cannot be said directly in Genesis, for example, because the ethnic politics of the Persian period militated against such explicitness.)

Having briefly located the quest for communicative intention against this background – bringing together considerations from poetics, pragmatics and reader theory – it remains now to deal with the challenges brought forward by structuralism and poststructuralism which threaten to undermine the very idea of authorial agency. These movements have been highly influential not just within literary criticism but within the human sciences generally, and a critical pluralism that wants to preserve intentionalist criticism as a coherent enterprise will need to defend itself against any theory which seeks to dissolve individual agency into larger structures of culture or cultural hybridity. Once again, it will be possible only to sketch in the theoretical issues that bear most closely on the present discussion.

First, it is necessary to differentiate between Ferdinand de Saussure's pioneering work in linguistics, *Cours de linguistique générale* (1916), and the applications of his work in anthropology, notably by Claude Lévi-Strauss in influential works such as *Structural Anthropology* (1963). In this latter work, Lévi-Strauss was inspired by the advances made in linguistics, in particular in the science of phonology, which had succeeded in reducing the sounds used in all known languages to a small number of binary phonetic contrasts. Lévi-Strauss argued, by analogy, that it was possible to analyse social phenomena, like marriage and kinship, across various traditional societies and reduce them to a small number of structural principles (cf. Rogerson 1978: 102–14). In recent studies of Genesis, for example, there has been much discussion of an idea introduced by Lévi-Strauss, that the ideal marriage from the point of view of the groom would be with a daughter of the mother's brother, i.e. matrilineal cross-cousin marriage (see Donaldson 1981; Oden 1987: 106–30; Prewitt 1990). This is a possible reading of

INTRODUCTION

Genesis 27–8, discussed above, in which Jacob is advised to find a wife from among the daughters of his mother's brother.

Naomi Steinberg (1993: 8–14) has rightly questioned whether there is really sufficient evidence to sustain such an hypothesis in the case of Genesis. She suggests, on the contrary, that the final text of Genesis reveals the ideal to be a form of 'patrilineal endogamy' in which both the father and the mother descend from Abraham's father, Terah. The system is called 'patrilineal' since the line of the father defines the bounds of the lineage, but it has a 'collateral', or sibling, feature that includes women. Rebekah, like all the 'proper' wives, also stems from the patrilineage of Terah, since her father Bethuel is the son of Nahor. Thus, the collateral patrilineage of Terah looks like this:

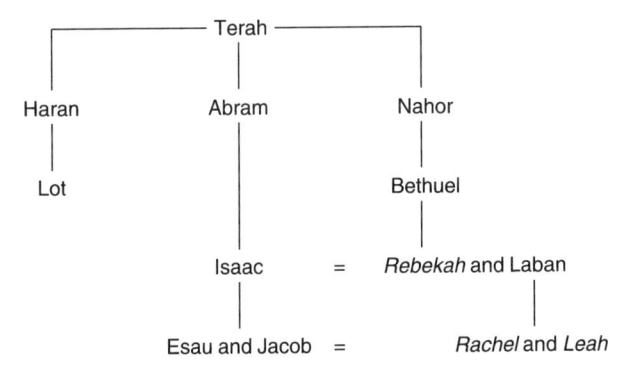

```
                  ─── Terah ───
        │              │              │
      Haran          Abram          Nahor
        │              │              │
       Lot             │            Bethuel
                       │              │
                     Isaac    =    Rebekah and Laban
                       │              │
               Esau and Jacob    =    Rachel and Leah
```

Figure 1 Patrilineage of Terah

I will examine the implications of this argument in due course, but the important question arising at this point is methodological: what kind of interpretative question is answered by Steinberg's thesis? And in precisely what sense does her thesis differ, as she claims, from the kind of structuralism descended from Lévi-Strauss?

Steinberg distances herself from Lévi-Strauss by distinguishing social 'structure' from 'social organization'. In aligning herself with studies of social organization, she means to place a greater emphasis on the 'individual decisions made in adapting to external circumstances' while, at the same time, abstracting a pattern that reflects reiterated individual choices (1993: 9–10). She implies that structuralist anthropology operates without sufficient attention to the complex realities of individual agency, and cites Raymond Firth in support of her perspective:

A structural principle is one which provides a fixed line of social behaviour and represents the order which it manifests. The concept of social organization has complementary emphasis. It recognizes adaptation of behaviour in respect of given ends, control of means in varying circumstances, which are set by changes in the external environment or by the necessity to resolve conflict between structural principles. If structure implies order, organization implies working towards order.

(Firth 1964: 61)

This passage from Firth, and Steinberg's use of it, reflects the tension in recent social theory between social structures and individual agency. Firth is careful here to affirm the 'complementarity' between his position and any stronger emphases on structure that would make individual agencies redundant. Whether he succeeds in maintaining such an eirenic balance we may leave as an open question. It may be possible to sustain this idea of complementarity if structuralism is seen as having an extremely abstract *depth of focus*, on analogy with comparative grammar, rather than a detailed focus on the intricacies of individual agency and particular speech-acts. At least in biblical studies, even where structuralist interpretations have begun from particular texts, it seems that their purpose has been to suggest a wider context of oppositions and schema within which an author is unwittingly implicated (e.g. Barthes 1977). But structuralism is not alone in this regard: other schools of social thought also have tended to relegate the discourse of actors to the margins of analysis, whether they have emphasized the systemic unity of societies, or whether they have viewed societies as the product of fundamental socio-economic conflicts (Mayes 1989).

There has, however, been a marked tendency in recent social theory to give more attention to individual agency, or at least to intentional action (Handel 1993). Mary Douglas's reading of Numbers and James Scott's account of covert resistance provide examples of anthropological work which promises a *rapprochement* between the social sciences and the older humanism of biblical scholarship with its focus on matters of language, text and authorial intention. It is doubtful, however, that Steinberg's work on Genesis can be read as part of this quest for a more balanced account of agency. In the end, she replaces one structure with another: matrilineal cross-cousin marriage is replaced by patrilineal endogamy, providing a new 'norm' for Israelite marriage which is never articulated as such in the primary

INTRODUCTION

literature. The goal of Steinberg's analysis still seems to be a structural principle which is then used to formulate a highly generalized account of how the patrilineal endogamy, while unknown to the agents involved, serves as a defence of community boundaries in the exile (Steinberg 1993: 142–7; cf. Mullen 1997). Steinberg's thesis does not explain, for example, why Abram should be commanded by Yahweh in Genesis 12.1 to leave his father's house, nor does it deal adequately with all the evidence of exogamous marriage (cf. Lemche 1985: 272–5).

To be fair, it is important to recognize that there is a range of interpretative goals within the human sciences, and intentionalist criticism cannot be aligned with all of them. Anthropology and sociology attempt to explain social relations and processes on a large scale, and such attempts can never be restricted to the evidence that comes from the discourse of individual actors. It is not just that social scientists have to collect a large number of communicative acts before they have a statistically significant sample. The methodological issues are more complex. Some aspects of social life never come to expression in discourse, and in this respect it simply does not matter whether discourse is understood as the product of intentional action or (as in extreme versions of poststructuralism) as an anonymous intertextuality within which an individual's subjectivity is completely dissolved (so Foucault 1972: 55, 122). Even where intentional action turns out to be influential, individuals are always constrained by the conventions and institutions of their milieu, and actions regularly have consequences which are quite unintended. Intentional action is not simply the aggregate of psychological states. These issues are taken for granted in the recent social theory that attempts to recover a balance of structure and agency (notably Giddens 1984; 1987).

But even given that the human sciences are working with a much larger canvas than is the intentionalist literary critic, it is always possible to study events and social processes in a way that highlights 'what it was like for those involved' (Runciman 1983: 42). This is a logically separable issue *within* the disciplines of anthropology and sociology, and it is a focus on this issue that suggests the need for co-operation between the human sciences and literary criticism (Runciman 1983: 236–42; Rogerson 1985: 255). What was the actor's point of view? Or to put the question into the plural: what were the actors' points of view, and how did they interact?

This brings us back to the earlier suggestion that we should distinguish carefully between the *linguistic* structuralism of Saussure and the *anthropological* structuralism Lévi-Strauss (cf. Thiselton 1992:

80–141). Building on an analogy with Saussure's phonology, Lévi-Strauss aimed to analyse social phenomena across various traditional societies, and to reduce them to a small number of structural principles. This kind of comparative anthropology produced results which were never intended to be intelligible to the anthropologists' informants. That was not the aim. Another linguist, Kenneth Pike, built on Saussure's phonology for a quite different purpose, and Pike's work has been important in shaping another school of social theory which distinguishes between *emic* and *etic* goals of interpretation.

Pike (1964) derived his terms from the linguistic disciplines of phonemics and phonetics: phonetics attempts to describe systematically all the sounds of human speech, irrespective of whether native speakers of particular languages would recognize the scientific metalanguage of the linguist (it was this aspect of Saussure's work which most interested Lévi-Strauss). Phonemics, on the other hand, describes the significant differences between the sounds of speech *as perceived by native speakers in their own linguistic system*. Pike applied this distinction to the study of human action, suggesting that some kinds of socio-scientific explanation need not be understood in native categories – e.g. if it seems that a society lacks the concept of economy, it does not follow that they are never influenced by economic forces (cf. Runciman 1983: 13). *Emic* social science, however, defines its goal in terms of describing 'native points of view'. Pike's distinction has generated a great deal of discussion, and it is now clear that any emic–etic contrast must be conceived as a continuum, rather than as a dichotomy; interpreters necessarily betray the categories of their own culture (Taylor 1985). But it is still viable to distinguish between forms of social explanation that seek primarily to satisfy only scientific communities and forms of description which are actor-oriented.

A pluralist can promote both programmes of research as complementary. And a pluralist, such as myself, who is interested in authorial intention could form an alliance with *emic* social science, without attempting to give this interpretative interest any methodological or ethical privilege. There are, however, some problems attached to actor-oriented research which need to be recognized. The author of an ancient text can be regarded as a kind of informant from a foreign culture, but, as anthropologists have made clear, it is always necessary to be aware of informant bias. For example, an actor's gender, or power, can have considerable bearing on how his or her discourse is to be interpreted (Ardener 1972; Keesing 1987). A woman's perspective on her society, for example, could be considerably different from the point of view of a male chief. And in the case of Genesis, it would be highly relevant to know whether the final editors opposed the ethnocentrism represented by the imperial governors, since the asymmetry of power would affect strategies of communication. A comprehensive actor-oriented interpretation of a society will seek to encompass the diverse voices that make up a culture.

I have mentioned, uncritically up to this point, terms like 'social system', 'culture' and 'linguistic system'. These are the presumed *wholes* of which the individual agent is seen as a part. But, clearly, there are substantial questions about the extent to which these wholes – whether individual societies, cultures, languages or even the individual self – can be considered a unity. Recent poststructuralist theory, both literary and socio-scientific, has consistently sought to undermine the assumptions of wholeness with regard to both corporate and individual agency. Precisely how are these wholes, whether of language, culture or the self, constructed?

One of the most important features of Saussure's work was his idea of 'synchronic' linguistic systems, and this idea represented an attempt to constrain the relevant context for interpreting a language. Synchronic interpretation (both in linguistics and in anthropology) began as an opposition movement to the nineteenth-century historicist idea that in order to understand any social phenomenon it is necessary to understand its place within a process of development. Saussure insisted, on the contrary, that it was necessary to understand words within the context of their contemporary linguistic system. The most relevant context was not the whole history of a word's usage (much of which is unknown to the average native speaker) but the range of possible options available to a speaker at any particular moment. Language, for Saussure, was like a game of chess: the semantic content of a term draws its significance from its relationship with other terms in the system. It is this system of relationships that has priority for semantics, not the ways in which language hooks on to the world, or the ways in which linguistic associations develop through time. Indeed, there is something of a consensus among contemporary linguists that language systems can, and normally do, change from generation to generation (see e.g. Hudson 1981). Thus, the English spoken by Australians in the 1990s cannot be understood simply on the basis of English-language antecedents in the 1930s, and Shakespearian English is even less relevant. The same is true of Hebrew: we cannot assume, for example, that the language of the Qumran texts is a reliable guide to the Hebrew of the sixth century BCE. By analogy with these insights in linguistics, anthropologists reacted against the evolutionary doctrine of 'survivals', arguing that social phenomena should be understood as part of their contemporary social system, rather than as a barely-understood 'survival' of a previous age.

The present book is a synchronic study insofar as it focuses on the intentions of the final editors of Genesis in the Persian period, considered against the background of the cultural options of the time. This implies that where the editors have used pre-existing sources they have used them for purposes that need to be understood in their immediate context. I am not denying the probability that some of these sources were composed much earlier than the Persian period; it is just that the historicist tendency to treat the sources as survivals of an earlier period is not sufficient for our interpretative purposes.

My concern has analogies also with Saussure's programme in that I am not concerned primarily with *referential* uses of language, in the straightforward sense of referring to events in the distant past. That is to say, even though the narratives of Genesis purport to describe events in the lives of Israel's progenitors, even before settled life in Canaan, these events are not at issue here. Rather, the primary concern is with the relationships between discourses of the Persian period. Following Slavoj Žižek, I will take the texts to be ideological, or political, even if they are quite accurate or *true* in relation to their referential claims – 'if true, so much the better for the ideological effect' (Žižek 1994: 7–8). What is at issue is not the asserted content but the way in which this content is related to particular social interests. Thus, the age of the stories about Abraham or Joseph, or whether they are historically accurate, are questions which are quite separate from the *social interests* served by the narratives in the Persian period. And it is these social interests which are the focus of this study.

The history of the composition of Genesis is extremely complex. The variation in the names for God is just one factor indicative of the complexity of textual pre-history, and I discuss more evidence of sources and editing in the chapters following. Precisely such complexity means that the final form of Genesis is not a unified whole, a point which has been taken for granted in critical studies of the Bible for more than a century. However, historical criticism has tended to resolve these complexities by reconstructing coherent layers of literary sources and subsequent editing, assuming that their authors and editors were themselves all characterised by a coherent subjectivity.[11] Given the assumption that all these agents were addressing particular situations and audiences, and that they all had coherent purposes in mind, it became for the historicists a matter of matching the particular layer of text with the relevant subjectivity.

INTRODUCTION

A great deal can be learned from this historicist style of scholarship, but it is burdened by some key assumptions which are highly questionable. First, the presumption of coherent agency has been undermined by poststructuralist theory in both literary criticism and the social sciences. Communicative interaction is commonly marked by incongruities, repetitions and contradictions, some of which may be deliberate and some not. Biblical scholars have too often credited the sources of Genesis with an extraordinary consistency (cf. Whybray 1987).

Second, there has been a common presumption that the key to an editor's intention is to be found in the peculiar additions made to the sources; the earlier material is merely 'traditional', and it has been left intact for reasons difficult to determine – either out of antiquarianism or out of some sort of religious respect for the tradition. The difficulty here is twofold: the editors were clearly not antiquarian or respectful enough to have left the material alone altogether, yet once any editorial intervention has been posited, it is impossible to know how much of the 'traditional' material has been lost. An interpreter can hardly presume to know what has been cut from the narrative by an ancient editor if what has been cut is, clearly, entirely missing. Moreover, it is no more plausible to assume that the key to an editor's intention is to be found in his additions than to assume the reverse: it would make eminently good sense for the editors of Genesis to have kept 'traditional' material because it suited their purpose; any additions to the text could simply have been designed to stitch together the sources that were most appropriate to their communicative purposes.

The presumption of the present study, on the other hand, will be that the activity of the final editors can be characterised as 'intentional hybridity'.[12] What is envisaged here is *neither* an organic hybridity wherein the complex pre-history of cultural elements is entirely unknown, *nor* a serial addition of traditions, all equally coherent and perspicuous. Rather, intentional hybridity is a blending of two or more voices, without compositional boundaries being evident, such that the voices combine into an unstable chorale – sometimes speaking univocally, but more often juxtaposing alternative points of view such that the authority of the dominant voice is put into question. Hybridisation takes the focus off particular editorial additions and allows a more holistic consideration of the texts – except that this notion of *holism* is poststructuralist to the extent that it expects complexity and contradiction, not unity. In the case of Genesis, the overriding ideologies have been juxtaposed with so many traces of otherness that the dominant voices can be deconstructed by those who have ears to hear.

THE CONTEST OF METHODS

The interpretation of Genesis presented in this book might be taken as the invention of a deconstructive reader whose concerns are entirely different from the theological and social intentions of the ancient editors. But postcolonial versions of deconstruction have got nothing to do with what Terry Eagleton has caricatured as a libertarian pessimism, blessedly free from the shackles of meaning and sociality (Eagleton 1991: 38; contrast Bhabha 1994: 183; and see Norris 1990). There are indeed forms of deconstructive criticism which advocate the 'free play' of textuality, but deconstruction is construed differently within postcolonial theory. My purpose here is to trace in the text of Genesis the patterns of incongruity, and my suggestion is that these patterns point to an ancient editorial agency which is contesting the privileged grasp of colonial power in the Persian period. The agency of resistance is not seen as the product of a pure, egalitarian and consistent consciousness (cf. Bhabha 1994: 187). On the contrary, the text of Genesis seems to reveal a hybrid inter-subjectivity, not necessarily perspicuous to itself, incorporating diverse cultural elements both from within Israelite tradition and from outside it. Older literary sources may well have been used without any knowledge of the origins of such sources. Against extreme forms of postmodernism, which would deny hybrid subjectivity any agency at all, the present study follows Homi Bhabha in assuming that some kind of agency is necessary in any resistance to a dominant culture.

Having suggested that Genesis can be read as an example of such subversive and artful hybridity, I turn now to explore this hypothesis in detail. The reading offered here is not a verse-by-verse commentary: there is little purpose in reiterating the details that can be found, for example, in Claus Westermann's magisterial three-volume work on Genesis (1984; 1985; 1986). But the reading does set out to be comprehensive in the sense that every chapter of Genesis is shown to be related, in some sense, to the aims of the final editors within the historical context of the Persian period. Not every interpretative possibility will be explicitly considered; the primary goal is to show how a particular configuration of hypotheses can illuminate the intentions of the final editors.

1

GENESIS 1–11

Creation and dominance

Dominance in Genesis 1–3

In the beginning, Elohim created the heavens and the earth.
And the earth, it was welter and waste,[13]
and darkness was on the face of the deep,
and the spirit of Elohim hovered on the face of the waters.
(Gen. 1.1–2)

When the world began, there was earth and water, undifferentiated and lifeless. The first sign of life came from the divine, 'hovering' perhaps like an eagle over its young.[14] *Elohim*, normally translated 'God', is grammatically plural, but the Hebrew verb for creating is here conjugated as singular. So is the divine singular or plural? Grammarians rule in favour of the singular, giving priority to the verb, but this is a short-lived solution to the question. The assumption of unity in the heavens is maintained for most of the chapter, but it is not sustained with absolute consistency. In 1.26 Elohim speaks in the plural, implying some kind of divine council: 'Let us make humankind in our image, as our similitude.' Indeed, there are more occasions in the primal history where the divine plural appears: 'The human has become like one of us, knowing good and evil' (3.22); 'Come, let us descend and confuse their language so that they will not understand the language of their neighbour' (11.7). So the question eludes a simple grammatical solution: is God one, or is God many? Is there differentiation in the heavens? How is God named, and what implications does this naming have for human beings?

The book of Genesis resists a clear answer to such questions. The name of God shifts from *Elohim* in the first creation story (1.1–2.3) to *Yahweh Elohim* in the second creation story (2.4–3.24) to simply *Yahweh* in Genesis 4, the personal name most clearly associated with Israel's God. Later in the book, we find *El Elyon*, *El Roi*, *El Shaddai* and a variety of other names, some of which perhaps amount to a reticence to give a name since the divine is spoken of only in relation to a particular family – the 'god of Abraham', the 'god of Jacob', and so on. The habit of interpreting these family-dependent names as pointing to a single God is usually supported by the Hebrew grammar, but not always. Thus, for example, in 31.53, when Jacob makes a covenant with Laban, there is an oath which implicitly distinguishes between the 'god of Abraham', Jacob's grandfather, and the 'god of Nahor', Laban's grandfather: 'May the god of Abraham and the god of Nahor . . . judge between us'. The verb 'judge' is plural here, and it implies that there are two gods at issue in this story.[15] I consider this variety of divine names later, but at this beginning point in Genesis it is worth noting that the mercurial language of the divine is not peculiar to the creation narratives.

It is significant also that 'Elohim' is actually a generic term for divinity, and thus it has no particular connection to Israel. Unlike many creation stories from the ancient world, there is no focus on the author's own people or temple. Nor is there an account of the creation of the gods themselves, a common feature of the mythological literature of the time. For example, the Babylonian *Enuma Elish* (the exiles in Babylon would have known this myth, even if some version of it had not made its way to Israel in earlier periods), begins by describing the birth of the gods from their progenitors Apsu and Tiamat. We find a great deal of colourful detail about the gods even before Marduk, the god of Babylon, slays Tiamat – the goddess of salt water – in a violent battle, dismembering her body to make the heavens and the earth. By comparison, Genesis 1 is extraordinarily peaceful in its representation of creation and extraordinarily reserved about the nature of divinity. Verse 26 indicates some form of divine sociality but no hint of disagreement: 'Let us make humankind in our image, as our similitude' (cf. 3.22; 11.7). The Hebrew Bible elsewhere contains several references to a divine council,[16] but the meaning of these texts is also elusive. There are a few references to violent creation motifs (e.g. Pss. 74.13–14 and 89.7–11; Isa. 51.9), but Genesis 1 is markedly free of such violence (Levenson 1987; Janzen 1994).

Having considered these wider contexts of comparison, what can be said about the significance of these verses as the beginning to a book which was finally edited in Israel during the Persian period of colonial administration? Clearly, Genesis 1 reveals a remarkable lack of the agonistic creation motifs which can be found both elsewhere in the Bible and elsewhere all over the ancient Near East. There is a pronounced reticence in speaking about the divine, which is reflected also in the use of a generic term, Elohim, rather than the proper name Yahweh – the God clearly associated with Israel. If the editors were setting out to promote an exclusivist religion, and a sharply defined ethnic identity (so Mullen 1997: 95, 98), then this would seem an unlikely beginning. On the contrary, the mood of the story implies more of an eirenic inclusivism; in the primordial creativity of Elohim, the identity of Israel is not a matter of contestation. We might infer, then, that wherever social identities become highly conflicted, this will be a matter of divine regret.

Some commentators, however, suggest that the theme of division is embodied not so much in the primal scene of 1.1–2 but in the acts of creation which begin in 1.3–5. With the creation of light comes a separation between light and darkness, and the key Hebrew word for separation in v. 4, *hibdil*, re-appears several times. Some have argued that *hibdil* is a cipher for social separation and that an Israelite exclusiveness is being secretly legitimised by the cosmic ordering (e.g. Kapelrud 1974: 185). But it seems to me that the evidence points in another direction: the use of *hibdil* refers not to the order of living creatures but exclusively to the cosmic ordering – the separation of light from darkness (v. 4), day from night (vv. 14 and 18), and the separation of water above the heavenly vault from the water below it (v. 7).

It might be thought that the mere repetition of *hibdil* is significant, but a number of phrases are used with an almost liturgical repetitiveness in the first creation story, and the vocabulary of separation is actually less significant than the divine exhortations ('Let there be light . . . ', 'Let there be a vault . . . ', etc., a speech pattern repeated eight times) and the celebratory refrain 'And Elohim saw that it was good' (vv. 4, 10, 12, 18, 21, 25). The latter refrain is expanded climactically in v. 31: 'Elohim saw all that he had made, and look, it was very good.' The vocabulary of separation is simply a small part of the dialectical oscillation between divine exhortations and the celebratory refrain.

Division is perhaps hinted at in the idea that the plants and animals were created 'according to their kinds' (vv. 11, 12, 21, 24, 25), and a hierarchy certainly arises with the creation of the species that exclusively is made in the image of Elohim:

> And Elohim said, 'Let us make humankind in our image,
>   according to our similitude,
> and let them rule over the fish of the sea and the birds of the
>   heavens, over the livestock,
> over all the earth, and over all the creatures that move on the
>   earth.'

So Elohim created the human in his image,
in the image of Elohim he created him,
male and female he created them.

And Elohim blessed them and said to them,
'Be fruitful and increase in number, fill the earth and subdue it,
rule over the fish of the sea and the birds of the heavens
and over every living creature that moves on the earth.'
(1.26–8)

But even here, where a basic distinctiveness of humankind is asserted, there is an element of continuity between humankind and other creatures. The first divine speech that contains an imperative is addressed to the creatures of the sea and the birds of the air – 'Be fruitful and increase in number' (v. 22). That is, the blessing for procreation has already been shared with these creatures. So when Eve celebrates at the birth of Cain by exclaiming 'With Yahweh I have made[17] a man' (Gen. 4.1), her expansive mood answers Elohim's exhortation of co-creation, but this exhortation to 'be fruitful' is not the exclusive preserve of human beings. In addition to the creatures of the sea and of the air, the earth itself is twice called upon to participate: 'Let the earth produce vegetation . . .' (v. 11), and 'Let the earth bring forth living creatures . . .' (v. 24). Not only is there no licence for Israelite separatism in Genesis 1, even the distinctiveness of the human species is undermined when humankind has to share the divine vocation of co-creation with the earth and with other creatures.

This is reinforced by the first covenant in Genesis – a divine promise encompassing *all* creatures, not just the human ones (Gen. 9.8–17). If Israelite seed is in any sense sacred, it is not Elohim's reproductive blessing that makes it holy. Indeed, the language of holiness is largely absent from Genesis, and this sets the book apart from the rest of the Pentateuch (Moberly 1992: 99–103). Holiness is attached only to the seventh day's rest (2.3), not to human procreation, and as the polemical Isa. 56.6–7 makes clear anyone can participate in Sabbath worship, not just native-born Israelites.[18] The creation narratives provide no warrant for the notion of 'holy seed', and the first covenant in Genesis is radically inclusive.

There is, however, no escaping the overt hierarchy asserted by the text: human beings are called on to rule the earth and to subdue it. The use of the verb *radah*, 'to rule', in vv. 26 and 28 probably alludes to royal ideology, and the language of the 'image of God' was commonly associated with pharaohs and kings in the literature of ancient Egypt and Mesopotamia (Bird 1997: 134–8). This idea is unparalleled in the Hebrew Bible. Indeed, in the hymn to leviathan in Job 41, it is specifically said that the great beast of the sea cannot be subdued (v. 9) and that 'he is king over all the children of pride' (v. 34). In short, the book of Job contests the idea that humankind can ever be fully successful in being kings over all the earth. Indeed, the 'image of Elohim' language is so unusual in the Hebrew Bible that we need to look more closely at the intertextual subtleties associated with Genesis 1.27–8.

When humanity as a whole is exhorted to rule over the other living creatures, this is best read as a polemical undermining of a role otherwise associated primarily with kings. The characteristic association of the phrase 'image of God' with Mesopotamian kings and Egyptian pharaohs has long been observed, but the implication of this comparison have often been under-analysed. If the health of the created order does not depend upon kings (whether Mesopotamian, Israelite or Persian kings), then the democratising tendency of 1.27–8 can be seen as anti-monarchic. Indeed, there is an anti-monarchic tone to Genesis, as I will show, which begins in chapter 1 but extends into the second creation story and beyond. The polemical intent is subtle, but the evidence for it accumulates as the narrative unfolds.

Within Israelite royal tradition, one frequently finds a connection between the ideal king and the fertility of the land, and in this respect the rule of the created order is specifically linked to the monarchy within the Hebrew Bible itself and not just in Egyptian and Mesopotamian literature. Psalm 72, for example, interweaves the expectation that the ideal king is one who defends the weak and afflicted (vv. 2, 4, 12–14) with the claim that this rule is characterised by prosperity and fertility (vv. 3, 6–7, 16–17). In Psalm 72, we even find the impossibly utopian expectation that the Israelite king 'will rule from sea to sea, and from the River to the ends of the earth' (v. 8), echoing the human vocation in Genesis 1. One could argue, therefore, that these aspects of Israelite royal ideology have also been democratised in Genesis 1, and it is interesting to notice both the continuities and discontinuities which the comparison invites: in Genesis 1.28, it is humankind as such who are to rule 'over all the earth', but there is no expectation that this rule will entail the subjugation of distant enemies and nations, as Psalm 72.9–11 suggests. In Genesis 1, the vision of human expansion over all the earth does not envisage social conflict.

Moreover, in spite of the exhortation to 'rule' and to 'subdue', even the potential conflict between humans and animals is somewhat muted. It is quite clear from vv. 29–30 that the editors of Genesis 1 envisage the primal condition to be vegetarian: humans, beasts and birds are given only green plants and fruit as food, and thus one might infer that violence between the species would be unnecessary. While it may be possible to interpret the verb 'rule' in the positive sense of care for the weak, as evidenced in Israelite royal ideology, the language of subjugation precludes a purely eirenic interpretation. Thus, the representation of even this utopian beginning is marked by a significant tension, which probably betrays the realities of daily experience in the ancient world.

Up until modern times, there have been many societies in which the threat presented by wild animals is a constant danger. This was especially true in ancient Israel, and one can find many prophetic judgements, for example, which draw on this fear. The theme is taken to almost comical lengths in Amos 5.19 where a day of judgement is compared to serial encounters with the face of death:

> It will be as if someone fled from a lion and met a bear,
> entered the house and rested his hand on the wall
> only to have a serpent bite him.

Conversely, prophetic announcements of hope often entail the utopian removal of such threats, such as in Isaiah 65.25, where the lion finally turns to eating straw and the serpent to eating dust (cf. Gen. 3.14).

The prophecies of Hosea are particularly relevant, as that book uses vocabulary strikingly similar to that of Genesis 1.27–8 when it suggests that Israelite violence and faithlessness has brought death to 'the beasts of the field, the birds of the heavens, and the fish of the sea' (Hos. 4.3). The point of this text is that the wholesale destruction of other species is an image of horror for the prophet; it is evidence of wrongdoing. In Hosea 2.18, the security of a new covenant with Yahweh envisages not only the end of war but a covenant with 'the beasts of the field, the birds of the heavens, and the creatures that move on the earth'. In other words, a holistic vision of human restoration requires the removal of both threats of war and threats from the natural world. Hosea's vision of peace in human society is integrally linked with a return to ecological utopia, and this is characteristic of prophetic hope (cf. Gowan 1986: 97–120). The first creation story reflects the tension between, on the one hand, this primal utopia and, on the other hand, the reality of a threat to human beings from other species.

The editors of Genesis may well have been aware of the tensions set up in the first story, and so have juxtaposed with it a second creation story which potentially undermines any inflated version of human supremacy which might have been envisaged by Genesis 1.27–8. Genesis 2.4–5 returns the reader to the time before plants were made, and displaces the anthropocentric perspective of the first story by saying that 'there was no human to work the land'. Not only does this form of words place the needs of the land before those of the human, but there seems to be a deliberate irony in the Hebrew text since the word for 'work' (*'bd*) is otherwise most commonly translated as 'serve', in the sense of 'work for'. A more pointed translation would be: 'there was no human to serve the land'. The same vocabulary is used in 2.15: 'And Yahweh Elohim took the human and put him in the Garden of Eden to serve it and to take care of it,' effectively reversing the vocation to rule and to subdue the earth. The irony is heightened in 2.7 where the human is created from materials of the earth: 'And Yahweh Elohim formed the human (*adam*) from the dust of the land (*adamah*) and breathed into his nostrils the breath of life.' The wordplay between *adam* and *adamah* is manifest, but beyond the wordplay lies the potentially subversive claim that the human is derived from soil.

This subversive hint becomes relevant to our understanding of the further wordplay in 2.23: after the creation of woman, the human (*adam*) says, 'She shall be called woman (*ishah*), because she was taken out of man (*ish*).'[19] Some interpretations of this speech suggest that there is here an implied claim to gender superiority in that the woman is said to derive from the man, displacing her role as co-creator and giving priority to the generative capacity of the male. (It makes no difference to this claim whether this was in some sense the man's 'intention' or whether the speech is an unconscious product of patriarchal ideology.) But two features of the narrative undermine such an ideology. First, Eve's speech in Genesis 4.1, 'With Yahweh I have made a man (*ish*)', is a peculiar form of words, partly because the use of *ish* to describe a child is unusual – it is used normally with reference to adults. The use of this particular word has a point, however, if Eve's speech is read as an ironic retort to the man: you claim to have made *ishah*, but I have made *ish* (so Pardes 1993). Second, the seeds of deconstruction have already been planted before Eve's speech in chapter 4, since the male rationale could be applied also to the claim that the human was made from soil (2.7; 3.19): if the man is superior to the woman, because woman was taken from man, then the land is superior to the man, because man was taken from soil.

This raises questions about the fact that the animals also were formed from the land; the vocabulary in 2.19, where the animals are created, is the same as in 2.7, where the human is created. Commentators have made much of the idea that the naming of the animals is an act of domination, and this is clearly one function of naming, especially when, for example, pejorative social labelling serves to make a claim on superiority. However, the act of naming something can be construed also positively, for example when some fresh experience can be expressed in language (like Hagar's naming of God in Gen. 16.13), or when naming is an act of resistance to ideological dominance (like Eve's naming of Cain, which subtly resists 2.23 by claiming that she has made *ish*).[20] Not all naming has the same social function. If we take the narrative on its own terms, the human's naming of the animals cannot have had an evil intent, since humankind has not yet acquired the knowledge of good and evil; the naming of the animals seems rather to be a celebration of diversity. Similarly, the human's naming of woman in 2.23 marks the celebration of an intimacy which is then reinforced in v. 24 by the idea of being 'one flesh'. The fact that 2.18–21 describes a quest for a 'helper' (*'ezer*) does not count against this interpretation: elsewhere in the Hebrew Bible the *'ezer* is frequently God (e.g. Pss. 33.20; 115.9–10); the fact that the human needs an *'ezer* is a sign of lack, not of superiority. According to this narrative, the human is equivalent to the animals in that they are all part of a kinship group which descends from the land. In the genealogical terms suggested by the introductory formula in 2.4a – 'these are the generations of the heavens and the earth' – the land is the parent. In Genesis 2, there is no 'ruling' to be found.

There is, however, a special intimacy between the man and the woman that differentiates them from the animals, and this is expressed by having Yahweh Elohim build the woman from a part of the man (2.22). A more significant differentiation for the context of the Persian period, however, would be v. 24: 'Therefore a man leaves his father and mother and clings to his wife, and they become one flesh.' The verb to 'leave', *'azab*, has been toned down in the translation, since it more often has the sense of 'abandon' or 'forsake'. The idea of 'abandoning' parents represents a potentially scandalous subversion of the conventional Israelite obligations to mother and father (Terrien 1985: 15). In a context where men were being urged to leave their foreign wives, however, the peculiar strength of this language may well be explained by reading the verse as suggesting a priority of commitments: the kinship bond with the wife stands above that of the parents, and in this sense, marriage comes before bloodlines. The notion of the 'holy seed' suggests the reverse – that marriage has to conform to the bloodlines.

The multiplication of ironies in the second creation story could well have been evident to the editors of Genesis, who were leaving clues for the perceptive reader or hearer: the juxtaposition of alternative points of view would place the dominant voices in question. Such 'intentional hybridity' need not leave explicit indicators of previously existing sources (Bakhtin 1981: 358–61), but the change in the divine name in chapter 2 does at least suggest a different source. 'Yahweh Elohim' is, however, an unusual combination of names; outside this narrative it occurs only once more in the Pentateuch, in Exodus 9.30. It may be that the editors have themselves constructed this combination in order to suggest a more inclusive view of God: the generic *Elohim* is now identified with the specifically *Israelite Yahweh* (cf. Genesis 14.18–22 where the priest–king of Salem names God 'El Elyon' and Abram responds by speaking of 'Yahweh El Elyon'). Yahweh was present in these primordial events, even if Israel was not.

A more telling sign of a change in the literary source is the fact that the second creation story has a chronology that is incompatible with Genesis 1. In the second story, the human is created first, then the animals, and the making of the woman happens only after the creation of the animals (2.22–3). The animals appear in the second story only because Yahweh Elohim has found something about creation which is 'not good' – the human is alone. In Genesis 1, on the other hand, animals are created first, and humankind are then created together, male and female. Everything about creation is 'good'. Also, the primal picture in Genesis 2.5–6 is of a dry land which is then watered by rivers. In Genesis 1.9, on the other hand, the dry ground (*yabashah*) is formed by dividing the previously undifferentiated waters of the earth.

The second creation story, moreover, was designed for entirely different purposes: it is primarily an explanation of how the first human couple came to be alienated from the eirenic conditions of the Garden of Eden. It seems that the editors have taken an existing story and juxtaposed it with Genesis 1 in a way that ostensibly just moves the plot of Genesis on one more step, but the seeds of subversion are, at the same time, being planted by the addition of the second narrative.

If the first creation story is concerned to affirm the likeness between Elohim and humankind, the second creation story denies it. Contrary to many traditional interpretations, the first humans are mortal from the beginning, and the tree of life mentioned in 2.9 receives hardly any attention at all: it appears again only in 3.22, when God contemplates the possibility that an evil humanity might *acquire* immortality. Admittedly, the humans possess the knowledge of good and evil after eating the forbidden fruit, and this is construed as a likeness to divinity, but this likeness was not part of the divine intention. Indeed, the possession of such knowledge was initially put forward by the snake (who speaks nothing but the truth) as simply a seductive possibility: 'You will be like Elohim, knowing good and evil' (3.5).

In 3.22, God resolves to keep the humans from getting any closer:

> And Yahweh Elohim said, 'The human has now become like one of us, knowing good and evil. He must not be allowed to reach out his hand and take also from the tree of life and eat, and live forever.'

This humbling of the humans is pointed up by the fact that, although *they* must first eat the fruit of a forbidden tree to gain wisdom, the talking reptile has wisdom to start with. The serpent is said to be *arum* ('shrewd'), and this is precisely the word used in the book of Proverbs to speak approvingly of the prudent (e.g. Prov. 12.16, 23; 13.16; 14.8, 15, 16; 22.3; 27.12). There are other resonances with Proverbs: in Genesis 3.6, the forbidden fruit is said to be 'desirable' (*nechmad*) for 'gaining wisdom' (*haskil*). Outside this narrative, *nechmad* occurs only in Proverbs 21.20 – to describe desirable food in the house of the wise – and *haskil* appears in Proverbs 16.23 and 21.11, with clearly positive connotations (cf. Mendenhall 1974). To fall prey to a wise reptile which 'creeps upon the earth' – as the RSV translates the phrase in Genesis 1.26 and 28 – is a cutting humiliation. While one can barely conceive of the first humans dominating the seas and the heavens, one might imagine that subduing the land animals was slightly more realistic. But Genesis 3 dashes even that notion: the one that creeps upon the earth wins out.

There are so many puzzles in the second creation story that we can presume it has passed through several re-tellings. There are traces of mythological motifs which are now opaque to the reader of the final text. The four rivers in 2.10–14, for example, have been the occasion of much scholarly speculation. The goddess Ishtar from ancient Mesopotamia was pictured holding a 'tree of life' from which four rivers flowed, and Ishtar's priestesses apparently dispensed divine favours through sacral prostitution – the *Epic of Gilgamesh* associates this cultic practice with the getting of wisdom, suggesting at one point that sexual knowledge makes a mere man 'like a god' (Gardner 1990). In the Sumerian myth *Enki and Ninhursag*, the marriage of the main characters takes place in the land of Dilmun, a garden of the gods which figures in several Mesopotamian narratives (Wallace 1985). But contrary to these ancient parallels, and to some traditional Christian interpretations of the Eden story, the final editors did not see the forbidden fruit as providing sexual knowledge, since sexuality is already presumed by Genesis 2.24: 'Therefore a man leaves his father and his mother and clings to his wife (*ishah*), and they become one flesh.'

So what kind of wisdom is dangerous and should properly have belonged to God alone? The negative light thrown on wisdom in Genesis is arguably to be seen more precisely as a critique of *royal* wisdom. There is, for example, a close verbal resonance between the second creation story and 2 Samuel 14.17, 20, where the shrewd woman of Tekoa ironically flatters king David by referring to his god-like wisdom: 'The king is like an angel of God in discerning good and evil.' The expression 'knowledge of good and evil' (Gen. 2.9, 17) is also used to characterize political wisdom in 1 Kings 3.9, where in a dream Solomon asks God for wisdom. The connections to royal material are indeed reinforced by the only other use of Eden motifs in the Hebrew Bible – Ezekiel 28, where the king of Tyre is indicted for imagining himself to possess divine wisdom (28.2). He did indeed possess wisdom, Ezekiel suggests (vv. 12, 17), but pride, violence and dishonest trade (vv. 16–18) had led to his expulsion from 'Eden, the garden of God' (v. 13).

Thus, the strongest intertextual links within the Hebrew Bible suggest that the negative view of wisdom in the Eden narrative can be explained by the same hypothesis I used to interpret the 'image of Elohim' in Genesis 1.27–8: the final editors of Genesis were covertly anti-monarchic. This reading does not preclude the possibility that the editors have used existing sources which were already anti-monarchic in tone; that may well be so. But the juxtaposition of the two creation stories has heightened the theme to the extent that every attempt at hierarchy has been de-stabilised. If the first creation story deconstructs a royal 'image of Elohim' by democratising it, the second creation story undermines any 'royal' aspirations humankind as a whole may have had by satirising the human failure to rule over even the creatures which 'creep upon the earth'. The only kind of 'rule' spoken about in Genesis 3 is the lamentable patriarchal rule of male over female (3.16), a symptom of alienation befitting the new-found royal knowledge. It is a symptom of alienation that characterises life outside the garden of Eden, and in this sense male rule is a sign of distance from God, not likeness to God.

What implications would have been drawn from the combined creation narratives in the fifth century BCE, the historical setting of the final editing? As I suggested in the Introduction, the king relevant in this period would have been the Persian king, represented by a governor. The anti-monarchic tendencies in both creation narratives can be read, therefore, as directed against the Persian king and his emissaries. Ezra is praised for his wisdom by the king (Ezra 7.25–6), but Genesis sees monarchic wisdom negatively. If there is a political allegory intended between expulsion from the Garden of Eden and events in Jerusalem in the fifth century, it is indicated by the fact that one of the rivers in Genesis 2.13 has the same name as the spring in Jerusalem, the Gihon, where Solomon was anointed king (1 Kgs. 1.33, 38; cf. 2 Chron. 32.30). Perhaps the mythological expulsion from the garden can be related concretely to the governor's powers of expropriation (Ezra 7.26; 10.8).

The wisdom of the Persian-sponsored governors dictated the divorce of foreign wives, and one can imagine the poignancy in such a context of a text which says: 'Therefore a man leaves/abandons his father and his mother and clings to his wife, and they become one flesh' (Gen. 2.4). As indicated above, this verse presents a conflict of commitments in a potentially subversive way. One can envisage also that the sending away of children with their mothers (Ezra 10.3) would have added a heavy weight to the text which reads: 'I will greatly increase your pains in childbearing; with pain you will give birth to children. Your desire will be for your husband, but he will rule over you' (Gen. 3.16). The wisdom characteristic of rulers occasions divisions not only between humankind and the land (Gen. 3.17–19) but within the family itself. Male dominance is represented as a distortion of the ideal, and aspirations to be 'like God' are seen in the second creation story to be inherently dangerous. The reader could then infer that any likeness between a 'holy seed' and God was equally problematic: as we have seen, the language of holiness is attached in Genesis 2.2–3 to the Sabbath alone, and not to procreation.

Dominance in Genesis 4–11

Having narrated the first failure to keep an explicit divine command, Genesis 4 takes up the theme of crime and punishment once again, but this time the divine expectations are not explicitly articulated. No prohibition against murder has been stated, yet we must assume that such a prohibition is part of 'the knowledge of evil' which humankind has now acquired. Cain is initially obedient to the divine vocation to work the land, which is reiterated even after the expulsion from Eden (3.23). His vocation is described in vocabulary which echoes Genesis 3: he 'serves' the land (4.3). Abel's work as a shepherd, on the other hand, is not foreseen by Yahweh Elohim. If some ancient animosity between agriculturalists and pastoralists has left its trace in the story, the final form of the text excludes the possibility that Yahweh favours the shepherd as such. At the beginning of the chapter, Cain is doing nothing other than what was divinely asked (3.23; 4.3), and in this respect his rage at not having his agricultural offering accepted by Yahweh is quite justifiable.

The reason why God prefers Abel's offering is simply not given. Attempts to demonstrate the inferiority of Cain's gift (he gives grudgingly, without purity of heart, etc.) assume that divine acceptance will always be the product of human performance. While this is often the case in biblical narratives, it is not always so. The fundamental preference for the people of Israel, for example, is not based on human performance, and Genesis 4 seems to be concerned precisely with the tension between an ungrounded divine preference and the consequences for the rest of humanity who are not so graced by God's favour.

The divine speech in 4.6–7 is, unfortunately, extremely puzzling in the Hebrew. Cain's resentment is the only unambiguous element of the text: he was angry, and his face 'fell'. The use of the word *s'et* ('dignity', 'honour', 'exaltation') in 4. 7 is unusual, and some have suggested that it refers to the 'lifting up' of Cain's downcast face: although v. 7 does not specifically mention Cain's face, one could translate Yahweh's words to Cain as: 'If you do rightly, will there not be dignity [in your face]?' The verb 'to do rightly' here (*ytb*) is related to the word 'good' (*tob*) in the phrase 'good and evil' (2.17 and 3.22), and this suggests that the knowledge contained in the forbidden fruit has been passed on to him: Cain knows what is good, and it is within his power to do it. This reading then gives this sense to 4. 7:

> at the door sin crouches,[21]
> and for you is its desire,
> but you can rule over it.

The syntax and vocabulary of lines 2–3 is almost identical to those of 3.16b, which could therefore be rendered in a strict parallel translation:

> for your husband is your desire,
> but he can rule over you.

The linguistic similarity perhaps draws attention to the fact that 'ruling' is a key theme, but 4.7 is making an entirely different point to 3.16b. The rule of male over female in 3.16b is a social distortion which arises from eating the forbidden fruit. Although the knowledge of good and evil has affected certain structural changes in the world, the narrative of Genesis 4 assumes that 'sin' (Genesis 2–3 does not use this term) is a threatening possibility that can be 'ruled' over: it can be controlled. Cain can still choose dignity, rather than sin.

The only other place in Genesis where *s'et* ('dignity', 'honour', 'exaltation') is used is in 49.3, where Jacob says to Reuben: 'You are my firstborn, my might, and the first fruits of my strength, superior in honour [*s'et*] and superior in power.' A semantic parallel such as this one between 4.7 and 49.3 would be insignificant were this parallelism not a piece of a larger puzzle in Genesis concerning genealogical superiority. A comparison between Cain and Reuben is instructive insofar as both are firstborn sons, and both therefore carry the honour of primogeniture. Perhaps this issue of honour is also hinted at in Abel's name (*hebel*), since although Eve does not explain Abel's name – as she does for Cain in 4.1, and for Seth in 4.25 – the word *hebel* has ominous overtones of 'meaninglessness', 'transience' and 'worthlessness' (e.g. in Ecclesiastes 1.14). Abel's life is indeed transient, but as a younger son he also enjoys less honour. Yahweh's exhortation to Cain in 4.7 suggests, however, that honour is to be found in doing what is right, not just in genealogical superiority.

The narrative of Genesis 4, then, seems to deconstruct in advance the highly structured patrilineal genealogies of 5.3–26 and 11.10–26. Taken sequentially, these two texts describe the descent from Adam to Abram, and they create the impression of an almost ineluctable order of primogeniture in which the only people in the world worth naming are the firstborn sons. The ordering is formulaic, so I may restrict myself to a single example: 'When Jared had lived 162 years, he fathered Enoch; after he fathered Enoch, Jared lived 800 years and he fathered sons and daughters' (5.18–19). The formula can be rendered almost mathematically:

> When a had lived x years, he fathered b; after he fathered b, a lived y years, and he fathered sons and daughters (where a and b are male personal names).

The formula suggests that the climax of a man's life is the birth of his first son, and this may be taken to represent a dominant ideology in Genesis. But the most important elements of these genealogies are to be found, as I will show, where the formula is *transgressed*. The story of Cain and Abel is the first in a number of cases – including that of

Reuben – where genealogical superiority counts for little. The fates of Cain, Ishmael, Esau and Ephraim illustrate that being the firstborn son is not sufficient ground for winning divine favour. On the contrary, divine preference is often focused otherwise than on primogeniture; and, indeed, such a representation of God would have been potentially destabilising.

Regardless, however, of the favour shown towards (the 'worthless' son) Abel's offering, Yahweh is still concerned with Cain. The elder brother is exhorted in 4.7 to do what is right, based on his prior knowledge of the difference between good and evil. The key question in 4.9, 'Am I my brother's keeper [*shomer*]?', probably has an ironic edge, since Abel was designated a keeper of sheep (*shomer* in 4.2). But Cain is sarcastically denying what he already knows: he is, indeed, expected to be his brother's 'keeper', even though he has not been explicitly told this. In short, the narrative envisages divinely sanctioned moral obligations to be operative, whether or not one enjoys the cultic favour of Yahweh.[22] In this sense, the narrative projects a moral framework that extends beyond any cultic particularism.

Although Cain fails to take up the challenge of integrity in Genesis 4, we soon learn that there is at least one person in the primeval history who does achieve righteousness, and whose integrity is 'complete': 'Noah walked with Elohim', we are told in 6.9, whereas Cain, after committing fratricide, 'went out from Yahweh's presence' (4.16). After his brother's blood cries out from the soil (*adamah*), Cain is driven from the land (*adamah*), which will no longer yield crops for him (4.10–12). This is poetic justice, not just because the killer has bloodied the land, but because Yahweh punishes Cain by taking away the work that has defined him up until this point. If he cannot 'keep' his brother, neither can he keep the land. If the first human was punished with painful toil on the land (3.17), Cain's punishment is intensified such that land will no longer yield food for him *at all*. In spite of his fears of becoming a restless wanderer, he takes up the life of the city-dweller (4.17), and his descendants are generally linked with the development of urban arts and culture, although one is said to have been a cattle nomad (4.20).

In any case, Cain's descendants do not work the land, and when we next hear of a 'man of the land [*adamah*]', it is in 9.20 when Noah plants a vineyard after the flood. In terms of characterisation, Noah is in some senses the inverse of Cain (cf. Spina 1992). The fresh relationship with the land is foreshadowed in Noah's birth speech: 'He will give us consolation in the labour and painful toil [*'itsabon*] of our hands from the land which Yahweh cursed' (5.29). This speech alludes to the consequences eating of the forbidden fruit in 3.17: 'The land is cursed because of you; through painful toil [*'itsabon*] you will eat of it.' But after the flood, Noah's vineyard also marks a connection to the land which is thematically the reversal of Cain's alienation from it. The 'keeper' of every species of bird and animal can lay claim to being a keeper of the soil as well. The righteous Noah is the ecological ideal.

Cain's descendants form a bridge to the flood narrative in that they illustrate the escalation of violence on the earth: four generations down the lineage, Lamech's life of murder and revenge is extreme (4.23–4). In 6.5 and 6.11, it is the scale of violence and corruption that becomes the reason for the flood; contemplating the rampant evil on the earth, Yahweh 'regrets' or 'repents' of having created humankind, and, indeed, 'he was pained to his heart' (6.6). The verb here for divine pain (*'atsab*) is related to the nouns used in 3.16 and 3.17: after eating the forbidden fruit, the woman was told: 'I will greatly increase your birth pains [*'itsbonek*]'; and to the man was said: 'Cursed be the earth because of you, with painful toil [*'itsabon*] will you eat of it.' Reading Genesis 3 and 6 in parallel like this shows that the consequences of evil cause pain for all three characters – Yahweh, woman and man, not to mention the serpent. When the flood arrives, God is among those who suffer, but the divine pain is a response to human violence.

The overture to the flood story is, therefore, to be found in the genealogies of 4.17–26 and 5.1–32. The succession of names in 4.17–18 is the patrilineage from Cain to Lamech that leads to the escalation of violence. The names in 4.25–6 overlap quite clearly with those in 5.3–8: the sequence of Adam–Seth–Enosh is first given in 4.25–6 but then repeated in 5.3–8. In the second case, the names are re-framed according to the formula mentioned above: when *a* lived *x* years, he fathered *b*; and after he fathered *b*, *a* lived *y* years, 'and he fathered sons and daughters'. The only deviation from this formula in 5.1–20 is where Adam's son Seth is said to be 'in his image, according to his likeness' (5.3). The vocabulary here is identical to that in the first creation story where humankind is made in the image of God (Gen. 1.26), and the phrase in 5.2, 'male and female he made them', matches 1.27. Clearly, there is an allusion to the image of God in the retelling of the genealogy, but what significance should be attached to this fact?

It seems that the genealogy in Genesis 5 is offering a construction of reality alternative to the one presented in Genesis 4. As I have said, the succession of names in 4.17–18 is the patrilineage that represents the escalation of violence: Cain–Enoch–Irad–Methushael–Lamech. The succession of names in Genesis 5, on the other hand, begins with Adam and Eve's younger son, Seth, and concludes with the sequence: Jared–Enoch–Methuselah–Lamech–Noah. Not only are the names *Enoch* and *Lamech* identical, but *Irad* and *Jared* are closely related, as are *Methushael* and *Methuselah*. It is almost as if these names are variations of a single oral tradition. Yet from the point of view of the final editors the two genealogies are dramatically different, and the crucial clues to the difference are to be found where the genealogical formula in Genesis 5 is broken, notably, in the cases of Enoch and Noah.

In addition to the formula already mentioned, Genesis 5 has one more element attached to each person named: 'altogether, *a* lived *z* years, and then he died' (this element is missing from the genealogy in 11.10–25). The only person who does not receive a death notice is Enoch, of whom it is said: 'Enoch walked with Elohim. And he was no more, for Elohim took him' (5.24). At the end of the succession of firstborn sons, Noah also breaks the formula in having three sons named, not just the firstborn. Noah's death notice – using the same formula – comes in 9.28–9, and in this sense the entire flood story, from 6.1 to 9.27, can be considered an expansion of the genealogy in Genesis 5.

Noah, we soon discover, was entirely righteous, and he also 'walked with Elohim' (6.9), just as Enoch did. From the editors' point of view, the line of violence passes from Cain to Lamech. Righteousness, on the other hand, exists only in the line descending from Seth, the younger son who is said to be the image of his father. It is in this line that we find the two figures with a significant proximity or 'likeness' to God: Enoch and Noah. Enoch is spoken of only cryptically, but Noah's integrity is explicitly said to be complete. Like Cain, he is a firstborn son, but it is not that genealogical honour which distinguishes him; it is his righteousness that marks him out. Not all patrilineages are the same: the one from Cain to Lamech is an entirely different construction from that extending from Seth to Noah. At the end of Genesis 5, then, the future of the earth is suspended between these two options.

Up until Genesis 6, the biblical narrative has made occasional use of mythological material, such as in the four rivers of Eden (2.10–14), but the flood story in Genesis 6–9 makes extensive use of ancient Mesopotamian traditions. The *Atrahasis Epic*, for example, contains a creation story in which humankind was created from clay, and made to work for the minor gods; but most strikingly the hero escapes a devastating flood in a boat filled with animals. The basic plot is therefore very similar to the biblical narrative, although there are significant differences as well: unlike the biblical concern with human integrity and righteousness, the deluge in the *Atrahasis Epic* is sent by

CREATION AND DOMINANCE

the gods to quell the human population and the noise it was making. While Genesis is reticent to give any description of the divine council, the divine mind is portrayed as univocally concerned with good, rather than evil, and with righteousness, rather than violence. The expansion of the human population is considered a blessing.

In the *Epic of Gilgamesh*, the reason for the flood is not clear, but some of the details are even closer to the Bible: the ship is to contain 'all living things' (XI: 27); after the flood, it settles on a mountain; three times birds are sent out to find dry land; a sacrifice is made; and a god promises never to forget the flood (XI: 140–69). Exactly the same sequence of events can be found in Genesis 9.1–10.17. But, once again, the similarity of the plot heightens the differences between the two accounts. Gilgamesh is a king, and we are told at the beginning of the narrative that he is one-third human and two-thirds divine. After the death of his friend Enkidu, he becomes obsessed with the possibility of immortality. The epic narrates his heroic journey to Dilmun, the garden of the gods, where he tries to discover how Utnapishtim and his wife became immortal after surviving the great flood. What he discovers is that before the deluge, and for no apparent reason, Utnapishtim was secretly forewarned by a minor god; after surviving the disaster, the high god had gone aboard the ship to grant the couple immortality – again, for no apparent reason. In the ceremony that granted the gift of immortality, the high god Enlil proclaims: 'Hitherto Utnapishtim has been but human; henceforth, Utnapishtim and his wife shall be like unto us gods' (XI: 193–4).

The curious fragment in Genesis 6.1–4, which speaks of divine–human hybrids, forms an intriguing preface to the biblical flood narrative, since, like Gilgamesh, these hybrids are 'men of renown', or 'men with a name', a mixture of humanity and divinity (6.4). Genesis 6.3 draws attention also to the issue of mortality when Yahweh says that the human is but 'flesh' and shall live only 120 years (6.3). The implication is that the divine–human hybrids are unacceptable: there has to be a clearer difference between the divine realm and the human realm. This text marks, then, the transition from the extraordinarily long lives mentioned in the genealogy of Genesis 5 to the more realistic life-spans after the flood. The people who lived before the flood are, however, not explicitly spoken of as partly divine; 6.1–4 is the fragmentary exception.

Likeness to God is a key issue both in the *Epic of Gilgamesh* and in Genesis, but in the biblical account the analogue to divinity has been defined primarily with respect to (1) the human rule over the other species of creation and (2) the knowledge of good and evil. The first

41

analogy has been subtly deconstructed by the second creation story: Genesis 2 has no concept of 'rule', and Genesis 3 sees dominance as a regrettable consequence of sin, a sign of distance from God, rather than proximity. A third analogical possibility, immortality, is briefly considered, but the way to the Tree of Life is barred. In short, the human can really be like God only by acting rightly, by ruling over sin (cf. 4.7), and this is far more important to the editors of the primeval history than are such ideologies of dominance as male superiority or primogeniture. The biblical emphases are, in this sense, without parallel in the *Epic of Gilgamesh*, in spite of the striking similarities.

Perhaps the closest thematic connection with *Gilgamesh*, however, comes after the flood, when the goddess Ishtar promises never to forget the horrors of the deluge (XI: 162–5). This comes close to the biblical covenant tradition which speaks of Elohim 'remembering' the covenant between God and 'all living creatures of every kind' (9.15–16). Admittedly, the specific sign of the biblical covenant, the bow (*qeshet*) in the clouds, does not appear in the *Epic of Gilgamesh*. But the biblical flood story is clearly a collage of mythological motifs turned to new purposes,[23] and the bow may have been derived from a number of other sources. For example, the *Enuma Elish* (VI: 84–92), mentions a bow placed in the heavens by the gods. This symbolizes a divine weapon, rather than a promise, but the Hebrew word *qeshet* ('bow'), also means a weapon elsewhere in the Hebrew Bible. The divine promise in Genesis 9 speaks of a deliberate putting aside of the deluge as a weapon of judgement (9.11). The bow is a symbol of divine memory, just as Ishtar promises to remember the consequences of the flood.

A heavy irony hangs, however, over Ishtar's promise to remember. Among the characters in the *Epic of Gilgamesh* she is perhaps the most notorious for faithlessness (Sarna 1966: 59). Early in the story, there is a somewhat comical narrative of her attempt to seduce Gilgamesh. He not only rejects her advances but provides a lengthy list of the lovers whom she has abandoned (VI: 1–79). Having been rejected, Ishtar plans her deadly retribution. Given this kind of characterisation, the reader is left wondering at the value of Ishtar's promises.

The biblical reflections after the flood, on the other hand, have about them a divine realism and authenticity consistent with the descriptions of God in earlier chapters. Even though 'the devisings of the human heart are evil from his youth', Yahweh promises never again to curse the soil or strike down all living things (8.21–2). Genesis 9 recapitulates the idea that there will never again be a universal flood (v. 11), but this time the promise is reframed in the language of covenant. There is nothing in the characterisation of God in Genesis 1–9 that would lead the reader to doubt the divine reticence to bring judgement. If anything, God has a history of mitigating punishment. 2.17 threatens immediate death as the consequence of eating the forbidden fruit, but the actual punishment amounts to the realities of everyday life: painful childbirth, painful toil, a distorted relationship between the genders, and (after Yahweh has provided proper clothing, in 3.21) exile from the Garden of Eden. In 4.10–12, Cain is driven from the land in an act of poetic justice; but then, in response to Cain's plea, Yahweh puts a mark of protection on the murderer.

After the flood, we find God making a series of compromises, but even given the divine tendency to mitigate punishment, the demand for justice is reiterated. Humankind is now permitted to eat animals, but both humans and animals will need to give an account of any blood which is shed (9.3–5). The call for the restraint of human violence is a moral principle based not upon the particularities of Israelite law, but on a broader, if not 'universalistic', foundation:

> He who sheds human blood, by humankind his blood will be shed
> for in the image of Elohim was the human made.
>
> (9.6)

The principle of 'blood for blood' is clearly designed to constrain violence, not to promote it, and it should be read against Lamech's principles of exponential violence in 4.24. All human beings share the analogy to God, and it can therefore function as the basis of human ethics as such. At the same time, there is a universalistic realism: 'the devisings of the human heart are evil from his youth' (8.21). This text suggests that there is a lowering of the divine expectation ever again to find the integrity that was found in Noah. Certainly, when Abram is set apart for divine favour in Genesis 12, no mention is made of his righteousness. (On the contrary, the second half of 12 gives an account of Abram's irrational fears and blatant self-interest, evidenced especially in 12.12–13. The first mention of Abram's righteousness comes in 15.6, long after the divine promise has been made, where his belief in Yahweh is 'credited to him as righteousness'. The issue there is Abram's trust, not his behaviour; he did not earn the promise.)

As in Genesis 1, the reference to the image of Elohim in 9.6b ostensibly reflects a basic difference between humankind and the animals: 9.2 even speaks of the 'dread and fear' (*mora'* and *chat*) which the human now inspires among all the other species,[24] and this excessive language parallels the call to 'rule' and 'subdue' the earth in Genesis 1. This time, the reiteration of the divine exhortation to 'be fruitful and increase in number' applies only to Noah and his sons (9.1, 7); ominously, the formula for procreation is not given to creatures of the sea and birds of the air, as it was in 1.22. Indeed, the language of 9.2 is almost the language of war. The 'dread' (*mora'*) felt by the animals resonates with the vocabulary used in Deuteronomy 11.23–5, a conquest tradition that fantasises about total dominance of the promised land and the dispossession of all the nations between the Mediterranean sea and the River Euphrates. Deuteronomy 11.25 has Yahweh promising the Israelites that 'the fear of you and dread of you [*mora'*] will fall on the whole land, wherever you go'. Similarly, the phrase 'into your hands they are given' – referring in Genesis 9.2 to the animals – is commonplace in conquest traditions, and refers to the subjugation of enemies (e.g. Joshua 8.7; 10.19; 24.8; Judges 3.28; 7.15; 8.3; 18.10). The overt ideology of Genesis 9.1–3, then, heightens the human dominance over animals that was expressed in 1.26–8.

Just as Genesis 1 was undermined by the second creation story, however, so the editors of Genesis 9 have structured the chapter to undercut the excessive language of the overt ideology. First, any killing of animals has to pay respect to their blood: it is not to be eaten because blood is the sign of life (9.4–5). The basic principle here is that life should not be taken thoughtlessly, and it applies to animals and humans alike. In the case of humans (9.6), a similar principle applies, except that human blood is set apart in the sense that the human is made in the image of Elohim. Genesis 9.6 is so poetically structured, however, that it may have been an existing element that the editors have placed between two texts which emphasize the unity of humankind and animals: blood is a sign of life in all living creatures (9.4–5), and the covenant theology that follows 9.6 emphasises precisely the unity of humankind and animals: Elohim's promise is made to all living creatures. Noah and his descendants are mentioned briefly in 9.9, but almost every verse that follows reiterates the concern for 'every living creature', 'all flesh' or 'the earth' (9.10–17).

We have thus begun to discern a pattern in the editing of Genesis wherein *overt ideologies of human dominance, male dominance or primogeniture are allowed to stand, but alternative perspectives are juxtaposed in such a way as to undermine the dominant ideology*. This pattern is arguably exemplified also in the next section of text, 9.18–10.32, which deals with the relationships between Noah's three sons – Shem, Ham and Japheth.

Noah's firstborn son, Shem, is destined to provide the lineage which leads to Abram (11.10–26), but before we get there the primeval history has one more contribution to make to the theme of dominance. The narrative opposition between Cain and Noah, both firstborn sons, suggests that despite all appearances to the contrary, primogeniture is less important than righteousness and integrity. Being of superior birth is not the primary issue. The crime and punishment story in 9.20–7, however, is not concerned to undermine the status of the eldest son, since it is committed by a younger son. The crime elicits a curse from Noah (9.25), just as Cain's fratricide had provoked a curse from Yahweh (4.11). Just as the curse against Cain was framed with poetic justice, so is this curse: slavery is a fitting punishment for a crime of dominance. The narrative in 9.20–4 makes clear that the perpetrator had taken advantage of his father's weakened state, and his brothers had not.

It is not clear from the narrative, however, whether Ham or Canaan committed the crime, nor exactly what the crime was. Initially it seems that Ham was at fault (9.20–4), but then Noah curses Canaan, the son of Ham, saying that he will be the slave of both his 'brothers', Shem and Japheth (vv. 25–7). The combination of traditions appears clumsy here, but it might be that the editors were intentionally putting a question mark against this curse of 'Canaan'. What, indeed, is conveyed by this label? Some sort of political allegory is evident, and perhaps the tradition in 9.26–7 dates back to a time when the Canaanites were dominated by an Israelite or a Judean monarchy. But the final editors of the Persian period were far removed from such a setting. Questions of ethnicity were being framed in new ways. Could this curse of Ham, or Canaan, simply be reinforcing the practice of ethnic stereotyping which was being promoted by the Persian governors? Or is it that the curse against Canaan is alluding to a dominant ideology that, once again, is about to be subverted?

The first clue to a deconstructive reading can be found in Genesis 9.27. This verse is inimical to any Israelite separatism, since it presents an eirenic picture of the descendants of Japheth living 'in the tents' of Shem. Exactly who these people were is not significant for my interpretation. The only descriptive category mentioned is that they were coastal peoples, which is suggestive of a connection with the Mediterranean. There is a range of theories about the identity of 'Japheth', all of which point in the opposite direction from a 'holy seed' which should not be mixed with other peoples'. In the 'Table of Nations' in Genesis 10, the descendants of Japheth (10.2–4) are manifestly separated from the descendants of Shem (10.21–31), yet Noah's blessing in 9.27 had envisaged the two lineages as happily engaged in social intercourse, if not genealogical hybridity. Only the 'sons of Ham' are problematic.

Whatever confusion hovers over the culprit in the crime against Noah, the reader is expected to see the curse of slavery as justifiable, and this suggests that the sons of Ham in 10.6–20 lie under a cloud of suspicion. Just as Cain's violence gave birth to more violence among his seed, so Ham's dominance may be reflected in some way among his descendants, including Canaan. So what is it that holds the Hamites together, including as they do Ethiopia, Egypt, Canaan, Babylon and Assyria? Stretching from Africa to Mesopotamia, they are radically diverse in geographical location and language group. Several commentators (e.g. Obed 1986) have rightly suggested that the Table of Nations in Genesis 10 is organized around socio-political, rather than ethnic, considerations. A unifying principle among the Hamites is urbanism, and this feature is reflected especially in the mythical Nimrod, son of Cush (or Ethiopia), who somehow founds the urban centres both of Babylon and of Assyria. Nimrod is an empire builder, indeed the prototype of empire builders. And the implicit suggestion from the editors of Genesis is that empire builders – like Ham – are guilty of crimes of dominance.

More than that, empire builders are guilty of improper ambition; the Tower of Babel episode in Genesis 11 is designed to show this, as we will see. Whatever the historical origins of this tower, the final editors have provided a link between Nimrod in Genesis 10 and the tower in 11: Nimrod's cities are located in Shinar (10.10), precisely the location of the tower project (11.2). The builders with grand designs want to build a city (11.4), just as Nimrod did; they are made of the same stuff as the empire builder. Those who built the Tower of Babel, we infer, were sons of Ham, even though Genesis 11 does not identify them as such.

Genesis 10 and 11 can hardly be a compositional unity, I must note in passing, since 11.1 begins by saying that 'all the earth had one language and the same speech', when the reality of linguistic diversity has already been asserted three times (10.5, 20, 31); indeed, the implication of this refrain is that there were different languages within each genealogical branch of the Table of Nations. Even the sons of Shem are envisaged as variegated in their 'clans and tongues, in their lands and nations' (10.31). Genesis 10 envisages the scattering of the peoples as occurring without any specific divine intervention, whereas 11 provides a watershed incident. As in the case of the juxtaposition of the two creation stories, the chronologies of chapters 10 and 11 do not quite mesh. Confronted with such problems, historicist scholarship has tended to isolate the constituent elements and treat them separately, but my interpretative interest is in the intentional hybridity of the final form.

Not only do the tower builders of Shinar attract the suspicion of being sons of Ham, but they use vocabulary that associates them with the divine–human miscegenation of Genesis 6. The purpose of the city and the tower is to make 'a name' (*shem*) for the builders, so that they would not be 'scattered over the face of all the earth' (11.4). The divine–human hybrids in 6.4 were also 'men of renown' or 'men with a name' (*shem*), and thus the description in 11.4 of a tower 'in the heavens' may well imply an improper quest for divine attributes. But the concomitant fear of dispersion can, at the same time, be read as a failure to fulfil the divine exhortation to fill the earth (Sarna 1966: 63–77). More generally, this fear can be explicated as a fear of linguistic and ethnic diversity (Anderson 1994: 173–8). Yahweh has grave doubts about homogeneity and forcibly makes the tower builders confront their fears: 'Yahweh scattered them from there over all the earth' (11.6–8). The intervention re-affirms the first vocation to fill the earth, and in this sense the ending of the Tower of Babel narrative does not amount to punishment; it is an affirmation of diversity.

This story would have had a particular relevance for the Persian period, in which we find the quest for an homogenous 'holy seed'. Yahweh, the editors are saying, desires diversity rather than homogeneity. The 'sons of Japheth' can dwell happily, for example, in the tents of Shem. The quest for genealogical superiority is mistaken. The only relevant likeness to God is found in righteousness, and in avoiding crimes of dominance. But at the same time, divine favour resists any simple explanation.

This last point is evidenced, once again, in the transition from the end of Genesis 11 to 12. As was the case at the end of the formulaic genealogy of Genesis 5, the last person in the sequence has three sons named, not just one (11.26; cf. 5.32). The account of Terah at the end of 11 introduces two issues that will be important in the following chapters, namely, Lot's relationship to Abram and Sarai's childlessness. The narrative also points out, however, that it was Terah's initiative to leave Ur of the Chaldeans 'to go towards the land of Canaan' (11.31). Ironically, this draws attention to the fact that Abram's journey to Canaan was not his own initiative; it was his father's. Thus, when we hear in 12.4 that Abram set out from Haran after receiving the divine command of 12.1 ('Leave your country, your people . . . '), his father had *already* taken him from his country of origin. Unlike Noah, Abram has no distinguishing marks of righteousness, and we are deprived even of the possibility of reading the journey to Canaan simply as a mark of obedience to Yahweh's command. The Persian editors have once again subtly contested the notion of the 'holy seed':

without any marks of integrity or holiness, Abram becomes the recipient of ungrounded divine preference. If he separated himself from the 'Chaldeans',[25] this was not – as surface appearance suggests in Genesis 12 – simply the result of divine command. It was because his father Terah had taken the initiative. This will make it all the more important for the careful reader to examine the intertextual nuances of the promises to Abram.

2

GENESIS 12–25

The making of nations

The promises to Abram in 12.1–3 belong to a series of divine promises, spread over several chapters, which mutate slightly with each reiteration. This first text, 12.1–3, connects to the previous chapters especially through the use of the key word 'name', *shem*. Yahweh promises Abram to 'make your name great' (12.2), taking up vocabulary from the Tower of Babel narrative, as well as from the story of the divine–human hybrids in 6.1–4: the tower builders wanted to make a name (*shem*) for themselves, so that they would not be scattered over the earth (11.4), and the hybrids were 'men of renown', or 'men with a name' (*shem* in 6.4). Unlike the heroes of Genesis 6 who could lay claim to greatness through their admixture of divinity, and unlike the tower builders who could lay claim to greatness through extraordinary achievements, Abram appears on the scene without any marks of distinction. He is not said to be righteous, nor is he said to be holy. Perhaps he carries the honour of being the oldest son of Terah (if we can presume from 11.26 that the first son listed is the eldest), but the editors of Genesis 1–11 have subtly rendered this an ambiguous honour, as I have shown. In Genesis 12.2–3, there are only two divine gifts which are going to make Abram's name: he will become 'a great nation' (*goy*), and he will be a channel of blessing. Like Yahweh's preference for Abel's offering, this divine favour is quite ungrounded. Genesis 12.1–2 effectively reverses the logic of the tower builders in Genesis 11: they wanted to make a name for themselves in one place, so that they would not be scattered over the earth (11.4), but Abram must first leave his birthplace before his name can become great.

The first words spoken to Abram are not a promise, but actually a divine command: 'Go from your land, your kin and your father's house to the land that I will show you' (12.1). The kinship terminology here would have been highly significant in the context of the Persian period, given the politics of identity at issue. 'Father's house' (*bet ab*) does not refer to a building, but rather to a patriarchal 'household'; this is the normal designation in the Hebrew Bible for an extended family, headed by the senior male. The *bet ab* was the smallest unit of kinship, while the tribe was apparently the largest. A 'nation' (*goy*) might unify a number of tribes, but *goy* is probably not to be thought of as a kinship term. Between the layers of the *bet ab* and the tribe was a network of extended families called the *mishpachah*, a term normally translated as 'clan' (the translation is sometimes disputed: according to anthropologists, most clans are exogamous, but this characteristic does not apply to the Israelite *mishpachah*). This middle unit of kinship is mentioned in 12.3 when Yahweh promises that 'all the clans of the earth' will be blessed through Abram. Genesis 12 does not resolve the conceptual puzzle of how a single nation can bless all the clans of the earth, but the puzzle is resolved to a limited extent in some of the subsequent divine promises which speak of Abram becoming the father of many nations, not just a single nation, as in 12.2.

Before his name becomes so distinguished, as we have noted, he must first leave his own birthplace. What is intriguing about 12.1, however, is that it deviates from the normal kinship terminology: rather than instructing Abram to leave 'your land, your *mishpachah* and your father's house', the text has another term instead of *mishpachah*: *moledet*. This latter word is relatively uncommon, but it appears again, significantly, in the narrative of Genesis 24 where Abraham instructs a servant to go back 'to my land and my kin (*moledet*)' to find a wife for Abraham and Sarah's son Isaac (24.4).[26] The servant returns to Mesopotamia and procures Rebekah, the grand-daughter of Abraham's brother Nahor. In effect, the story in Genesis 24 contravenes the divine command to Abram in 12.1 to forsake his old network of kinship. Using the apparently insignificant term *moledet*, the editors have linked the two chapters and planted a question in 12.1 about the legitimacy of Isaac's endogamous marriage to Rebekah. Nowhere in the wooing of Rebekah in Genesis 24 do we find that the marriage was God's initiative; in the detailed analysis below, it can be seen that all references to Yahweh are in the mouth of the characters, not the narrator. The editors have structured 12.1 so that it quietly undermines the ideology of endogamy in 24.

With the promise of blessing in hand, Abram sets out from Haran with his wife and nephew (12.4–5). Sarai and Lot have already been introduced in 11.29–31, since they belonged to Abram's 'father's house' when Terah moved from 'Ur of the Chaldeans'. Thus, at the beginning of 12, Abram has already left the land of his birth and is living in Haran. When Abram reaches Canaan, he receives a second promise, which this time directly mentions his 'seed' (12.7). By reserving this vocabulary for the second promise, the editors have taken the emphasis off the theme of seed, highlighting the promise of nationhood first. And the foundation of nationhood is apparently constituted by exogamy, not endogamy, since Abram was called to leave his kinship group, not to remain within it. This point of origin could be considered parabolic: the solidarity of nationhood stretches beyond the normal bounds of kinship. Once again, the emphasis of the text is subtly different from the ideology of 'holy seed'.

The divine promise in 12.6–7 is given in Shechem at 'the terebinth of Moreh', or possibly, 'the terebinth of instruction'. Unlike 12.1–3, this promise explicitly mentions both seed and land, and v. 6 blithely mentions that 'the Canaanite was then in the land'. The terebinth is mentioned as if it was already known to the audience, but, more importantly, commentators have long associated this particular tree with Canaanite religion (cf. the condemnation in Hos. 4.13 and Deut. 16.21 of worship associated with trees). The narrative is doubly ironic since this land promise is delivered in the very territory which is to be possessed by Abram's seed, at a site that was probably sacred to the original owners of the land. The narrator refrains from commenting on any potential conflict of interest between Abram's progeny and the prior inhabitants.

There is no hint in Genesis of the ideology of dispossession that governs the books of Deuteronomy and Joshua. On the contrary, Abram builds an altar to Yahweh in the same area as the sacred tree (12.7), and this is just the first of many cases where the religious practices of the Israelite ancestors flout the laws of Deuteronomy without so much as a cautionary remark from the editors. Deuteronomy 16.21 prohibits the juxtaposition of trees and altars, yet Abram builds an altar beside terebinths both here and in 13.18. Deuteronomy is concerned more specifically with the Canaanite worship of the goddess Asherah, but the cultic significance of trees is nevertheless relatively clear in Genesis, and in the narrative these trees are rendered compatible with the worship of Yahweh. The eirenic tone stands in stark contrast to the ideology of separation, both in the book of Deuteronomy and in the Persian period.

As if to reinforce Abram's lack of distinctiveness, the divine promises are immediately followed by a narrative illustrating his blatant self-interest. Framed by notes on a journey to Egypt (12.8–9 mirrors the return journey in 13.3–4), the second half of Genesis 12 contains a basic plot which is almost conventional: this is the first of three occasions in the book where we find an ancestor pondering the beauty of his wife, fearing death at the hands of strangers who might want to acquire her, and so resolving to pass her off as his sister. Abram adopts this strategy twice (12.10–20 and chapter 20) and Isaac once (26.1–12). Each telling of the plot is marked by peculiarities, however, and in this case the story is told in such a remarkable way that it almost inverts the exodus narrative. 12.10–20 is the only version that sets the events in Egypt and has the Pharaoh as the foreign protagonist. The oppressor, however, is clearly Abram, who imagines that his wife Sarai is expendable. Nevertheless, Yahweh afflicts the Pharaoh and his household with plagues, just as in the exodus story, and this is the only time that plagues are the means by which the foreign potentate comes to discover the wife–sister ruse. Sarai is released, and Abram then leaves Egypt with notable wealth (12.16; 13.2), just as the Israelites did when they escaped (Exod. 12.36, 38; cf. Gen. 15.14). He leaves Egypt wealthier, rather than wiser, since he expresses the same irrational fear of death in Genesis 20, and once again he imagines that Sarai is expendable.

Given the sending away of wives recommended in the Persian period, one wonders whether the editors of Genesis have repeated this plot in order to explore the motives for such actions. The narrator is clear about Abram's motives in the first story: irrational fear and self-interest (12.12–14). The second wife–sister episode expands the motives even more strikingly: Abraham imagines that 'there is surely no fear of Elohim in this place' (20.11), and the patriarch has to be taught that even foreigners receive divine revelation. No version of the story is a simple allegory of events contemporary with the editors, but there are nevertheless thematic links which may be inferred. Read in parallel, the two wife–sister episodes in Genesis 12 and 20 indicate that the fear of foreigners is groundless.

The foreign protagonist in the second story, Abimelech, is not only visited by God in a dream, but Elohim agrees with the king's self-defence that he was 'pure in heart' when he took Sarah (20: 5–6). The Hebrew for 'pure' here is *tam*, a word which is related to *tamim*, used in Genesis 6.9 to describe Noah's integrity. Noah is also said to be 'righteous' (*tsadiq*), a quality the king of Gerar lays claim to in 20.4: 'Lord, will you kill a nation even if righteous?'[27] Given Abimelech's innocence, a reader would be justified in finding the subversive implication in Genesis 20 that foreigners may, in some ways, have greater integrity before God than does Abraham. Even when Abraham protests in 20.12 that Sarah really is his sister, 'the daughter of my father though not of my mother', an educated Persian audience would have known that such a marriage was unlawful according to Leviticus

(18.9, 11; 20.17) and Deuteronomy (27.22). Not only is Abraham quite unjustified in his motives for giving up his wife, but his endogamy is effectively parodied as incestuous.

This unflattering portrait of Abraham's character is an important clue to how we should read the chapters concerned with Lot, especially 13–14 and 19. Genesis 13 deals with the separation of Abram and his nephew, and it has often been presumed that Lot's choice of living space on the lush plains reflects his greed, while the gracious and modest Abraham takes the hill country left over. But 12.13 has already revealed Abram's self-interest, and the narrative in 13.1–4 of the journey up from Egypt continues this theme: the text emphasises Abram's wealth, mentioning also silver and gold (13.3) even though 11.16 had described his possessions in terms only of flocks, herds and slaves. The reference to silver and gold may constitute a subtle allusion to wealth taken from the Egyptians by the exodus group (Exod. 12.35), but clearly we cannot configure Abram as a man committed to a Spartan lifestyle. He is a man of substance, and the only tension between his household and Lot's is occasioned by the accumulation of wealth (13.5–7). If there was a parting of the ways, chapter 13 assures us, it was purely on practical grounds, not theological ones. The fact that Lot locates himself ominously close to Sodom does not necessarily reflect a character flaw; it simply sets the scene for later events, in Genesis 19, foreshadowed already by 13.10 where the narrator mentions the destruction of Sodom and Gomorrah.

It does seem that Lot is quietly excluded from the divine promise concerning Abram's seed in 13.14–17, reiterated this time to emphasise the innumerable quantity of Abram's descendants and not just their possession of the land. One might want to put the case that Abram's choice of the highlands represents a separation from the unrighteous cities of the plain, and therefore the divine promise is implicitly grounded on his holy separatism. But such a reading is unlikely, especially if interpretation is focused on the final editing. We are told in 13.18 – ostensibly without further clarification – that after receiving the divine promise Abram moved to Hebron and built an altar to Yahweh by the terebinths of Mamre. This narrative forms a parallel with 12.6–7, where the altar is built in the vicinity of a sacred tree, but there is a yet more relevant connection with 14.13: there we are told that Abram was living 'at the terebinths of Mamre the Amorite, kinsman of Eshcol and Aner, who were Abram's confederates'. Whether or not this is an editorial addition to earlier tradition, as has been suggested, its relevance in the Persian period is manifest: far from Abram's living space being an indicator of separatism, the editors have made it clear that he was an ally of certain Amorites. If Abram's seed is considered to be holier than Lot's, it cannot be because Abram eschewed social intercourse with the prior occupants of Canaan. Moreover, this association with Amorites provides a rationale for the events in Genesis 14.

The traditions in chapter 14, regarding a Canaanite rebellion against their imperial overlord, do not constitute a flowing narrative, but we are focused here on the implications of the present shape of the text, regardless of any stylistic imperfections or historical implausibility (cf. Westermann 1985: 194). Three of the Canaanite kings mentioned in 14.2–4 come from cities already connected with Lot in 13.10: Sodom, Gomorrah and Zoar. It comes as no surprise, then, that Lot should be implicated in the Canaanite rebellion. Genesis 14.4 indicates that the Canaanites had been subject to only one of the four Mesopotamian kings listed in v. 1, but the narrative implies that the oppressors of the far north-east have banded together to re-assert the rights of imperial rule. They sweep down the entire length of the country east of the Jordan river and then swing back to engage the Canaanite kings in the 'Valley of Siddim', apparently a valley subsequently flooded by the Dead Sea (14.3). The wealth of Sodom and Gomorrah is carried off, along with Lot and his possessions.

When Abram enters this conflict, it is on the grounds of his kinship with Lot (14.14). Thus, the solidarity of kinship is maintained even after the divine promise of 13.14–17 apparently excluded Lot. As in the case of Cain and Abel, the editors are concerned with the implications for those left outside the focus of divine favour. In this case, however, the question at issue is how those who receive ungrounded divine attention (Abram) should behave towards those who, ostensibly at least, do not receive it (Lot). Not only does Abram act on Lot's behalf, he acts in concert with others who are entirely outside his network of kinship, a feature of Genesis 14 which is sometimes overlooked. A significant role is played by Abram's Amorite confederates – Mamre, Eshcol and Aner (14.13 and 24) – and although they also may have had relatives affected by the imperialist incursion (v. 7) the editors have left us with the impression that it is primarily the Amorites' alliance with Abram that is the source of their commitment to the rescue operation. This alliance undermines any suggestion of the patriarch's separatism. In the context of the Persian period, readers may well have been struck by the fact that Abram stands with the peoples of the land against the imperialist invaders from Mesopotamia.

Abram's relationship with the Sodomites is, however, more complex than the case of the Amorites. In his dialogue with the king of Sodom in 14.21–4, the patriarch insists that he himself will take no share of the booty, but his Amorite confederates should have their share. Given that Abram has accepted ill-gotten gains from the Egyptians in chapter 13, one wonders at the motives for this self-denial. Some commentators have suggested that Abram wishes to distance himself from the injustice of the Sodomites, mentioned in 13.13, but from a narratological point of view it is important to notice that the information regarding the Sodomites in 13.13 has been conveyed by the narrator only to the audience: it is not at all clear that Abram is in possession of this information. Indeed, his defence of Sodom in Genesis 18 suggests that he does not know the scale of wrongdoing in the city.

One of the most striking features of chapter 14 is the language used of God when Abram says to the king of Sodom, 'I have raised my hand to Yahweh, El Elyon, maker of heaven and earth, and have taken an oath . . . ' (14.22). The narrative flow of this section of the chapter has been somewhat disrupted by the appearance of Melchizedek, king of Salem, in 14.18–20; the conversation with the king of Sodom begins in v. 17 and resumes in v. 21, and that may have been the original sequence of the narrative. But if so, the significance of the divine names in v. 22 would not have been highlighted in the way that they are now. Melchizedek is described as priest of El Elyon, and he blesses Abram in the name of El Elyon. Even though the king of Salem has played no role at all in the preceding story, he supplies the crucial divine name that Abram takes up in v. 22. We know from ancient sources other than the Bible that the divine name 'El' and the epithet 'Elyon' derive from Canaanite religion (cf. Smith 1990: 21–2), yet Abram has unhesitatingly linked them with the specifically Israelite divine name *Yahweh*.

Abram's actions might be taken as a kind of political allegory for later events since, although Melchizedek's city is here called Salem, Psalm 76.2 identifies Salem with Zion, i.e. Jerusalem. Genesis 14.18–20 thereby provides the only link between the Israelite ancestors and the all-important capital of the Davidic dynasty. But if we are to read the narrative within the context of the book of Genesis itself, Melchizedek provides the first link to the promise of blessing in 12.2–3: according to the logic of the first divine promise, whoever blesses Abram will themselves be blessed. Not only does 14.18–20 make Melchizedek the first candidate for this reciprocal blessing, but the narrative makes explicit that the priest–king from Salem blesses Abram in the name of a Canaanite deity. The mutuality obtaining between Melchizedek and Abram takes place regardless of any religious differences.

The *final* form of Genesis 14, however, has Abram replying in v. 22 not to Melchizedek but to the king of Sodom. The patriarch is thereby appropriating the language of Canaanite religion, even in a context where the narrator has warned the reader (in 13.13) of Sodom's injustice. If there is any reticence on Abram's part towards Sodom, it is not motivated by a general ideology of separatism: the roles of Melchizedek and the Amorite allies speak decisively against such a reading. Any question about Sodom is not likely to be focused on matters of religion or ethnicity. It may be that conventions of politeness would be transgressed if Abram were to accept the generous offer from the king of Sodom in v. 21: 'Give me the persons, but take the property for yourself.' Abram does not want to be indebted, and so he accepts only the portion of the booty that is for his Amorite friends (v. 24), presumably returning to the Sodomites the rest of the property that was theirs in the first place. In any case, the editors have represented Abram as scrupulously fair towards the Sodomites, perhaps because his nephew Lot lived in their vicinity.

The next chapter reiterates the divine promises to Abram with a number of important permutations. In spite of the fidelity expressed towards Lot in Genesis 14, the promise in 15.4 stresses that Abram's heir will come from his own body. Any ambiguity about Lot's exclusion in 13.14–17 is now resolved: in 15.2–3 Abram names a member of his own household as the potential heir, Eliezer of Damascus not Lot, and this is precisely the source of Abram's complaint to Yahweh: 'Look, you have given me no seed.' Chapter 15 provides the first instances of the patriarch expressing doubts about the divine promises, and in spite of the use of prophetic-sounding formulae in 15.1 and 4 ('The word of Yahweh came to Abram in a vision'; 'Then the word of Yahweh came to him') the narrative is more of a spirited dialogue than it is a collection of oracles. Both before and after the reference in 15.6 to Abram's trust in Yahweh we find arguments with God: the patriarch complains about his lack of descendants (v. 3), and he questions how he can know that his seed will inherit the land (v. 8). If the mysterious covenant ceremony in 15.9–21 is supposed to answer Abram's rational doubts, then it is perhaps relevant to take note of his laughter in 17.17–18, where the very thought of having a child produces only amusement in the aged patriarch. It seems that Abram's trust in God is characterised neither by extraordinary righteousness, nor by pious acquiescence. His is not a faith that allows incongruity to pass without comment. Nevertheless, this audacious faith is 'attributed to him as righteousness' (15.6).

The editors have planted at least two other incongruities in Genesis 15 upon which Abram does not comment. Within the covenant ceremony in his dream, the patriarch is told that his descendants will return to the promised land only after four generations, 'for the iniquity of the Amorites is not yet complete' (15.16). This peculiar rationale for delaying the fulfilment of the divine promises appears nowhere else in Genesis, and perhaps its nearest parallel is actually in Deuteronomy 9.4, where the wickedness of the indigenous nations justifies dispossessing them of their land. Given that it was precisely Amorites who were Abram's closest allies in Genesis 14, and not the other groups of people mentioned in 15.19–21, the final editors have provoked a puzzle about the exact nature of this Amorite guilt. Moreover, 15.18 has so inflated the extent of the promised land ('from the river of Egypt to the great river, the Euphrates') that questions would surely have arisen in the minds of an astute audience in the Persian period: there never was a time when Israel dominated all the territory from the Nile to the Euphrates, and the formulation of this divine promise is so extreme that one begins to wonder at the editors' motives. While many commentators have found an appropriate comparison with the extent of Solomon's kingdom described in 1 Kings 4.21, the wording there has Solomon's territory extending to 'the border (*gevul*) of Egypt', not 'the river (*nahar*) of Egypt'. The difference in Genesis 15.18 is a subtle one, but it stretches the bounds of credulity just one step too far for those who are not blinded by ideological self-importance.

It seems to me that 15.7–21 has the marks of a dominant ideology that, at first glance, is being allowed to stand, but which on closer inspection reveals fissures cracked open by the surrounding narratives. Abram's dealings with the Amorites and with the king of Salem are indicators of a much broader pattern wherein the ancestral religion embodies an eirenic inclusivism rather than an ideology of dispossession. Just as the human dominance envisaged by Genesis 1 is undermined by Genesis 2–3, and the primogeniture of Genesis 5 undercut by the preceding chapter, so also the occasional expressions of ethnic separatism in Genesis are deconstructed by a broader pattern of intertextual subtleties. The vague allusions to the ideology of dispossession in chapter 15 are elsewhere ignored, and the divine promises are often developed in ways consistent with compromise and inclusivism (cf. Moberly 1992: 79–104; Habel 1995: 115–33).

However, as postcolonial theory would lead us to expect, stories of dissent can rarely be turned into tales of pure, egalitarian, rebel consciousness; more often than not, we have to deal with the ambiguities of solidarity and betrayal (Guha 1983:39–40; Bhabha

1994: 187). Genesis 16 is marked by just such ambiguities. Having been the victim of Abram's blatant self-interest in 12, Sarai exhibits her own form of self-interest in 16.1–2: she is childless and wants to be 'built up' through her Egyptian slave, Hagar – presumably one of the slaves whom Abram acquired in Egypt on Sarai's account (12.16). Abram readily complies with the suggestion, perhaps thinking that Hagar will be the conduit for the divine promise recorded in 15.4; the fruit of such a union would be seed from his own body. However, he noticeably fails to resist Sarai's complaints when the plan turns sour and she claims – with an economical grasp on the truth – that it is all Abram's fault (16.5). Sarai had apparently miscalculated the implications of social credit: the making of a child was giving status to Hagar in a way that was starting to counter-balance her standing as a slave. Sarai was determined that no stigma of childlessness was going to undermine her own superiority, so she takes her complaint to the man of the house, saying of her slave Hagar that 'when she saw that she had conceived, I became slight in her eyes'. In spite of the possibility that the child is the fruit of the divine promise, Abram simply replies, 'Do to her what is good in *your* eyes.' What is good in Sarai's eyes is, according to 16.6, to make her slave suffer (*'anah*).

Hagar then flees from her mistress, and her cry is heard by Yahweh as she sits in despair by a well in the desert. Yahweh responds by giving the slave her own promise of uncountable seed (16.10) and says to her, 'I have heard your *suffering*' (16.11). The noun translated as 'suffering' in 16.11 (*'aniy*) is related to the verb *'anah* which, as indicated, is used in 16.6 to describe Hagar's mistreatment under Sarah, but this verb is used also in reference to the harsh treatment to be inflicted on Abram's descendants (15.13). In effect, the choice of vocabulary links Hagar's experience with the experience of the exodus generation. The wording in 16.11 resonates especially with a divine speech in Exodus 3.7, where Yahweh says: 'I have indeed seen the *suffering* (*'aniy*) of my people who are in Egypt, and their cry I have heard.' Thus, Yahweh hears both the voice of Hagar, the Epytian slave, and the voice of the slaves under Pharaoh. In effect, the inversion of the exodus story that began with the first wife–sister episode in 12.10–20 is continued in the Hagar story in chapter 16. The oppressors are now both Abram and Sarai, and the victim is no longer Sarai but an Egyptian woman.

While we are told in Genesis 12.8 and 13.4 that Abram 'called on the name of Yahweh', Hagar goes one audacious step further in 16.13: she 'called the name of Yahweh "El Roi"', meaning perhaps 'God of seeing'. Her explanation of this divine re-naming is unfortunately preserved in very obscure Hebrew, and some commentators have suggested reconstructing the text in line with Moses' experience of seeing Yahweh in Exodus 33.17–23. The narrator, however, provides another explanation in Genesis 16.14: 'Therefore the well was called "The Well of the Living One who sees me".' This turns the emphasis away from Hagar's seeing God to God's seeing Hagar. The narrator's interpretation seems to provide the grounds for Hagar to return to the mistress who does 'what is good in her eyes'; whatever Sarai's construction of the good, El Roi sees things differently.

The question of 'point of view' is one of the crucial factors in the interpretation of Genesis 16. While the malice of Sarai and the indifference of Abram seem relatively clear, the perspective of the narrator is not so evident. And as we observed in the transition from the first creation story to the second one, the view of the editors cannot simply be identified with that of the narrators; the voice of the narrator within the context of a dominant ideology may be subtly undermined by the narrator's voice in another text.

In Genesis 16.8–9, the narrator represents the divine voice as initially breath-takingly oppressive: the woman is addressed as 'Hagar, slave of Sarai', ironically reminding her of her social status even after she has fled. But, in terms of narratology, the very fact that a woman is addressed by the divine makes her unique within the patriarchal traditions. Certainly, Hagar is not given a single word of direct speech when her concubinage, and its consequences, are negotiated between Sarai and Abram in 16.1–6. As in the case of Genesis 1, the dominant ideology is stated first: the *status quo* is ostensibly re-instated when the messenger of Yahweh instructs Hagar to 'return to your mistress, and suffer at her hand' (16.9), recalling Abram's dismissive comment to Sarai in v. 6: 'Your slave is in your hand; do to her what is good in your eyes.' But then that dominant ideology is undermined by what happens next: Hagar receives Abram's promise of uncountable seed, she is instructed to name her child *Ishmael* (which means 'El hears'), and she names Yahweh as El who 'sees', implicitly contesting the way the world is viewed through Sarai's eyes.[28]

The narrator does not even comment on Hagar's return. We simply hear that Ishmael is born 'to Abram' (Sarai's desire to be 'built up' is not mentioned), and it is Abram who names his son, not Hagar. Once again, in 16.15, the narrator speaks as if it is the male head of the household whose power is supreme. The secret reality is that the naming of Ishmael was earlier transacted between God and the slave-woman, and the name reminds her that El hears her suffering.

After the birth of Ishmael, Abram's attitude seems to change: when Sarah pushes the patriarch to drive Hagar away in Genesis 21 he is no longer indifferent. Sarah's intentions seem 'evil in his eyes because of his son' (21.11). Unfortunately, there is no evidence in the narrative that this change of heart has anything to do with a new-found respect for his concubine. In fact, no conversation is ever recorded between Abram and Hagar, and the focus of attention after Hagar returns in chapter 16 is precisely her son, or rather, as indicated by the wording of 21.11, 'his son'. Abram's concern with Ishmael is expressed already in Genesis 17, where the patriarch's response to the reiterated divine promises is to put forward the practical suggestion that the divine favour might pass through Ishmael and not through a son who is, as yet, only a figment of Elohim's imagination (17.17–18). The idea that Abram and Sarai would have a son in their old age is simply a source of mirth; the patriarch falls down laughing at the very thought of it (17.17).

The theme of laughter becomes, indeed, the connecting thread through the next few chapters, weaving its way even into the final expulsion of Hagar in Genesis 21. Abram's extroverted hilarity in 17.17 is followed Sarah's inward laughter in 18.12, and the theme is reinforced in 18.15 where Sarah (their names change to 'Abraham' and 'Sarah' in chapter 17) denies her suppressed amusement. The repetitions draw attention to the verb 'to laugh', which then forms the basis of the name *Isaac (yitzchaq)* in 21.3: *yitzchaq* means 'he laughs', and hence Isaac's name recalls for both his parents the incongruity of his birth. Isaac is the incarnation of divine humour – childbirth at an impossibly old age – and Sarah's meditation in 21.6–7 elaborates the theme: 'Laughter has Elohim made for me; whoever hears will laugh at me.'

This speech is followed, in 21.8–9, by tragic echoes of the past: the next person who laughs is actually the very one who was earlier named 'El hears': Ishmael. The Yahweh who heard both Hagar's suffering in 16.11 and Sarah's inward laughter in 18.12–15 has been the ultimate source of both of Abraham's sons, Ishmael and Isaac, yet the divine connection is hidden from Sarah's eyes. The sight of Ishmael 'laughing' provokes her to assert in 21.9–10 that Hagar's son will not share the inheritance of her son Isaac. Some translations have Ishmael 'mocking' in 21.9, rather than 'laughing', but not only is this negative connotation an unnecessary imposition on the Hebrew, but it obscures the verbal connection between the catalyst for Sarah's malice – Ishmael's laughter – and Isaac, the name of her own son. Even though, incongruously, she has been blessed with a son in her old age, it seems that she still can't take a joke.

Unlike the parallel events in Genesis 16, when Sarai takes her concerns to Abram, this time the presenting issue is not Hagar's lack of respect, but purely a question of inheritance. Once again, it is worth pausing here to reflect on the possible connections between this story and divorces of foreign women prescribed by the imperial governors of the Persian period. As already indicated above, Kenneth Hoglund's work on Ezra and Nehemiah suggests that such a prescription would have clarified the administration of property, since land tenure based on purity of birth could exclude competing land claims, i.e. what appears on the surface as a theological issue actually accords well with issues of social control. The property claims of those who returned from Babylon, for example, may well have been made on the basis of genealogical connections demonstrating prior ownership, and these claims would inevitably have come into conflict with those who had never gone into exile and who are represented, moreover, as having inter-married with the 'people of the lands' (Ezra 9.1). If Sarah's complaint to Abraham in Genesis 21.9–10 can be read as in some sense a political allegory of these events, then it is noticeable that the narrator has allowed Sarah's speech to render the driving away of a foreign woman in purely economic terms. There is no theological veneer to be found. Hagar and Ishmael's fate is determined solely by the question of inheritance. Interpreted in this way, the story is not primarily about Sarah as a vindictive woman; it is more generally about the politics of dispossession. Hagar's fate stands for the dispossession of many others who have inter-married, and if she is to be taken as exemplary then the name of her son indicates divine concern with all such suffering. But before I examine the question of the editors' intentions in chapter 21, there is need first to take account of more of the material in Genesis 17–20.

Genesis 17 re-iterates the divine promises in the language of *covenant*. Although this word was first used in a patriarchal promise in 15.18 (cf. 9.8–17), there are several important differences between chapters 15 and 17. The first difference is to be found in the divine names. The narrator opens 17 speaking of 'Yahweh', as was the case in 15, but the divine speech to Abram in v. 1 has a different self-designation: 'Yahweh appeared to Abram and said to him, "I am El Shaddai".' In other words, the name *Yahweh* is not actually revealed to the patriarch at this point; the narrator reveals it only to the reader.

The meaning of the name *El Shaddai* is disputed, but it is clearly associated with the Canaanite divine name 'El', used previously in the combinations 'El Elyon' (14.18–22) and 'El Roi' (16.13). Here, however, unlike the latter case, the narrator does not provide an interpretation of 'Shaddai'. It seems sufficient to observe that this is a trace of an archaic epithet, the origins of which have been lost.

Commentators routinely draw attention to the parallel text in Exodus 6.2–3 which even denies that the name 'Yahweh' was known in this early period:

> Elohim spoke to Moses, and he said to him, 'I am Yahweh. I appeared to Abraham, to Isaac and to Jacob as El Shaddai, but by my name Yahweh I did not make myself known to them.'

Accordingly, Genesis 17 belongs to the traditions of Genesis which scrupulously keep the specifically Israelite divine name in the background (contrary to 12.8; 13.4; cf. 4.26). 'Yahweh' here appears only in v. 1, in the narrator's discourse. Elsewhere in 17, the narrator speaks of 'Elohim'. It seems that the editors of Genesis may have introduced 'Yahweh' into 17.1 simply to provide a link with the immediately preceding narrative: 16.13 provides a parallel case where the narrator speaks of Yahweh whereas the main character, Hagar, knows God by another name, El Roi. In short, the editors have used the name Yahweh to identify the God of Hagar with the God of Abram, in spite of the fact that this divine identity is not clear to the characters in the story. Divine reality, one could say, exceeds nominal constructions.

Another significant feature of 17.1 is that this is the first occasion on which Abram is exhorted to be 'blameless' (*tamim*, also used in Gen. 6.9 to describe Noah's integrity). Moreover, this divine demand might be construed even as providing the condition of the covenant promises that follow. The conditionality is not made explicit, but it is perhaps suggested by the juxtaposition of clauses: 'Walk with me and be blameless, and I will grant my covenant between me and you, and I will multiply you very greatly' (cf. 18.19). This expansion of the basic promise is remarkable in that, as we have seen, Abraham has been represented up to now without distinguishing features of righteousness. Even his 'belief', mentioned in 15.6, is framed by his doubts (vv. 3 and 8). Genesis 15.6 is the 'exception that proves the rule': whatever belief Abram might have possessed was 'attributed to him as righteousness', i.e. it was not itself righteousness.

While this new element of divine exhortation in Genesis 17 cannot be denied altogether, it should not be over-estimated. First, there are no formulaic corollaries here, such as one finds in Deuteronomy 28; Genesis does not say: 'If you are blameless, then you will receive the promised goods; if you are not blameless, you will not receive them.' The implications of the divine demand in Genesis 17 are not explicated in any detail. Just as Abram first received divine promises without any rational grounds, so also the possibility remains that continuing divine favour is not predicated upon absolute human integrity. If absolute integrity were required, then one would think that the covenant would have been lost when for the second time the patriarch attempted to pass his wife off as his sister, simply to save his own skin (20.11–12).

Even within 17, the editors have rendered Abraham's obedience somewhat ambiguous. The obligation laid on him by Elohim's covenant is specified in only one respect: every male of the household is to be circumcised, both those born in the household[29] and those bought from 'any foreigner – those who are not of your seed' (17.9–14). Verses 23–7 read like a textbook fulfilment of the requirements in vv. 9–14: beginning with his son Ishmael Abraham circumcises every male of his household, including the foreigners.

However, between these two sections lies the most problematic part of the chapter, vv. 15–22. First, there is a parallel promise to Sarah: she will become the mother of nations and of kings, just as Abraham is to become the father of nations and kings. Their change of names in vv. 5 and 15–16 highlights the innovation that although Abraham was promised descendants as numerous as the dust of the earth (13.16) and the stars of the sky (15.5), this extraordinary fecundity could still be interpreted within the framework of the single 'great nation' mentioned in 12.2. Now that Abraham and Sarah are set to become the father and mother of many nations, it is no longer possible to restrict this covenantal promise to the people of Israel. The catch for Abraham, however, is that if Sarah's inclusion within the covenant means that she herself must have a son, then the status of Hagar's son is thrown into question. Abraham therefore intercedes on Ishmael's behalf (v. 18), only to be assured that Hagar's son will become a 'great nation', but outside the covenant with Sarah's son. This divine reassurance (vv. 19–21) is precisely what makes the conclusion of the chapter so problematic: if circumcision is the 'sign' of the covenant (v. 11), and the covenantal line is to go through Isaac – not through Ishmael – why have the editors so blithely placed the 'obedience' of vv. 23–7 at the end of the chapter? The first person circumcised is Ishmael, the son excluded from the covenant.

The standard historicist response to this kind of problem is to reconstruct the layers of the text so that the first layer of the narrative is seen to be coherent, while the clumsy additions have rendered the final text illogical (e.g. Grünwaldt 1992: 27–70). This kind of interpretative response has its own legitimacy, but it leaves one of the most interesting questions unexplained: why would anyone want to add a contradiction to a text? This question can be avoided only by assuming that the editors were intellectually less gifted than the authors of the earliest traditions, an assumption which is often unjustifiable. It seems much more likely that the editors had a purpose in view, but this purpose could not be conveyed by a perspicuous logic since the issue at stake lay at the heart of a dominant ideology of the Persian period. The ostensibly simple 'obedience' of Abraham in 17.23–7 is exploiting the tensions within the final text: the circumcision of Ishmael contradicts the exclusivism of vv. 19–21 by holding to the inclusivism of vv. 9–12. If every male of the household is to be circumcised, as suggested in the first part of the chapter, then that should include Ishmael. Moreover, if Ishmael is to be the father of a 'great nation' (v. 20), then that reflects a partial fulfilment of the promise that Abraham is to be the father of many nations (v. 5). In short, the editors have smudged the edges of the covenant tradition.

The rite of circumcision in Genesis 17 is therefore much more inclusive than one might have thought. Any reader familiar with the narrow interpretation of the 'holy seed' in Ezra 9.1–2, for example, would have been struck by the wording of 17.12:

> For the generations to come every male among you who is eight days old must be circumcised, including those born in your household or bought with money from a foreigner – he who is not of your seed.

If this text is implying that *all* slaves are to be bought from foreigners, then it presumes the legal background of Leviticus 25.39–46, rather than Deuteronomy 15.12–15 (the Deuteronomic slave law permits the buying of Hebrew slaves, but the Levitical law prohibits this, permitting only the purchase of foreign slaves). But whatever the legal presumption, Genesis 17 is clearly envisaging that foreigners would be circumcised, and in this sense the covenant is seen as broader than Israelite kinship. It would include those born outside the line of Ezra's 'holy seed'.

Indeed, in the setting of the Persian period, circumcision could no longer have the same significance as it had during the exile: the Babylonians did not practise circumcision, and therefore the rite would have been a distinctive mark of social identity for Israelites living in Babylon, but the distinctiveness of this mark of the covenant would have been lost as soon as the Israelites moved back to the promised land. As indicated by a text in Jeremiah, Israel's neighbours, including the Egyptians, Edomites, Ammonites, Moabites and 'all who live in the desert', also practised circumcision (Jer. 9.25–6). If we can include the Ishmaelites among these desert dwellers (cf. Gen. 21.20–1), then the people listed in Jeremiah 9 include not just the exclusive people of the covenant but also all peoples represented in Genesis as related to Abraham. Ezra 9.2, we should remember, prohibits inter-marriage specifically with Egyptians, Ammonites and Moabites, three of the peoples listed in Jeremiah 9.25–6 as circumcised. In short, the logic of the exclusivism in Ezra 9.2 cannot be based on the sign of the covenant in Genesis 17. And it may be no accident, therefore, that immediately following Genesis 17 we find two inter-related chapters which conclude by explaining the origins of two of the other circumcised peoples: the Ammonites and Moabites. If Genesis 17 explains how Ishmaelites come to be circumcised, then chapters 18–19, one could say, provide the Abrahamic link to these other peoples similarly distinguished by the practice of circumcision.

Both Genesis 18 and 19 begin with narratives of hospitality towards divine visitors who come in human guise. In the first case, Abraham receives three guests who look like 'men' (18.2), but much of the conversation takes place with only one of them, whom the narrator identifies as Yahweh (18.1, 13, 17, 20, 22, 26, 33). Abraham, however, has a different point of view: he addresses the visitor only as 'my lord' (*adonay* in 18.3, 27, 30, 31, 32). The other two visitors are identified in human terms simply as 'the men', e.g. in 18.16, 22, where they set off towards Sodom. It is these two 'messengers' whom Lot receives in 19.1, when they arrive in Sodom. They are again called 'the men' in 19.10–12, 16, and, as in the case of Abraham's conversation in chapter 18, Lot also addresses the visitors as 'my lords' or 'my lord' (19.2, 18). The messengers eventually save Lot and his daughters from the fate of Sodom, and it is the daughters who, in 19.37–8, are destined to become the mothers of the Ammonites and Moabites 'of today' (the narration here betraying its historical distance from the events being described, as in 12.6 and 13.7).

Abraham argues vehemently for the preservation of Sodom in Genesis 18, bargaining Yahweh down to a deal that would save the city if only ten righteous people could be found there. The bargaining with Yahweh would be almost comic, were it not that the fate of an entire city was at stake. The argument with God demonstrates, however, that Yahweh is bringing judgement on the basis solely of the Sodomites' injustice, and not for any other reason. The narrative in Genesis 19 serves to illustrate that the entire city is eager to abuse Lot's visitors – 'all the men from every part of the city, young and old' (19.4).[30] The key to chapters 18–19 lies in Abraham's question in 18.25: 'Will not the judge of all the earth do right?'[31] The answer of these narratives is a resounding 'yes': judgement will fall only on the guilty, not on the innocent, and it will fall only after due process. Even though the narrator has already informed the reader (13.13) that 'the people of Sodom were very evil offenders against Yahweh', divine probity requires that there be an investigation into whether the outcry against Sodom is entirely justified (18.21). The unified aggression of the Sodomites in chapter 19 then confirms the previous witness against them.

We are left, however, to ponder the question of why God saves the mothers of Ammon and Moab. A mechanical system of reward and punishment might suggest that Lot and his daughters were saved because they were righteous, but this is never asserted in the narrative. In fact, Genesis 19 offers two different accounts of the divine motivation: v. 16 speaks of Yahweh's 'compassion' for Lot's family, while v. 29 states: 'When Elohim destroyed the cities of the plain, he remembered Abraham, and he sent Lot out.' Neither explanation imagines that Lot or his daughters possessed any notable virtues, and in this sense the reader may conclude that chapter 19 locates the origins of Ammon and Moab in an act of divine grace. Even if we read v. 29 to imply a restriction of divine preference (God 'remembered *Abraham*', not Lot's family for their own sake), this must be construed in the widest possible sense to include kinship relationships excluded from the covenantal promises.

We should not, however, over-simplify the idea that Lot and his daughters lack any virtues worthy of divine attention. There has been an unjustifiable tendency to depict them in a consistently negative light. Some commentators argue, for example, that the quality of Lot's hospitality in 19.1–3 is inferior to Abraham's in 18.1–8. But Genesis 19.3 says that Lot had to press the messengers to accept any hospitality at all, since they initially refused it, and the narrator indicates that they are given not just a humble meal, but a 'feast' (*mishteh*). Much more problematic is the significance of v. 8, where indeed Lot's hospitality is taken to a shocking extreme: he resists the baying crowd outside his house, who want to subject the two visitors to sexual humiliation, by offering his two virgin daughters instead. Even in the Hebrew Bible, the social standing of daughters was not so negligible that they could be disposed of as mere chattels; the honour of a virgin daughter had considerable significance within the cultural framework of the patriarchal family (as is made plain by the case of Dinah, in Genesis 34). But the Hebrew idiom of Lot's offer of his daughters has a chilling familiarity: 'You can do to them what is good in your eyes.' The vocabulary here is identical to that used by Abram when he turns Hagar over to Sarai, to suffer at the hand of her mistress (16.6). The case may not be comparable, in that the abuse of Hagar did not take the form of sexual humiliation, but it is probably no accident that the chapter immediately following this incident in Sodom recalls how, for the second time, Abraham regards his wife's sexual purity as dispensable. Genesis 20 contains the second wife–sister episode, in which Sarah is taken into the harem of a foreign king. In short, by ordering the narrative in this way, the editors have quietly suggested that Lot's weaknesses are not dissimilar to Abraham's. Any differences between them may simply be a matter of degree and not of kind.

Genesis 19 shares some remarkable features with another story, in Judges 19, in which the men of Gibeah threaten a visiting Levite. The points of similarity are striking: the evil men of the city surround the house; they demand that the visitor be brought out so that they may 'know him'; the host protects the visiting male, but offers his own virgin daughter and the visitor's concubine so that the crowd may do to them 'what is good in your eyes' (Jud. 19.22–4). The story in Judges is the more horrible, however, since there is no divine deliverance: the crowd accept the concubine and rape her all night, while her 'lord' (*adonay*) remains safely indoors (Jud. 19.25–7). It is not necessary, for my purposes, to examine the parallel narrative in Judges within its wider literary context, but the relationship between Genesis 19 and Judges 19 is relevant insofar as the final editors of Genesis would have known the material in Judges. An audience in the Persian period may well have seen some analogy between the two narratives, and we can reasonably assume that nuances of the Genesis version have been conveyed through a subtle intertextuality. The similarities between the two texts are relatively clear, but what about the differences?

Apart from the major theme of divine deliverance in Genesis 19, it seems that another key difference is suggested in v. 9 where the men of Sodom say to Lot: 'This one came here as an alien, and he sets himself up as judge! Now we will do more evil to you than to them.' Ironically, this speech follows Lot's appeal to the crowd as 'my brothers' (v. 6). The same rhetorical appeal to brotherhood is used by the host in Judges 19.23, but in Genesis the theme of foreignness is developed further.[32] Both narratives are about power and social status, rather than lust, and this is indicated by the fact that the gender of the victim is almost irrelevant. In both chapters, the crowd is determined to humiliate a stranger (cf. Stone 1995), but only Genesis actually expresses this explicitly. The words spoken by the men of Sodom (v. 9) betray a social attitude according to which the resident alien (*ger*) has to maintain a clearly subordinate position, or suffer the consequences. Up to this point in the Genesis story, Lot has enjoyed a measure of peace and stability alongside the Sodomites, as long as he did not challenge the social hierarchy. Now that he seeks to defend two strangers, whose social status is even lower than his own, he is to suffer the same aggression that the visitors have attracted.

The implications of this inter-textual comparison turn our attention away from Lot's character flaws (which, in any case, he shares with Abraham) to the characterisation of the Sodomites. A long line of biblical commentators have assumed that the sin of Sodom in Genesis 19 can be understood as 'unnatural desire' incited by the beautiful young messengers (e.g. von Rad 1963: 212–13). But in his influential commentary on Genesis, Gerhard von Rad had to concede that this interpretation is at variance with 'the popular Israelite conception of Sodom's sin' which can be derived from Isaiah 1.10; 3.9; Jeremiah 23.14; and Ezekiel 16.49, none of which speak of 'unnatural desire'. If there is a common theme in these prophetic allusions to Sodom, it would be oppression of the weak. The texts in Isaiah and Ezekiel are concerned with matters of justice, while Jeremiah 23.14 condemns the abuse of prophetic power. The reading offered here, that Genesis 19 is focused on the humiliation of foreigners, actually accords better with the other references to Sodom in the prophetic literature: the common thread is the perception of the Sodomites as people who abused power. From the editors' point of view, it seems that Genesis 19 is not just concerned with the narrow issue of sexual violence, for the text specifically highlights the abuse of strangers. This emphasis fits well within the politics of the Persian period, we may note, especially insofar as the idea of the 'holy seed' had been implicated in an abuse of power directed at aliens.

In focusing on the characterisation of the Sodomites, however, we should not ignore the horror of Lot's willingness to sacrifice his daughters. The narrative in 19.30–5, where Lot's daughters seduce their own father, can be considered poetic justice – a fitting fate for someone willing to bargain away his daughters' sexuality. But it does not follow that this narrative concerning incest, in 19.30–5, amounts to a negative depiction of the origins of the Ammonite and Moabite nations. The elder daughter makes clear that the circumstances are extreme:

> Our father is old, and there is no man on the earth to lie with us. . . . Come, let us give our father wine to drink and let us lie with him, so that we may keep alive seed from our father.
>
> (19.31–2)[33]

As we shall see, Genesis 38 provides a narrative of similarly extreme circumstances where a daughter's incestuous initiative turns out to be fully justified, and on the same grounds: it preserved the seed of the family. The patriarch who is deceived in this latter case is none other than Judah, and he has to confess of his daughter-in-law that 'she is more righteous than I' (38.26). Moreover, in the very chapter that follows Lot's incest, we find the curious repetition of the wife–sister motif within which Abraham protests to Abimelech that Sarah really is his sister, 'the daughter of my father though not of my mother' (20.12). As I have already noted, such a marriage would be considered incestuous according to Leviticus 18.9, 11; 20.17 and Deuteronomy 27.22. In short, Abraham suffers from the same flaw as Lot, although Lot's incest is framed by mitigating circumstances (as is the case in Genesis 38).

Taken out of context, then, the story of incest in Genesis 19 could easily feed ethnocentric prejudices, but once again the editors of Genesis have elsewhere provided clues to a more nuanced perspective on the story. Lot's daughters become the mothers of Ammon and Moab, and it is quite justifiable to read this as an extravagant fulfilment of the promise that Abraham would become the 'father' of many nations. It is Abraham's *patronage* that ensures the salvation of Lot's family from the destruction of Sodom. This is not the result of Abraham's *righteousness*, any more than it is a result of Lot's righteousness; all the main characters are riven with moral ambiguity. But a divine extravagance conspires with the complexities of human agency to found two of the circumcised nations listed in Jeremiah 9.26 – Ammon and Moab.

I have already touched on the opening section of Genesis 21, where we find the birth of Isaac and the malice of Sarah against Ishmael. The next section, concerning the expulsion of Hagar and Ishmael, can be construed in a way similar to chapters 18–19. Once again, the narrative explains the birth of a nation marked by the ambiguity of circumcision. Like the Ammonites and Moabites, Ishmaelites are excluded from the covenant, but included under the patronage of Abraham. In this sense, they are still part of the fulfilment of the divine promises.

The divine speech in 21.12–13 is extraordinarily ambivalent towards Hagar and Ishmael. Their names are not actually mentioned, and Elohim appears both to capitulate to Sarah's malice and to appeal to Abraham's vanity: 'Listen to her voice, because your seed will be known through Isaac.' At this initial stage, the divine argument seems disturbingly superficial, but the conclusion of the speech is more thought-provoking: 'But the slavewoman's son, also, I will make a nation, for he is your seed.' There is a slight shift of emphasis here towards Ishmael's well-being (if not Hagar's), and Abraham's interests are more understated: Ishmael is to become a nation because he is the seed of the patriarch, but this apparently will be something of a secret reality since Abraham's name will be associated with Isaac. Any pride in the slavewoman's son can be derived, therefore, not from the fame of the Ishmaelites but only from Abraham's knowledge that he had a seminal role in their origins. This seems to be enough for him, and the next day he sends away Hagar and the boy, with the most meagre of provisions, to wander in the wilderness of Beersheba. As in Genesis 16, not a single word of dialogue is recorded between Abraham and Hagar.

At the level of plot, the parallels between chapters 16 and 21 are striking: Hagar wanders in the wilderness; Elohim hears the voice of suffering; and a divine promise is delivered to her near a well. The details, however, are different: the wilderness is this time specified as Beersheba; God hears the voice of the lad, rather than of Hagar; and the divine promise is less enigmatic. It is not just that Ishmael will be a 'wild ass of a man' (16.12); this time, it is said that he will become a 'great nation' (21.18), using the vocabulary of the first divine promise to Abram in 12.2. Abraham and Hagar do not speak directly to each other, but Elohim speaks to both.

From the perspective of the final editing of Genesis, one needs to take account also of the fact that the promise to Hagar in chapter 21 is framed by the encounters between Abraham and the king of Gerar. When the last part of 21 deals with the 'covenant' between Abraham and Abimelech, it does so in a way that invites comparison with the divine promise of an Ishmaelite nation. But before such a comparison can be made, we need to review some of the details of the Abimelech narratives in order to see how the positioning of the Hagar episode affects the sequence of the material in chapters 20–1.

As noted above, Abimelech is the second victim of the wife–sister ruse, and he is shown to be pure in heart (20.5–6) – ironically, the very quality demanded of Abraham at the beginning of the covenant tradition in 17.1. Abraham, on the other hand, is shown to be flawed – on two counts: the patriarch's marriage is irregular, and he is proven wrong in his assumption that 'there is no fear of Elohim' among the inhabitants of Gerar. Genesis 21.22–34 continues the story with Abimelech's request to Abraham: 'Swear to me by Elohim that you will not deal falsely with me' – quite a reasonable request given the events of Genesis 20. Abraham then raises the matter of a disputed well, and a deal is struck without much rankling. The agreement is symbolized with seven lambs, and the subsequent naming of

'Beersheba' plays ambiguously both on the oath-making and on the Hebrew word for the number seven.

There are two aspects of the narrative, however, which call for more reflection. First, vv. 27 and 32 use the term 'covenant' to describe the agreement between Abraham and Abimelech, a word which has been given considerable theological weight in the previous chapters of Genesis. Second, 21.31 suggests that Beersheba is named here for the first time, to mark this covenant associated with a well. Genesis 21.14, however, already mentions Beersheba as the place where Hagar wanders after her expulsion. It is in Beersheba that she sees a well, immediately after receiving the divine promise, and the attentive reader might wonder whether this should be taken as the very same well that Abraham names in 21.30–1. A simple historicism would deal with these questions by suggesting that:

(1) the episodes in 21 are out of chronological order;
(2) the traditions are so separable that there is no need to conflate two wells to make one; and
(3) the term 'covenant' (*berit*) is so broad in its meaning as to be in no need of attempts to load it with theological significance.

The agreement between Abraham and Abimelech is not supposed to carry overtones of the divine promises recorded in chapters 15 or 17. Taken individually, all of these points have relevance. However, the unique configuration of factors in the final editing of Genesis 20–1 is just too suggestive to ignore.

The sequence of episodes can be schematised as follows:

- *20.1–18*: the purity of Abimelech, and the errors of Abraham;
- *21.1–21*: the expulsion of Hagar, and the divine promise at the Beersheba well;
- *21.22–34*: the covenant between Abimelech and Abraham at the Beersheba well.

Given the importance attached to the divine covenants in Genesis 15 and 17 (not to mention 9.8–17), one cannot help noticing that the Beersheba covenant is only a human agreement. Conversely, it is striking that the promise of a 'great nation' was precisely the first of the series of promises, given to Abram, that climaxed in the language of covenant. In passing on this promise to Hagar and Ishmael, Elohim devolves it to descendants of Abraham who were ostensibly separated from the privileged covenant lineage in 17.19–22. Just as 17.23–7 seems to deconstruct the separatism of the previous verses, so also the editing of chapter 21 seems to imply that the promise to Hagar is potentially the beginning of an alternative covenant. The divine gift of a 'great nation' stands in the Abrahamic tradition that finally led to an explicit covenant, and surely the divine–human axis of the promise to Hagar is more important to the editors than the human–human axis of the other promises made at the Beersheba well.

All of this is implied rather than spoken, but the evidence for a complex editorial intention is accumulating. Just as Genesis 18–19 explores the divine preference which lies behind the founding of Moab and Ammon, chapter 21 does the same for the Ishmaelite nation. Taken together, 18–21 deconstructs the exclusive covenant of 17.18–22, as does Abraham's puzzling circumcision of Ishmael at the end of chapter 17. The horizon of divine concern is far greater than an exclusivist interpretation of the covenant tradition might imply, and the narrative of Genesis has thus far demonstrated that at least the Moabite, Ammonite and Ishmaelite nations have been blessed through Abraham, if not actually 'all the clans of the earth' (12.2).

The next chapter, Genesis 22, contains one of most enigmatic passages in the entire Hebrew Bible (cf. Derrida 1995). The near-sacrifice of Isaac takes us beyond the limits of the decent, law-abiding, religion: to kill one's own son is entirely contrary to the laws of Israel. While there are fragmentary clues which point to child sacrifice in early Israelite experience (see Levenson 1993b), such an act would be unthinkable to an audience in the Persian period. The story in Genesis 22 defies domestication within any conventional code of obedience to divine command. Taken as a free-standing narrative, the text may well permit a great number of interpretations, but there are primarily two questions that lie behind the present reading.

1 Why, in the final editing, does the 'sacrifice' of Isaac follow the expulsion of Ishmael?
2 What does this test of Abraham's faith have to do with the identity politics of the Persian period?

The narrator conveys crucial information to the reader in 22.1: what is about to happen is a test. The fact that this is withheld from Abraham until the very end of the story is not a product of the storytellers' cruelty: it can be read simply as indicative of the fact that the narrator has the benefit of hindsight. The historical distance from the events being narrated has been conveyed at several points in the story (cf. 12.6; 13.7; 19.37–8), and 22.1 can be taken as another case in point.

The narrator could have chosen to heighten the drama by not informing us that the command to sacrifice Isaac is a test, but this kind of manipulation of the reader is eschewed. We are told, even before the unthinkable divine command is given, that this horror is retrospectively known to have been a test.

If, however, the reader has been spared the full scale of the horror, Abraham has not. He does not know that he is being tested, and the divine command is represented as a chilling display of exclusivist ideology, tortuously trying to cover up the reality of the one excluded. The staccato syntax at the beginning of v. 2 points to much larger problems of identity: 'Take now your son, your only one, whom you love, Isaac, and take yourself to the land of Moriah and offer him up as a burnt offering . . . '. Classical Jewish commentary has explicated the problem here exquisitely by expanding the biblical narrative with a dialogue between Abraham and Elohim (see Genesis Rabbah 55.7, and Silbermann 1929: 93):

> 'Your son.' He said to Him, 'I have two sons.' He said to him, 'Your only one.' He said, 'This one is the only one to his mother, and this one is the only one to *his* mother.' He said to him, 'Whom you love.' He said to him, 'I love them both.' He said to him, 'Isaac.'

The Rabbis could have avoided this complexity by resorting to the fact that Ishmael has already been sent away in the previous chapter, and in this sense he is already out of the picture, but the rabbinical retelling of the story has not availed itself of such an easy solution to the problem. There is indeed a profundity to this rewriting which surpasses much of the modern scholarship on the chapter. The sequence of identity descriptions in 22.2 has opened up all the old wounds: Abraham has two sons, not one, and indeed it is precisely Elohim who emphasizes in the previous chapter (21.13) that Ishmael is Abraham's seed. Moreover, whatever elements of self-interest may be reflected in Abraham's advocacy of Ishmael in 17.18, and in his negative response to Sarah's exclusivist concern with Isaac in 21.10–11, it is never suggested in the narrative that Ishmael is not loved by his father.

One wonders why the editors have allowed the divine voice to contradict itself within such a short stretch of text. It is surely no accident that the difference between 21.13 and 22.2 turns on the significance of Ishmael. Elohim's positive reference to Ishmael as Abraham's seed in 21.13 is all-too-swiftly occluded by the divine command in 22.2. Moreover, the editors have chosen not to provide a simple identification of Isaac at the beginning of 22 (along the lines, perhaps, of 'Take your son, the son of the covenant'). Evidently the story in chapter 22 was not originally attached to the expulsion of Ishmael in 21, and the editors may simply be preserving a traditional form of words in 22.2; but such a diachronic hypothesis does not exhaust the question of why the editors have structured Genesis 21–2 the way they have. The idea that they have juxtaposed the stories for purely antiquarian reasons, without regard to the narrative tensions they have created, seems implausible. Taken together with all the other evidence of subtle editing in Genesis, the significance of chapter 22 may well be suggested by its literary context.

In both chapters, 21 and 22, Abraham is called on to sacrifice a son. In 21, the sacrifice comes at Sarah's initiative, not God's; it is she who wants to cut off Ishmael's inheritance by sending him away, and Abraham sees Sarah's agency as evil (21.11). Elohim's part in the drama is restricted to comforting Abraham, assuring him that Ishmael is his seed and that the slavewoman's son will become a great nation. In 22, the sacrifice is Elohim's initiative. In both stories, Abraham's silence is excruciating. There is no dialogue at the sending away of Hagar and Ishmael, and, in the second story, the narrator provides a great deal of concrete descriptive detail before the silence between Abraham and Isaac is broken: the journey is done, the wood is cut, the young servants are instructed to wait behind, the fire and the knife are in the father's hand, and in the most poignant detail of all, the wood is carried by Isaac, the intended victim (22.6). Only after all these details are recorded is silence broken, and then the dialogue is Isaac's initiative: 'My father . . . . Here is the fire and the wood, but where is the sheep for the burnt offering?' Even at this point, the father can speak only by using a misleading metaphor: 'God will see to the sheep for the offering, my son.' There is no dialogue, then, as the altar is built and the wood laid out; Isaac is bound, he is placed on the altar, and finally the father takes the knife in his hand as the narrator confirms the patriarch's intention – 'in order to slaughter his son' (22.10). There is no argument with God, as in the case of Sodom, and the narrator does not even portray Abraham's repulsion, as in his response to Sarah's directive to drive out the slavewoman and her son. There is neither an expression of anger against God, nor a pious speech of acquiescence: just silent obedience.

At the highpoint of the horror, a divine messenger calls out from the heavens, just as when Hagar was at breaking-point in 21.16–17. Hagar is sitting 'a bowshot' away from Ishmael, unable to watch her child die, and the heavenly messenger assures her that God has heard her son's weeping. Elohim heard the crying voice of the innocent victim, as the reader would expect from the earlier naming of 'Ishmael' in 16.11. In chapter 22, on the other hand, Abraham has the instrument of death in his own hand; he could not have been closer to his son. This time when the divine messenger calls out from the heavens, it is not in response to the weeping of the innocent victim, the son near death. The narrator has chosen not to focus on any human despair, whether of parent or of child. This cannot be because the Genesis narrator has no interest in human emotions, since feelings of anger and despair are powerfully depicted elsewhere. But these emotions are simply not the focus in the immediate context. What is at issue, apparently, is solely the extraordinary obedience of Abraham:

> Because you have done this thing and have not held back your son, your only one, I will greatly bless you and will greatly multiply your seed, as the stars in the heavens and as the sand on the shore of the sea, and your seed shall seize the gate of their enemies. And all the nations of the earth will be blessed through your seed because you have listened to my voice.
> (22.16–18)

This divine speech, however, leaves some significant questions hanging: why is it, for example, that the editors have retained the reference to Abraham's 'only' son – reiterating 22.1 – when the intertextual connections with the Ishmael narratives are so clear? Not only do we find the common themes linking chapter 22 to the expulsion of Hagar in 21, but when Abraham names the place of Isaac's deliverance *Yahweh Yireh* ('Yahweh sees'), in 22.14, this naming scene parallels Hagar's naming of God in 16.13–14 ('El who sees me'). The theme of divine sight permeates both 16.13–14 and 22.14, linking Hagar's experience of divine perception with Abram's. Moreover, in both chapters the naming scenes are associated with the divine deliverance of Abraham's sons, as well as with divine promises. These connections make it all the more puzzling to find that Yahweh's promises in 22.16–18 mention Abraham's 'only' son. The divine speech seems to be written within the terms of reference defined by an exclusivist ideology, one which would regard Isaac as the only relevant son since he is the one circumscribed by the covenant in 17.18–22. Given the numerous allusions to Ishmael in chapter 22, this ideology cannot be identified with the final editors' point of view. It seems much more likely that the joining of Genesis 21 and 22 is designed to subvert such exclusivism.

The concluding verses of 22 seem to be relatively insignificant, and we may not expect them to contribute much to the discussion of the weighty issues of covenant theology. But Genesis 22.19–24 may indeed be related to the subversive editorial intentions evidenced by the juxtaposition of chapters 21 and 22. The reference to a journey in 22.19 and the genealogical notes in 22.20–4 seem innocuous, but there are at least two points worth noting. First, after the dramatic test of faith, v. 19 says that Abraham returns to Beersheba, the very place where, according to 21.14, the divine promise concerning Ishmael was delivered to his mother Hagar. Historicist scholarship may treat this as the collocation of originally separate traditions, but for the careful reader of the final form, this geographical irony is simply too great to dismiss. Even if the character Abraham can succumb to the fiction that he has only one son, the reader cannot forget that Beersheba is the site where Elohim promised that Abraham's other son would become a great nation. Ishmael is the son confirmed by Elohim as the seed of Abraham (21.13), and Ishmael is the son whom Abraham himself circumcised, marking him with the sign of the covenant (17.23–7). As the son of an Egyptian, he is the product of an exogamous marriage, but the editors have planted numerous clues to suggest that this is no impediment to divine blessing.

The second feature of 22.19–24 worth noting is that the genealogical details provide the identity of a certain Rebekah, who is destined, in Genesis 24, to become Isaac's wife. Rebekah, we discover here for the first time, is the grand-daughter of Abraham's brother Nahor. In line with the exclusivist ideology of the divine speeches in chapter 22, the marriage of Isaac and Rebekah is foreshadowed as endogamous. In short, the son explicitly circumscribed by the covenant, Isaac, is associated already in 22 with endogamy. Yet 22.19 implies that Isaac lives with his father in Beersheba, the very place where the son ostensibly excluded by the covenant received a divine promise. In short, the names of Hagar and Ishmael are mentioned nowhere in chapter 22, but their ghostly presence is everywhere. The reader is faced with a choice: either hear their voices, or else read with the exclusivist ideology of Genesis 22 and ignore them. The editors of Genesis, it seems, have provided several reasons for hearing them.

In the historical setting of the Persian period, the inter-textual connections of 21 and 22 would have had quite clear social implications. The model of holiness promoted by the imperial governors suggested that all foreign women should be sent away, including Egyptians (Ezra 9.1–2). The expulsion of Hagar and her son can, in this sense, be read as one paradigm of holiness. Yet, as I have agreed, a careful reading of the final form of Genesis suggests that the editors thought otherwise. While not explicitly attacking the ideology of endogamy, they have arranged the narratives such that Hagar and Ishmael emerge as effectively equal recipients of divine grace. God hears the voice of suffering, no matter how ambiguous the relationship to Abraham. Exogamous marriages are thereby covertly defended. The exclusivist ideology of the divine speeches in 22 can pass without question only if one is willing to deny the reality of Ishmael's existence and his status as Abraham's son; clearly, Isaac is not Abraham's 'only' son. In effect, the narrow conception of covenant is condemned, not just as dishonest but as blind to the wider actions of God in the world. The reader is invited not to succumb to the paradigm of holiness suggested by Ezra 9.1–2.

Nevertheless, the detail and the drama of Genesis 22 cannot simply be dismissed as exclusivist ideology. There is a theological profundity in the chapter, and it deserves further reflection. By this point in the narrative, we should remember, Isaac has become the focus of all Abraham's hopes. However difficult the sending away of Hagar and Ishmael, this concubine and her son have become peripheral – in the context of the narrative – to the making of Abraham's fame (21.12). If a test of faith is in any sense a test of self-interest, then the expulsion of Hagar and Ishmael pales into insignificance beside the sacrifice of Abraham's focal claim on the future, Isaac. The editors seem to have used the narrative of Genesis 22, even with its exclusivist ideology, to address the most rigorous question for piety: Will Abraham follow God's instructions only because the rewards of progeny and land are so desirable, or is God intrinsically worthy of obedience? The question is never framed in such philosophical terms, but by putting the life of Isaac at risk the narrative has indeed evoked precisely this issue (cf. the parallel issue in Job 1.9).

In effect, the editors have placed two tests of faith side by side in Genesis 21 and 22. The first, the sacrifice of Hagar and Ishmael, is the kind of test proposed by the imperial governors of the Persian period. Yet this test does not actually touch the core issue of self-interest: if the quest for purity is simply a means to gain divine rewards, then God has not been honoured as intrinsically worthy but only as the giver of desirable goods. Genesis 22, on the other hand, implies that the only true test for disinterested piety would be to sacrifice Isaac – the medium through which all the future gifts of progeny and land would be grasped. Given the system of rewards and punishments outlined elsewhere in the legal traditions of Israel (e.g. in Deuteronomy 28), it is appropriate that Abraham's supreme test of faith should involve an act that is contrary to the law. If his obedience to God was meant to foreshadow mere legal obedience, then once again the issue of self-interest would not have been addressed: since keeping the law is also a means to acquiring divine blessings, no test of legal obedience could demonstrate that Abraham was capable of disinterested piety. Keeping the law does not entail the conviction that God is intrinsically worthy of obedience. While none of this is stated explicitly in the book of Genesis, it seems to me that there is enough evidence to suggest that the editors have undermined Ezra's test of piety (which represents purity in marriage as obedience to the law) by proposing a more profound theological test in the narrative of Genesis 22. Not only does the sacrifice of Isaac strike at the heart of Abraham's conception of the good life, but there is no evident connection between this kind of sacrifice and the rewards one would expect from obedience to the law.

The paradox of Genesis 22, however, is that all Abraham's rewards are reiterated as a result of his extraordinary obedience. In this willingness to lose his future, he gains it. The narrative does not reshape the nature of faith in the direction of other-worldly benefits; the divine speech in 22.16–18 promises the same benefits as before – uncountable progeny, land, and blessings to all the nations of the earth through the seed of Abraham. The narrative affirms two contraries without any attempt to reconcile them: the most radical faith is characterised by resignation before God so extreme that the foundation of Abraham's piety lies beyond even ethics and law, yet such obedience bears precisely the same fruit that the law also offers (e.g. in Deuteronomy 28.1–14). Whatever else it might say, this enigmatic narrative in Genesis implies that obedience to the laws of Israel is not the only form of life that God recognises and rewards.

Among the rewards mentioned in chapter 22, however, the promise of land is one that is articulated only obliquely and in an unfamiliar vocabulary: 'your seed shall possess the gate of their enemies' (v. 17). This promise seems to be at odds with the generally eirenic tone of Genesis, and a reader familiar with Deuteronomy might infer that this verse implies the dispossession of the prior inhabitants of the promised land. It is striking, therefore, that the very next chapter of Genesis focuses on a group called the 'Hittites', who are represented as 'the people of the land' (Gen. 23.7). In the two Deuteronomic lists of peoples marked for extermination under the laws of conquest, the Hittites feature first in both cases (Deut. 7.1; 20.17).

One might expect that Genesis would foreshadow, in some sense, the demise of the Hittites. Yet instead of providing an example of Abraham's military potential against this people group – as was the case in chapter 14 when Abraham's confederacy moved against the Mesopotamian kings – Genesis 23 does the reverse: it tells the story of how, when Sarah dies, the patriarch negotiates with the Hittites, in the most polite and respectful way, for a burial site. He begins by emphasising his social status as a resident alien (23.4), but this self-description is rejected by the Hittites, who prefer to call him 'lord' and a 'prince of Elohim' (23.6; cf. v. 11). This is not the language one would expect from enemies, and the editors of Genesis may therefore be planting the question whether the Hittites belong to those enemies mentioned in the divine promise of Genesis 22.17. Just as Genesis 14 inverts the Deuteronomic expectation that the Amorites would be Israel's enemies (the Amorites also are marked for extermination in Deut. 7.1 and 20.17), so also Genesis 23 questions whether the Hittites should be seen as enemies. As if to draw attention to this connection, the conclusion of chapter 23 actually mentions Mamre, the very place where Abraham is said to live with his Amorite confederates in 14.13, 24:

> And then Abraham buried Sarah his wife in the cave of the field of Machpelah near Mamre, which is Hebron, in the land of Canaan. And the field and the cave that was in it passed over to Abraham as a burial site from the Hittites.
> (Gen. 23.19–20)

While some commentators have suggested that the Hittites inflate the price of the property, the narrator chooses not to comment on such a possibility in these closing remarks to the chapter. The emphasis seems to be exclusively on the legality of the transaction: Abraham has acquired this land, a small foothold within the wider framework of the land promise of 15.18–21, by peaceful negotiation.

If Abraham is in any sense a paradigm of faith for later Israelites, then the characterisation of his dealings with other people groups may also be exemplary. This, surely, is a reasonable assumption to make about the intentions of those who finally edited the book of Genesis in the Persian period. Yet what we find in Abraham's character is extraordinarily different from the politics of identity, for example as set out in Deuteronomy and in Ezra: Abraham acts in concert with Amorites to defend the rights of the prior inhabitants of Canaan (Gen. 14); he pays tithes to the king of the Jebusites (Gen. 14.18–20);[34] he shares the promised land with Lot, the ancestor of the Ammonites and Moabites (Genesis 13 and 19); and he buys land from the Hittites by peaceful negotiation. Hittites, Amorites, Jebusites, and Canaanites are all marked for extinction by Deuteronomy (7.1 and 20.17), while Ezra

9.1 adds to these four groups both the Ammonites and the Moabites as people to be excluded from any pure marriage. The 'holy seed' is profaned by marriage exchanges with all these peoples, according to Ezra; and, according to Deuteronomy's laws of conquest, four of these groups deserve only death. Abraham's example seems to stand against all such exclusivist theologies.

Abraham's character, however, is too ambiguous for him to function as a simple model of the editors' social ideals. The narrative of Genesis represents him as frequently flawed, especially if he is viewed from the perspective provided by Deuteronomy's theology. Given that Abraham's own marriage to Sarah would be considered incestuous in Deuteronomic terms (Deut. 27.22; cf. Gen. 20.12), it is intriguing to notice that Genesis 24 takes up the question of a proper marriage partner for Isaac. Following as it does Abraham's extraordinary obedience of 22, and his scrupulous dealings with the Hittites in 23, we might expect chapter 24 to represent Abraham in similarly positive terms. Marriage within the kinship group would cohere with the model of piety proposed by Ezra and Nehemiah, and perhaps the editors have adapted the narrative concerning the wooing of Rebekah in order to allude to this dominant ideology of the Persian period. But as I have already indicated, Abraham's recommendation of endogamous marriage in Genesis 24 is highly ambiguous in its significance.

Clearly, there are overt and frequent expressions of piety within the narrative. At the beginning of the chapter, Abraham recounts Yahweh's promises, emphasising that Isaac should not return to the family's homeland in Mesopotamia (24.6–8). When the servant has travelled to Mesopotamia, he repeats Abraham's story to the kin, claiming Yahweh's providence in the meeting of Rebekah at the well. The servant asks God for a sign and worships Yahweh in gratitude when the sign seems to be given (vv. 12–14, 26–7). All of this piety is then reiterated to Rebekah's brother Laban, in vv. 34–48, who immediately responds by saying that Rebekah can be taken as a wife, for 'Yahweh has spoken' (vv. 50–1). However, in spite of all the God-talk in the mouths of the characters, it is strikingly evident that Yahweh does not speak at all in chapter 24. There is no direct speech from the deity, as is so frequently the case in earlier chapters, and the narrator never claims that any of the characters have accurately represented the divine point of view. In short, the wooing of Rebekah is not given a direct divine blessing, and the question therefore arises whether the editors actually endorse the celebration of endogamy that appears on the surface of the text. As will become evident in later chapters in Genesis, not all explicit claims on piety can be taken seriously.

THE MAKING OF NATIONS

When Abraham first says to his servant in v. 4 'Go to my land and to my kin (*moledet*)', the form of words ironically inverts the divine command delivered in 12.1: 'Leave your land and your kin (*moledet*).' In 24.7 Abraham seems to emphasise the promise of a new land, rather than the command to leave the old kinship group, and he obscures his own agency and responsibility by saying that God 'took me from my father's house and from the land of my kin'. In speaking here of 'the *land* of my kin', rather than (as in 12.1) the kin themselves, the patriarch is able to preserve the appearance of obedience: Isaac should never return to Mesopotamia, the servant is told, but a wife should ideally come from there. This idea is never asserted in a divine speech, nor suggested by the narrator. Noticeably, when the servant recounts Abraham's story back in Mesopotamia, he omits both the command to leave the kinship group and the promise of new land, preferring to mention only how Abraham's travels have brought him wealth and divine blessing (24.35). In 24.37–41, the servant three times mentions his master's wish that a wife be found from within Abraham's own 'clan' (*mishpachah*), rhetorically suggesting a continuing fidelity to the old kinship network when this would actually contravene the divine command in 12.1.

The characterisation of Laban is also highly significant, especially when we consider his later dealings with Jacob. In 24.29, we are introduced to Laban as the brother of Rebekah (interestingly, Laban's name is missing from the genealogy in 22.20–4, which mentions only Rebekah, as the daughter of Nahor's youngest son). His kinship status is thereby represented as dependant primarily on his connection with Rebekah. One wonders whether this subverts in advance his haughty reference to genealogical superiority in 29.26, when he tricks Jacob into marrying his eldest daughter first: Laban himself gains a genealogical foothold in Genesis only by being related to the daughter of a youngest son. More significant in the context of Genesis 24, however, is what the narrator reveals about Laban's character when Rebekah returns home from the well: 'When he saw the nose ring and the bracelets on his sister's arms, and when he heard the words of Rebekah his sister . . . ' (24.30). The extravagant gifts are what first draws Laban's attention; this suggests, subtly, that Rebekah's brother is a man attracted by wealth. Perhaps Abraham's servant senses this, since it is precisely the patriarch's wealth that the servant chooses to mention first when he tells Abraham's story in 24.35–41. Thus, despite Laban's pious-sounding response in vv. 50–1, the narrator has left several clues that piety is a mask in Genesis 24 for other, more self-interested, motives. The pursuit of endogamy is not what it seems to be.

The next chapter, Genesis 25, deals with the death of Abraham and questions of inheritance, and it is marked by a complexity similar to that of 24: the surface of the narrative embodies a dominant ideology, but several hints indicate a more subtle sub-text. The sons of Keturah, Abraham's second wife, are listed in vv. 1–4, but they are apparently left without any inheritance, since v. 5 indicates that Isaac was the sole heir. The sons of Abraham's concubines are then mentioned, but not given names; they were given 'gifts' – rather than a proper inheritance – before the patriarch died, and they were sent away from Isaac (v. 6). The rewards of the covenant, the narrative ostensibly suggests, are exclusive; of all the sons, Isaac was the only one of real significance. Daughters are not even mentioned.

Yet there are some features of the text that potentially undermine this overriding message. First, it is important to notice that if Isaac was the sole heir, then this would have been regarded as irregular by an audience familiar with the law of primogeniture in Deuteronomy 21.15–17: that law certainly stipulates a double share for the oldest son – even when he is the son of an unloved wife – but not exclusive rights to the inheritance. Abraham's eldest son is actually Ishmael, and one might even wish to assert that he is the son of an unloved wife, but covenantal theology has ostensibly overridden his rights as firstborn. Nevertheless, even if Isaac has taken on the status of the firstborn, his inheritance is disproportionately large.

Second, we discover that Abraham was not buried by his only significant son, but by both Isaac and Ishmael (v. 9). After their father's death, v. 11 suggests that Isaac 'then settled near Beer Lahai Roi'. This is an extraordinary irony, since it was precisely there that Ishmael's mother received her first divine promise (16.11–14). The connection is reinforced by the list of Ishmael's descendants, provided next in 25.12–18, which concludes by saying that Ishmael's progeny 'lived in hostility towards all their brothers'. The Hebrew is somewhat obscure, but the greater part of this phrase is identical to that used in 16.12, so we can at least assume that there is a deliberate allusion here to Hagar's first divine promise. Even if it is only Isaac who lives in Beer Lahai Roi, the reader cannot forget the significance of that place for Ishmael. The ideology of covenantal superiority is thereby undercut by this ostensibly innocent geographical reference that reminds us of another divine promise.

Genesis 25 in one sense marks the end of the Abraham story: he is buried along with Sarah in 'the cave of Machpelah near Mamre', a detail which recalls both the legitimate purchase of land from the Hittites as well as Abraham's Amorite confederate Mamre (14.13, 24). But in another sense, Genesis 25 illustrates how Abraham's identity lives on in the diversity of his descendants. The sons of Keturah (vv. 1–4), as well as the sons of the unnamed concubines (v. 6), form a penumbra around the social spheres headed by Ishmael and Isaac. The latter part of the chapter is divided up according to a formula which is frequently used in Genesis: 'These are the generations of Ishmael, son of Abraham' (v. 12); and 'These are the generations of Isaac, son of Abraham' (v. 19). The stylized Hebrew vocabulary here (*'elleh toledot*) has appeared for example in Genesis 2.4; 6.9; 10.1; 11.10, all decisive points in the unfolding of history. In this case, the headings precede both genealogical and narrative materials, which point to separate national identities under Abraham's patronage.

Genesis 25.13–16 lists the 'twelve princes' of Ishmael, fulfilling the promise of 17.20 that Ishmael would become the father of twelve princes and of 'a great nation'. Nevertheless, Ishmael's displacement by the covenant ideology of the previous chapters is here reflected in fully material terms: all the inheritance goes to Isaac (v. 5), just as Sarah wished (21.10). This overturning of primogeniture is reflected also in Yahweh's speech in 25.23, which predicts that there are 'two nations' in Rebekah's womb, and 'the older will serve the younger'. The rest of the chapter illustrates the beginnings of how this divine speech is fulfilled: the younger brother, Jacob, manipulates his older brother Esau – the father of the Edomites – into selling his 'rights as firstborn' (*bekorah*, v. 31). The text does not make clear exactly what these rights are, but they may include not just a double share of inheritance (as required by law in Deut. 21.15–17) but also a general claim on honour and social status (as reflected in Gen. 43.33; 49.3–4; cf. 1 Chron. 5.1–2).

Hence, both Ishmael and Esau are examples of how the status of a firstborn son can be displaced (cf. the case of Reuben, in Gen. 49.3–4, who loses his status by taking advantage of his father's concubine, an event reported in 35.21–2). One should not infer, therefore, that Genesis has a consistent preference for younger sons: the logic of primogeniture in the genealogies of 5.3–26 and 11.10–26 are, at the very least, evidence that the theme is treated ambivalently. The story so far has dealt with this issue in a number of distinct ways; and, if we consider also the material in Genesis 1–11, a number of points have emerged that relate more generally to the theme of dominance. For example, the narrative opposition between Cain and Noah, both firstborn sons, suggests that primogeniture is less important than righteousness and integrity. Similarly, the crime and punishment story in 9.20–7 that leads to the 'curse of Ham' (and thus to the indictment of empire builders), is not concerned to undermine the status of the eldest son, since it is committed by a younger son. Abraham himself is probably to be seen as a firstborn son.

The overt ideology of the Abraham story might suggest, however, that the social priority given to the firstborn (Ishmael) is properly replaced by a divine covenant with the first son born within the context of an endogamous marriage (Isaac). Yet, as I have argued, the sub-text of the narrative repeatedly throws into question any notion of *covenant* that is rigorously exclusive. The benefits of the promises to Abraham flow outwards to Lot and his daughters, as well as to Hagar and Ishmael, and Abraham's own endogamous marriage is effectively parodied as incestuous. Isaac's endogamous marriage to Rebekah is never divinely endorsed, and even within the context of this 'proper' marriage Rebekah's younger son has, already in Genesis 25, begun to supplant the eldest.

In Genesis 25, the displacement is less a matter of divine initiative than it is the result of Jacob's own cunning and Esau's weakness of character. The concluding comment to chapter 25 suggests that Esau actually 'despised his rights as firstborn'. This judgement from the narrator invites a comparison with the story of Cain: just as Cain lost his privileges through his own unjust actions, so Esau lost his rights through short-sighted self-interest. In both cases, the agency is purely human. The divine attitude to Jacob's cunning has not yet been made clear, but this concluding episode to 25 foreshadows the patterns of trickery which permeate the next section of Genesis. We can at least infer, however, that the editors of Genesis are rarely content to leave any claim on superiority unchallenged, whether the claim be on superior birth, or on the exclusive favour of the covenant, or on the purity of endogamous marriage. The only ideals left intact at this stage of the story are the integrity of Noah and the extraordinary obedience of Abraham in Genesis 22. But even these ideals have a critical edge: they both imply that integrity before God need not be restricted to obedience to the laws of Israel.

These conclusions would carry a number of implications for the audience in the Persian period, even though we can only formulate the implications as hypotheses. Quite apart from the fact that we are dealing here with narrative, and not abstract argument, the political context required that critical ideas be expressed only indirectly. First, contra Ezra and Nehemiah, endogamous marriage is not seen as a holy ideal that ensures divine blessing; divine blessing flows extravagantly over the covenant's borders to include Ishmaelites, Ammonites and Moabites, and the endogamous marriages of the protagonists (Abraham and Sarah; Isaac and Rebekah) are called into question. Second, even if 'pure' marriages were a legal ideal in the Pentateuch, legal integrity is not the only form of obedience acceptable to God. Third, the 'rights of the firstborn' (*bekorah*) are fragile; they cannot, for example, be used as an excuse to abuse power. Paradoxically, genealogical superiority is revealed to be as much a vocation as it is an accident of birth. Insofar as Abraham achieves any real integrity it is in his fair dealings with other people groups, and in his radical willingness to sacrifice self-interest. It is these virtues that the editors seem to respect, not aggressive claims on inheritance rights. If the imperial governors have used the ideologies of endogamous marriage and superiority of birth as strategies for asserting property claims, then the Abraham narratives have unmasked the politics of self-interest that underlie such claims.

3

GENESIS 26–36

On tricksters

Genesis 26 begins with the third of the wife–sister ruses, and the similarities with chapters 20–1 are so striking that one wonders what the editors are seeking to achieve in retaining this variant of the tradition. Very little has changed, except that Abraham's role is now played by Isaac. The son is the very image of the father, it seems. Not only is Abimelech still king of Gerar, but even 'Phicol the troop captain' appears in both narratives (21.22; 26.26). The divine speech in 26.2–6 reiterates the promises to Abraham and confirms that they have now been passed on to Isaac. Then Isaac replicates Abraham's anxiety that the beauty of his wife might lead to his own death, and so he tells everyone in Gerar that she is his sister (26.7). This time the trick is not revealed to Abimelech in a dream, but it is discovered nonetheless: the king happens to see Isaac and Rebekah 'playing' or 'laughing' together (the verb is the same as the one used of Ishmael's laughter in 21.9), and this mirth must have had enough erotic overtones to betray that they were not merely siblings. Abimelech is again depicted as righteous, and he cautions Isaac for allowing even the possibility of wrongful sexual relations. This time there is a more extended narrative concerning disputes over wells, but after another covenant with Abimelech is made (26.28; cf. 21.27), the naming of a well is, for the second time, associated with the name *Beersheba* (26.33; cf. 21.31).

As I have said already, Beersheba is first introduced in Genesis as the place where Hagar receives the promise of nationhood (21.14–18). In alluding to Beersheba again, the editors bring to mind the 'quasi-covenant' with Hagar which has chronological priority over the two subsequent covenants – the one made between Abimelech and Abraham, and this new one between Abimelech and Isaac. Historicist scholarship tends to treat the references to Beersheba as indicative of alternative traditions, but if the final editors were not simply unreflective antiquarians then we must assume that they were aware of the prior mention of Beersheba. Not only does the promise to Hagar have chronological priority in the narrative, but since the promise is the fruit of divine initiative we can infer that it has theological importance for the editors. When, in 26, Beersheba is 'named' for the second time, once again in relation to a merely human covenant, the reiteration heightens the memory of Hagar and Ishmael. Even if the privileged line of descent runs through Isaac, as indicated by the divine speech in 26.2–5, the editors have provided no evidence that the divine blessings promised to the Ishmaelites are thereby revoked.

Another striking feature of Genesis 26 is the peculiar reference to Abraham's obedience to Yahweh's 'commandments, statutes and laws' (v. 5). The vocabulary here is specifically legal, and it is common in the book of Deuteronomy. Yet there are two questions arising at this point: first, according to the chronology of the narrative, no divine statutes have yet been given; the divine law will be given to Moses only after the exodus from Egypt. Second, the paradigm example of Abraham's obedience does not conform to Deuteronomic law: if Isaac had died, then the patriarch would have committed murder. And it is only the offering of Isaac, a potentially illegal act, that provokes the narrator of the earlier chapters to commend Abraham's obedience (22.16–18).

Many commentators have suggested that 26.5 inadvertently betrays the theological framework of an editor influenced by Deuteronomy, but there are other ways of interpreting this verse that do not require us to assume mental laziness on the part of the editors. Such gross incongruities may, for example, point to a narrative strategy of 'intentional hybridity':[35] the text may well be alluding to a 'Deuteronomistic voice' (which construes obedience in legal terms only), but that voice is being undermined by the juxtaposition of the surrounding narratives. In speaking of 'statutes and laws', 26.5 emerges as anachronistic with regard to the story-world; moreover, the legal interpretation of Abraham's obedience is quite implausible to the attentive reader. The authority of the Deuteronomistic voice is thereby undercut without any overt theological argument. This interpretation is strengthened by the fact that the reader of chapter 26 is reminded specifically of Abraham's moral ambiguity by the replication in Isaac of his father's typological weakness of character — Isaac passes off Rebekah as his sister, just as Abraham twice did to Sarah. As was the case in Genesis 12, no sooner has a patriarch received a divine promise than he is expressing irrational fears and a lack of integrity, even to the extent of risking his wife's sexual purity.

Genesis 26.34–5, then, provides the bridge into the next chapter, and these verses also allude to issues of marriage purity. Exactly what is being said about marriage, however, is arguably more complex than what has often been thought. The narrator tells us that Esau's Hittite wives were a source of bitterness for Isaac and Rebekah, and commentators have often assumed that this implies a negative attitude towards exogamous marriage. But even if this is true of Isaac and Rebekah in chapter 27, the narrator never expresses this view. Genesis 26.34–5 mentions only the tensions created by these particular daughters-in-law; the text does not give voice to a general ethnocentrism, nor does it cite divine commands prohibiting marriage outside the kingship group. The narrator is at this point extremely reserved. Even when Esau discovers that his parents dislike the local women, and he tries to compensate by marrying Ishmaelites, the narrator takes an entirely neutral stance in reporting these events (28.6–9).

Just as 26.5 alludes to a dominant Deuteronomistic theology, so the reference in 26.34–5 to Hittite wives may be read as part of a narrative strategy of 'intentional hybridity'. The text would certainly appeal to ethnocentric dispositions, but it does not follow that the editors themselves endorse such ethnocentrism. On the contrary, the unfolding of the narrative in chapter 27 points to another interpretation. But already, in 26, the wife–sister episode illustrates Isaac's indifference to the sexual purity of his wife when he perceives his own safety to be at stake. In other words, Genesis 26 reveals in advance that Isaac's commitment to endogamy is superficial, and the ideal of marriage purity is thereby deconstructed by one of its key advocates – the patriarch himself.

Rebekah's speech in 27.46 certainly reads as if her only motive is the quest for endogamy:

> I am disgusted with my life because of these Hittite women.
> If Jacob takes a wife from Hittite women like these, women
> of the land, what will life mean to me?

But the interpretation of this verse needs to take account of the complexities of the whole situation, and the question of 'point of view'. Once again, the language expresses only xenophobia, not a divine vocation to marry within the kinship group, and this speech does not come from the narrator; it comes from the mouth of a trickster. Rebekah is the one who initiates the scheme to trick Esau out of his father's blessing, and she participates fully in the deception: she allays Jacob's fears, cooks the food, takes Esau's clothes, dresses Jacob, attaches the animal-skins to her youngest son's hands and neck, and places the food in his hands (27.11–17). This list of actions serves to emphasise her agency.

Moreover, when she hears of Esau's murderous resolve, she conceives of the plan for Jacob to flee to her brother Laban (vv. 42–5). Her speech to Isaac in 27.46 is an extraordinarily successful case of indirect communication.[36] She plays on Isaac's dislike of Esau's Hittite wives, exploiting the ethnocentric possibilities inherent in 26.35 without any explicit condemnation of Esau. Genesis 27.38 says that Isaac wept aloud when he discovered the wrong done to his oldest son; this particular 'blessing' was a ritualised testament for the firstborn, and it could not be revoked (27.34–7). Remembering that Esau was also Isaac's favourite son (25.28), Rebekah's defence of Jacob has to be tactful in the extreme. She does not suggest to Isaac that Jacob should take refuge with her brother; in fact, she does not even mention her brother. She simply expresses her disgust at the possibility of an exogamous marriage, and allows Jacob to fill in the gaps. She creates the illusion that the patriarch has all the agency, in the same way that she created the illusion that Isaac was blessing the son of his own choice. Rebekah's quest for endogamous marriage can then be read as a ruse designed to obtain paternal permission for Jacob's flight. The ruse is uncannily successful: Isaac instructs Jacob to take a wife from among the daughters of Laban (28.1–2). The very least we could say of Rebekah is that she is a woman of mixed motives.

The reticence of the narrator to comment on all this trickery is one of the factors that make it difficult to determine the editors' view on these events. If we consider the evidence of Genesis 29, however, then we certainly find a case of poetic justice (cf. Sarna 1966: 183–4): Jacob works for Laban for seven years, earning the right to marry the younger daughter of the household (Rachel), yet, under the cover of darkness, Jacob is tricked into marrying the elder (Leah). In defence of his ruse, Laban drives home the irony: 'It is not done, in our place, to give the younger in marriage before the firstborn' (29.26). His choice of words, with its direct mention of 'the firstborn', is noticeably different from v. 16 where the sisters are introduced by the narrator as 'the greater' and 'the smaller'. Thus, the plot of chapter 27 is inverted in 29: in the first case, Jacob cheats the firstborn out of his blessing, while in the second case he is himself tricked into marrying a firstborn. This irony was dramatically expanded in the traditional Jewish commentary, Genesis Rabbah:

> And all night he [Jacob] called out to her, 'Rachel,' and she answered him. In the morning, '. . . look, it was Leah.' He

said to her, 'Why did you deceive, daughter of a deceiver? Didn't I call out Rachel in the night, and you answered me!' She said: 'There is never a bad barber who doesn't have disciples. Isn't this how your father cried out Esau, and you answered him?'[37]

Moreover, the divine actions in chapters 29–30 also seem to be motivated by poetic justice. In 29.31 the narrator tells us: 'When Yahweh saw that Leah was not loved, he opened her womb, but Rachel was barren.' There follows in 29.32–30.21 a long list of children born to Leah and two concubines before, finally, we are told that 'Elohim remembered Rachel: Elohim listened to her and opened her womb' (30.22; cf. 30.2). Jacob's sons are listed in their order of birth, and the only daughter to be mentioned is Dinah, a child of Leah:

Leah	*Bilhah*	*Zilpah*	*Rachel*
(1) Reuben (29.32)	(5) Dan (30.6)	(7) Gad (30.11)	(11) Joseph (30.24)
(2) Simeon (29.33)	(6) Naphtali (30.7)	(8) Asher (30.12)	
(3) Levi (29.34)			
(4) Judah (29.35)			
(9) Issachar (30.18)			
(10) Zebulun (30.20)			
Dinah (30.21)			

It seems that the divine point of view even converges, to some extent, with Laban's: the favour of childbirth is initially bestowed on the elder wife, and the younger wife has to wait for the birth of her first child. It is almost as if Rachel is punished for Jacob's subversion of the order of primogeniture. Jacob, we should note, denies all responsibility for Rachel's plight when (in 30.2) to her plea for a child he replies angrily: 'Am I in the place of Elohim who has withheld from you the fruit of the womb?' The narrative certainly envisages children as divine gifts, but 29.31 shows that God acts partly in response to human agency: Leah is favoured because she is not loved by her husband. Jacob's denial of all responsibility therefore rings hollow.

These factors might seem to suggest that God is sanctioning the customary privileges of the firstborn. Yet such a conclusion would be premature, especially considering the leadership role which is to fall to Joseph in the final part of the Genesis story. It has been noted already that the rights of the firstborn are fragile: Reuben, for instance

– the first son born to Jacob – loses his rights through his own moral weakness (49.3–4; cf. 1 Chron. 5.1–2). The same is true of Cain, in Genesis 4. More importantly, in the immediate context of Genesis 25–9, Yahweh has already, in 25.23, disclosed to Rebekah that the nation descended from her elder son would be subject to the nation descended from her younger son. When Jacob receives the firstborn's blessing, to be lord over his brothers (27.29), his cunning places him exactly where the divine voice had already predicted he would be.

It does not follow, however, that the divine prediction of 25.23 – which inverts primogeniture – should be regarded as part of the core covenantal blessings. The divine promises to Isaac in 26.2–5 do not speak of lordship, but only of land, progeny and blessings to all the nations. These promises have essentially the same content as those which are already found in the Abraham traditions, and they are recapitulated in Jacob's dream at Bethel (28.13–15), again without any mention of Jacob's lordship over his brothers. In short, the dominance of the firstborn is not a part of the covenant tradition. God does not provide a generalised sanction for the customary privileges of the firstborn, so the divine favour shown to Leah can be attributed only to the particularities of the Jacob story.

Indeed, it seems probable that the complexities of trickery and counter-trickery in Genesis 27 and 29 have an additional layer of irony, which is implied by the editors' intentional hybridity even if not made explicit. If, as some commentators have suggested,[38] 'proper' marriages in Genesis are contracted with the household of Bethuel (Abraham's nephew in Mesopotamia), then Rebekah, Rachel and Leah derive from the appropriate lineage; the marriages of Isaac and Jacob are endogamous. But since, against this view, the divine command in 12.1 urges Abraham to leave his kinship group, we might infer that all these endogamous marriages will turn out to be, in some sense, problematic from the divine point of view. Admittedly, there is no explicit divine judgement against these 'proper' marriages, but neither should we expect the editors to articulate this overtly, since to do so would put them too clearly at odds with the endogamous ideal proposed by the imperial governors of the Persian period. On the contrary, any divine judgement would need to be implied rather than asserted. And indeed, not only does Genesis 12.1 imply that Isaac's marriage to Rebekah is not divinely sanctioned, but any reader familiar with Leviticus would know that Jacob's marriage to Rachel is contrary to the laws of Israel: 'Do not take your wife's sister as a rival wife and uncover her nakedness while your wife is living' (Lev. 18.18).

Accordingly, the ironies of chapters 27 and 29 might be read as a kind of implied divine judgement insofar as the trickster, Jacob, suffers counter-trickery at the hands of his kin back in Mesopotamia. As we have already seen, Rebekah also is implicated in this theme, since her sly initiative is crucial in chapter 27. It is only fitting, then, that her brother Laban should share her cunning character. The editors seem to be implying that there is not, in fact, much purity to be found within the ostensibly desirable kinship group. Rebekah's character is passed on to Jacob who, in turn, gets a dash of Mesopotamian cunning from Laban. In effect, if the characters choose to play by the conventional social rules of endogamy, then the divine point of view seems to be that they cannot be so selective: the conventional social order includes primogeniture, and they should play by those rules as well. If the protagonists retain the cultural ideal of endogamy, then they have to suffer the family trait of trickery.

A possible objection to this interpretation is that the category 'divine judgement', however subtly implied, is just not relevant to these trickster tales. This literature belongs to the genre of traditional folklore, and such literature is governed by different norms of storytelling. Folkloric texts often contain the theme of trickery, and, as many scholars have suggested, this theme appeals to an 'underdog' audience which has no other means of combating the dominant culture. Thus, we should not expect the representation of God in folkloric texts to cohere with the God who upholds ethical standards in some of the other Genesis traditions (cf. Niditch 1987: 49–50). In the case of folklore, the ethics of developed theological perspectives should not be imported anachronistically.

While this kind of argument is appropriate to an historicist concern with the origins of oral traditions, it does not apply straightforwardly to the task of interpreting the aims of the final editors of Genesis. The historicist would have to assume that the editors were mere antiquarians who had no interest in the coherence of their work, antiquarians who simply juxtaposed the folklore traditions with the other narratives in Genesis without giving much thought to the incongruities thereby generated in the rendering of the divine character.

There is, however, another possible interpretation. It may be that the editors conceived of a spectrum of wrongdoing. Within the narrative world of Genesis, not all misdeeds are of the same gravity: the Sodomites' mistreatment of foreigners earned them unambiguous judgement, whereas the typological patriarchal weakness of passing off a wife as a sister receives no condemnation from the narrator, only reprimands from a righteous foreigner. Some misdeeds could therefore be spoken of directly, but in other cases it may have been inadvisable to do so. Accordingly, the divine demand to leave the Mesopotamian kinship group might be subject to the lesser sanctions of poetic justice. Certainly, in a context where the Persian-sponsored governors were promulgating the values of ethnic purity and holiness, any critique of endogamous marriage would need to be formulated with the utmost subtlety.

In line with this interpretation, it is intriguing to note that all the key Mesopotamian characters emerge as somewhat devious and self-interested, including Jacob. However, this lack of integrity does not disqualify Jacob, or his mother, from their privileged place within the covenantal lineage. As in the case of Abraham, the divine point of view is not so optimistic as to expect absolute integrity; only Noah lived up to that standard (Gen. 6.9; cf. 8.21). The covenant tradition, in summary, entails neither the dominance of the firstborn, nor the expectation of complete righteousness. The covenanted family is characterised more by the trait of trickery than by personal integrity.

The second half of Genesis 30 is full of devious initiatives once again, and the cycle of trickery continues. Jacob expresses his desire to separate from his uncle by asking to be sent back to his 'place' and to his land (30.25). The choice of the word 'place' (*maqom*) echoes Laban's retort in 29.26; 'It is not done, in our place, to give the younger in marriage before the firstborn.' Both the retort in 29.26 and the request in 30.25 make clear that Jacob really belongs elsewhere. Geography takes precedence over genealogy, one could say, but the text does not make clear whether Jacob's sense of place derives from his birthplace or from the divine promises of land in 26.2–5 and 28.13–15. It is worth noting, however, that the narrative which frames the divine promises in chapter 28 actually contains the word *maqom* six times (in 28.11–12, 16–19). The place at issue there, Bethel, is the specific site of Jacob's dream after he leaves Beersheba. In the dream, Yahweh promises such innumerable progeny that they will spread out to the 'west, east, north and south', a form of words that leaves the scope of the promised land unspecified, but which envisages Bethel as the centre of Jacob's 'place'.

Jacob's request is markedly reserved in 30.25, insofar as he initially asks only to take with him his wives and children, while quietly stressing all the work that he has done over the years for his uncle (30.26). Perhaps this is only a conventional form of polite understatement, since his uncle readily acknowledges that he should pay his nephew wages. Jacob once again takes an excessively modest line, asking for nothing, but then immediately requests a small number of animals – those with unusual markings. We can assume that most of the sheep were white, not dark, and that most of the goats were plain-coloured, not speckled, so by asking for only the dark sheep and the speckled goats Jacob's negotiating strategy still has the appearance of restraint. Laban can hardly disagree with such a modest bid, and so assents to the proposal (30.34).

While the tone of Laban's speech is polite and agreeable, his actions in 30.34–6 are clearly intended to minimize the wealth that Jacob may take with him. Yet, again, Laban's self-interest emerges: he removes the animals which were potentially Jacob's and gives them to his sons, who are to keep the flocks at a significant distance from Jacob. In v. 35 the goats which are removed are described not just as speckled but as having 'white' (*lavan*) marks on them, and this evokes some verbal irony: the word for 'white' is in Hebrew identical to the name 'Laban'. In any case, Jacob is left tending the flocks without markings, i.e. the animals that the agreement set aside as Laban's.

The rest of Genesis 30 contains the sort of narrative one would expect in folkloric trickster tales. The 'underdog' has to rely on his magical powers in order to claim the wages that his uncle rightfully owes him. In all the watering troughs, Jacob places branches with pieces of bark peeled back to reveal the white (*lavan*) inner core. By some sort of sympathetic suggestion, the narrative implies, the animals bore speckled and spotted young. The logic of the rest of the story in 30.37–43 is not entirely clear, but the text is sufficiently coherent as to suggest that Jacob's wealth comes as the result of his own cunning initiative. The narrator does not suggest any direct divine involvement, but the implication seems to be that Jacob deserved his wealth, and the suggestion of poetic justice is reinforced by the use of the word *lavan* (white/Laban).

Genesis 31 then describes the parting of ways that has become almost inevitable. Not just Laban himself, but also his sons, his daughters, and even the voice of God, all confirm that it is time for Jacob to leave. The divine speech at this point echoes previous speeches, but it also brings to mind the sense of place indicated by 30.25, where Jacob first asks to be sent back to his land. Yahweh says to Jacob in 31.3: 'Return to the land of your fathers and to your kin (*moledet*), and I will be with you.' At first glance, this appears to invert the language of the command to Abraham in 12.1: 'Go from your land, your kin (*moledet*) and your father's house to the land that I will show you.' But these divine commands to Abraham and to Jacob are entirely compatible: 'the land of your fathers' is now Canaan, the land promised *to* the fathers, Abraham and Isaac. The only relevant kin are apparently those of the immediate family in Canaan. The divine speech here reinforces the fact that the realities of place have taken precedence over the old kinship ties in Mesopotamia, which are represented in particular by Laban and his sons. Yahweh's directive, in effect, encourages Jacob to return to his immediate kin, among whom we must include his brother Esau, and the encounter with Esau will become a dominant theme in the following chapters.

The position of Rachel and Leah is ambivalent in that they are related both to Laban and to Jacob. But here they make clear that they now belong with Jacob: 'Do we still have any share in the inheritance of our father's house? Why, we have been treated by him as foreigners' (31.14–15). This speech brings the whole quest for endogamous marriage to a tragic conclusion: Jacob's marriages within the kinship network in Mesopotamia have finally led to complete alienation.

Rachel and Leah are influenced in part, it seems, by Jacob's persuasive speech in 31.5–13. A noteworthy feature of the rhetoric at this point is the claim on providence: in spite of the difficulties put in his way by Laban, Jacob claims that the 'Elohim of my father has been with me'. In particular, whatever Laban decided should be the markings that determined Jacob's ownership of an animal (whether spotted, brindled or speckled – the vocabulary is somewhat confused), Elohim intervened and made sure such markings appeared. This divine intervention, Jacob asserts, was revealed to him in a dream. The preceding narrative in chapter 30, however, makes no mention either of such divine intervention or of a dream. Indeed, by claiming that only Laban decided on the markings that would determine ownership of an animal, Jacob underplays his own initiative in suggesting the criteria of ownership (e.g. in 30.32). The patterns of animal reproduction are represented in Genesis 30 as entirely the product of Jacob's own cunning. Similarly, Jacob exaggerates Laban's malice by claiming that his uncle changed his wages 'ten times' (31.7). Only in 31.13 does Jacob refer to the events evidenced in the preceding narrative: first, the language of divine self-revelation – 'I am the El of Bethel' – does recall Jacob's encounter with God at Bethel in 28.10–22. Second, the divine directive – 'Return to the land of your kin (*moledet*)' – does correspond to what the narrator tells us is the content of Yahweh's speech in 31.3. In short, Jacob has inflated the facts in order to persuade his wives that the 'Elohim of my father' is behind his success.

Interestingly, Rachel and Leah's response to Jacob in 31.14–16 begins with a focus on property, but it has theological implications as well. They suggest that their father has wrongly disinherited them, and on that ground they believe that anything Elohim has taken away from their father belongs rightly to them and to their children. Perhaps this is also the reason why Rachel steals the household gods (*teraphim*) in 31.19. She seems to be treating them merely as property, an impression reinforced later in the chapter. After Jacob's family leaves, without informing Laban of the departure, he discovers that his household gods are missing and comes in pursuit of both his daughters and his gods, catching up with them in the high country of Gilead. Laban calls the gods 'Elohim' in v. 30, not *teraphim*, so it may be that the latter term is viewed negatively by the narrator. Rachel hides the *teraphim* by simply sitting upon them, a humiliation of the divine images which is heightened by her claim that she does not wish to move because she is having her period (31.35). This incident might well have been seen as comic by an audience from the Persian period who knew the Levitical law that anything a menstruating woman sat upon would be considered unclean (Lev. 15.19–20). The household gods could hardly be treated with greater indignity, and in this sense, the episode illustrates Rachel's willingness to compromise the religion of her father.

The encounter between Jacob and Laban in the high country of Gilead marks a decisive parting of the ways. Laban emphasises that he has the power to do Jacob harm (31.29), and he refuses to concede his nephew's rights to the flocks and even his rights to Rachel, Leah and their children (31.43). But Laban has been cautioned by Elohim in a dream (31.24, 29), and he proposes a covenant as a final settlement. The covenant symbols, a pillar and a mound of stones, mark a boundary between the families (v. 52). The rupture in the relationship is conveyed even by the fact that the mound of stones is called 'mound of witness' in two languages: Jacob names it in Hebrew, '*Gal-ed*', but Laban uses the Aramaic '*Yegar-sahudatha*'. The linguistic difference is foreshadowed already in 31.24, where the narrator speaks, for the first time, of 'Laban the Aramean'.

The differences suggested by language and borders indicate that this narrative is not simply a story about a family schism. When Laban speaks in v. 53 of 'the Elohim of Abraham' and the 'Elohim of Nahor' he implies also religious differences: he invokes the Elohim to 'judge between us', and the verb for 'judge' is conjugated in the plural. Laban's perspective, therefore, is that there are several gods who are relevant to this covenant (cf. 31.29). Jacob, on the other hand, swears by 'the Fear of his father Isaac' (v. 54). The divine name is unusual (it is otherwise used only in 31.42), but we can conclude that Jacob's invocation of divinity is more limited; he refers only to the religion of his father. Taken together with Rachel's treatment of

Laban's Elohim, the narrative implies that endogamy is no guarantee of religious solidarity.

Laban then returns to 'his place', and Jacob begins the journey back to his father's house. The fact that Jacob is immediately met by 'messengers of Elohim' reminds us of how messengers of Elohim appeared to him in the dream at Bethel, when he first left his family to take refuge in Mesopotamia. Jacob named the place where the messengers first appeared 'house of El' (28.19), whereas here the appearance of the messengers elicits the name 'camp of Elohim' (32.2).

The identity of Elohim was a key feature in the earlier dream episode (Genesis 28), and it becomes so again in chapter 32. In the dream, the divinity was named as Yahweh (28.13) – 'I am Yahweh, the Elohim of your father Abraham and the Elohim of Isaac' – and Jacob mentioned the name Yahweh twice after he awakens (28.16 and 21). More importantly, the naming of God is the focus of Jacob's vow in 28.20–2:

> If Elohim will be with me and will watch over me on this journey I am taking and will give food to eat and clothes to wear so that I return in peace to my father's house, then Yahweh will be for me Elohim.

Jacob is the only patriarch to place conditions on the divine in this way, which is a noteworthy point in itself, but what is more important in the context of chapter 32 is that these conditions seem to have been abundantly fulfilled. Jacob is returning to his father's house not just with basic food and clothing but with considerable wealth. And, as he has said to Laban, 'If the Elohim of my father – the Elohim of Abraham and the Fear of Isaac – had not been with me, you would surely have sent me away empty-handed.' Yet, at the beginning of 32, Jacob speaks only of the camp of 'Elohim' and not of Yahweh. Jacob does address Yahweh in his prayer in 32.9 (in parallel with 'the Elohim of my father, Abraham, Elohim of my father Isaac'), but subsequently no mention of Yahweh is made in Jacob's dialogue, and he interprets the mysterious wrestling match at the Jabbok as a divine encounter with Elohim (32.30).

In short, Jacob never stabilises his conception of God. In spite of all the evidence of divine providence in his experience, he continues to struggle and to bargain his way through every significant interaction, whether with human beings or with the divine. Genesis 32 shows Jacob to be full of restless anxiety, first, in the planning of his meeting with Esau, and second, in the encounter with the unnamed figure at the

Jabbok. Before the meeting with Esau, for example, he divides his family and flocks into two 'camps' (32.7, 10), and the choice of words here echoes the 'camp of Elohim' in 32.2. One might think that the word-play was intended to invoke the memory of divine presence – the 'messengers of Elohim' who appeared both at the beginning and at the end of Jacob's journey to Mesopotamia. Yet the reason for the division of Jacob's group into two camps is actually fear: if Esau should attack the first camp, the second would have a chance to flee (32.8). Jacob, it seems, is never satisfied with the evidence of divine providence.

When he hears that his brother is approaching with 400 men, he fears the worst. He sends messengers to Esau, instructing them to adopt a tone of self-abnegation: they are to address his elder brother as 'lord', while the younger brother is to be spoken of as a 'servant' (32.4–5, 18–20). Having already divided his family and flocks into two groups, he assembles a 'gift' (*minchah*) for Esau of over 550 animals, thinking that this would placate his brother (32.20). The word *minchah* can mean 'gift', 'tribute' or even 'sacrifice', and it is used four times in 32.13–21. But when Jacob actually meets his brother, there is a very significant change in the vocabulary: he calls the gift a *berakah*, a word normally translated 'blessing' (33.11). In effect, the gift becomes compensation for the blessing Jacob had stolen from Esau. The narrative of 32 is doubly ironic since the stolen blessing (chapter 27) was specifically designed for the firstborn, and it included Isaac's exhortation to 'be overlord to your brothers' (27.29). Yet here, in 32, Jacob repeatedly elevates his elder brother and humbles himself, by using the language of 'lord' and 'servant'. This irony subtly underscores the fact that it is only Isaac's blessing that mentions the dominance of the firstborn. Yahweh's promise to Jacob, on the other hand, makes no mention of such dominance (28.13–15; cf. 26.2–5). By implication, Genesis 32 raises the question of whether Isaac's blessing has been effective, and indeed the whole chapter deals paradoxically with the theme of dominance and submission.

Before the meeting of the two brothers, the reader is told of a mysterious wrestling match between Jacob and an unidentified figure, whom the narrator introduces simply as 'a man' (32.24–7). They wrestle all night, with neither gaining the upper hand. Jacob's hip is dislocated, yet at daybreak the man still has to ask to be released. In reply, Jacob – the one who has become known as the thief of the firstborn's blessing – asks for yet another blessing. But instead of immediately granting a blessing, the man changes Jacob's name to 'Israel', anticipating Elohim's renaming of Jacob in 35.9–10. Unlike the later name change, 'Israel' is here provided with an etymology: 'for you have struggled with Elohim and with men, and you have won out' (32.28).

The etymology obviously carries a larger symbolism, one which extends beyond the immediate narrative context of Jacob's nocturnal wrestling with a solitary man. The episode arguably functions as a parable for Jacob's whole life, which has been characterised by struggle, deception, quests for blessing, and bargains with a divinity who seems to be identifiable by no single name. It is striking, then, that the man refuses to give his name, yet Jacob interprets the encounter by saying 'I saw Elohim face to face' (32.30). The narrator does not affirm Jacob's identification of the strange assailant, perhaps because the very idea of wrestling with God became inconceivable as the tradition was passed down. But the editors have at least preserved this traditional story in a way that anticipates the later name change, from Jacob to Israel, and the later renaming is specifically said to be the initiative of Elohim (Gen. 35.9–10). In any case, Jacob names the place 'Peniel', which means 'face of El', and he limps away to face his brother.

There are so many thematic connections between chapters 32 and 33 that the encounter with the god-like adversary at the Jabbok is surely to be read, in some symbolic sense, as an anticipation of the encounter with Esau. When Jacob says to his brother, 'for to see your face is like seeing the face of Elohim, but you have accepted me' (33.10), his words recall Jacob's overwhelming surprise in 32.30: 'for I saw Elohim face to face, but my life was saved'. Israelites commonly thought that it was not possible to see God and live (Exod. 33.20; Jud. 6.22–3; 13.22), so Jacob's dialogue in Genesis 33 is meant to evoke a similar assumption: he no more expected to survive the meeting with Esau than he expected to survive a fight with God.

The word 'face' is clearly the key term linking 33.10 and 32.30, but it also figures in 32.20 where Jacob provides the reason for sending the *minchah* (gift/sacrifice) on ahead to Esau. This earlier verse could be literally translated: 'For he said, "I will cover (*kipper*) his face with this gift which I am sending before my face."' The verb *kipper* is often used in sacrificial contexts to mean 'atone for', and although this cultic meaning is rightly avoided in most translations, the editors might well be hinting at such cultic overtones. Jacob's gift/sacrifice is in some sense designed to atone for his wrongs, and he hopes therefore that he will be able to look on Esau's face and live. Thus, to summarise: the *minchah*, which Jacob sends in 32.13–21, is designed to 'cover his brother's face', and the choice of language has specifically theological overtones. The theological theme becomes more overt when the frightening struggle at the Jabbok is interpreted as a 'face to face' encounter with Elohim, but this episode in turn has clear thematic links with Jacob's speech to Esau in 33.10: 'To see your face is like seeing the face of Elohim, but you have accepted me.'

However, in spite of all Jacob's anxieties, Esau's arrival is depicted as wholly peaceful. As was the case in chapter 32, Jacob adopts the language of 'lord' and 'servant' (33.5, 8, 13–15), but Esau addresses him only as 'my brother' (33.9). Esau initially refuses the extravagant gift, but his brother presses him until he accepts. From the elder brother's point of view, the reconciliation is authentic; there is no evidence of residual animosity. Esau wants to travel together with his brother, but Jacob makes excuses, suggesting that he will follow at 'the pace of the children' until he catches up with Esau in Seir (33.14). Mentioning the children gives Jacob's alternative suggestion the aura of homely honesty, but in fact the suggestion is deliberately misleading. Instead of travelling south to his brother's homeland of Edom, Jacob travels west – first to Succoth in the Jordan Valley, and then on to Shechem, where he buys a field within sight of the city.

The reader is given very few clues as to why Jacob behaves so uncharitably. One might have thought that Yahweh's command to Jacob in 31.3 ('Return to the land of your fathers and to your kin') should have included a more significant reconciliation with Esau. Moreover, it would have made sense for him to return to Bethel, where he received his own promise of land from Yahweh (28.13–15). Instead, he returns to the site where his grandfather Abraham first received a promise of land, Shechem (12.6–7).

Instead of setting up an altar to Yahweh at Shechem, Jacob sets up an altar to 'El, God of Israel'. The divine name here does resonate with Jacob's naming of 'Peniel' ('face of El') in the preceding chapter (32.30), but one could still ask why Jacob does not provide names which contain a reference to Yahweh. It may be that the use of the name 'El' is designed to link Jacob not just with Yahweh, conceived specifically as the God of Israel, but with El, the high God of the Canaanites (Westermann 1985: 529), i.e. Jacob's God appears under several names and one of those names is shared with the people of the land. Beyond that, the association with a site in the Abraham story seems to evoke the model of Abraham's dealings with the indigenous inhabitants: as we have seen, Abraham had no difficulty linking the divine names 'Yahweh' and 'El' (14.22), and his actions in respect of land claims were always just and fair.

If the altar Jacob built to 'El, God of Israel' is meant to evoke the example set by Abraham, then the narrative in Genesis 34 represents another model, one marked by deceit and by violence. Genesis 34.1

begins on an expansive note with Dinah visiting 'the women of the land', but the narrative turns quickly to the theme of ethnic conflict. This is another case where the text takes on a peculiar significance if it is considered in the context of the Persian period, as I will argue.

Genesis 34 is usually taken to be a crime and punishment story, beginning with Shechem's rape of Dinah. But the Hebrew text of 34.2 is somewhat ambiguous: when Shechem saw her, 'he took her, lay with her, and debased (*'nh*) her'. The agency of the male protagonist is clearly represented in these verbs, and Dinah's point of view is occluded, but it does not follow that Dinah must be seen as unwilling. The idioms of 'taking' and 'lying with' do not necessarily indicate violence in Hebrew, so the only significant point of interpretation turns on the verb *'nh*.[39] This certainly means 'humiliate' or 'shame', but it need not mean 'rape' (Bechtel 1994). Other verbs are normally used when violence is indicated. The language in 34.2–3 more likely concerns shame rather than violence, and the shame at issue is not just Dinah's personal experience, since it relates to the cultural identity of her entire family (cf. 34.13–14). It is the honour of the family that is at stake, and, as it turns out, it is only the actions of Dinah's brothers that are unambiguously violent.

But even if this chapter really does begin with a case of rape, then an educated audience in the Persian period would have known that such a case is covered by the legal prescriptions contained in Deuteronomy 22.28–9. Under this law, which pertains to women who are not pledged to be married, the sexual intercourse between Dinah and Shechem was only seriously problematic for Jacob's family if there was no prospect of marriage. The sanctions envisaged were less severe than those concerning adultery. Functioning entirely within patriarchal cultural assumptions, the law requires that fifty shekels of silver be paid to the woman's father and that the couple never divorce. The woman concerned is completely deprived of legal agency, but a descriptive interpretation needs to focus here on the cultural assumptions of the biblical material; it is precisely these patriarchal assumptions that are relevant to whether or not the editors saw Simeon and Levi's actions as an appropriate response to the crime.

When Shechem indicates that he loves Dinah, and that money is no object (34.12), he is in effect showing willingness to abide by the terms of the Deuteronomic law. (Deuteronomy would have been known to the Persian audience of the story, even if that law has not yet appeared in the story world.) Thus, the violence perpetrated against the Shechemites by Simeon and Levi would be regarded as clearly disproportionate in the eyes of any reader familiar with the laws of Israel.

Moreover, Simeon and Levi act in a manner which is arguably contrary to another law relating to religious matters. Exodus 12.48–9 stipulates that if strangers wish to celebrate the Passover festival, then males must first be circumcised. Once this condition is fulfilled, there is no impediment to solidarity in worship. Hence, even this religiously focused law is consonant with Hamor's speech in Genesis 34.8–10, where Shechem's father preaches a gospel of peaceful inter-marriage and the sharing of land and property. By deceitfully disabling the men of the city through the circumcision bargain, Simeon and Levi take the sign of the divine covenant in vain, a particularly grievous crime for the ancestor of the tribe whose vocation is to be focused on worship (cf. Moses' blessing on Levi in Deut. 33.10).

In an illuminating article, Lyn Bechtel argues that the narrative of Genesis 34 reflects two distinct attitudes in the Jacob group. Dinah, and her father Jacob, are interested in interacting with outsiders who agree to respect their values and customs. Significantly, the only specific reference to Dinah's agency is the mention of her desire to visit 'the women of the land' (34.1). Simeon and Levi, on the other hand, 'are threatened by the impure outsiders and want to maintain strict group purity' (Bechtel 1994: 36). Some scholars insist on seeing Simeon and Levi as noble and righteous (notably Sternberg 1985: 469–73), but this line of interpretation requires not only that Jacob's criticism of Simeon and Levi in 34.30 be seen as cowardly, but also that his negative 'blessing' on them in Gen. 49.5–7 be dismissed as the ravings of an old and flawed patriarch. Admittedly, the only overt condemnation of the brothers' violence is placed on the lips of Jacob, so one could indeed think that the editors have not actually provided their point of view on the events in Genesis 34.

But there is at least one more clue that commentators often fail to note: according to Genesis 46.10, Simeon had a Canaanite wife. For a reader attentive to the nuances of the final editing, this introduces a fatal flaw to the argument that Simeon and Levi are justified in their ethnocentrism (cf. Sternberg 1992: 481). Simeon emerges as a man given to extravagant violence and, hypocritically, he is quite capable of exogamous marriage himself. While it may have been too much to impugn the primary ancestor of the priesthood in this way, Simeon's marriage effects a guilt by association. Jacob and Dinah have the editors' indirect blessing. The subtleties of the narrative have seduced those readers who wish to justify ethnocentrism, even where it leads to violent excesses. The editors, on the other hand, have left a number of clues which point to the alternative interpretation, i.e. that they favour the openness of Dinah, Jacob and Hamor, not Simeon and Levi's violent quest for purity. The dominant perspective, which legitimates ethnocentrism, has been quietly undermined.

The next chapter, Genesis 35, might seem to be thematically quite unconnected to the Dinah story. Even literary critics attuned to the final form of the text have concluded that this chapter is simply 'a collection of miscellaneous notices about Jacob and his household' (Alter 1996: 195). But there are hints in the organisation of 35 which provide more evidence that Simeon and Levi are being displaced as a result of their action against the Shechemites. An overview of the material suggests the following scheme:

BETHEL tradition (35.1–7)	[altar built]
Death of Deborah, Rebekah's nurse; burial in Bethel (35.8)	
BETHEL tradition (35.9–15)	[pillar set up]
Death of Rachel, giving birth to Benjamin (35.16–20)	[pillar set up]

Disgrace of Reuben (35.21–2)

GENEALOGY of Jacob's twelve sons, beginning with the eldest, Reuben (35.23–6)
Death of Isaac, buried by Esau and Jacob (35.27–9)
GENEALOGY of Esau's descendants (36.1–43)

Apart from the two sections of Bethel tradition, which are theologically focused, chapters 35 and 36 are concerned with deaths and genealogical matters. More specifically, the issue of genealogical superiority is implicitly being raised.

The genealogy of Jacob's twelve sons in 35.23–6 reiterates information already provided in 29.32–30.21, where the sons are listed in the order of their birth. Here, however, the issue of superiority is to the fore, and hence the sons of the high-status wives (Leah and Rachel) are listed before the children of the concubines (Bilhah and Zilpah).

> The sons of Leah:
> Reuben the firstborn of Jacob, Simeon, Levi, Judah, Issachar and Zebulun.

The sons of Rachel:
Joseph and Benjamin.

The sons of Rachel's maidservant Bilhah:
Dan and Naphtali.
The sons of Leah's maidservant Zilpah:
Gad and Asher.

(35.23–6)

Within the binary division of the mothers' social status, the order of birthing is then reinstated as a principle of organisation: Reuben is listed first, then Simeon, Judah, Issachar and Zebulun – even though Issachar and Zebulun were, according to Genesis 30, born after Bilhah and Leah's sons. Rachel's sons, Joseph and Benjamin, are listed next, in spite of the fact that they are the youngest of the twelve.

The ordering is heavy with irony, since we have just been told that Reuben disgraced himself by sleeping with Bilhah, his father's concubine, and hence his status as the firstborn has been significantly weakened (cf. Gen. 49.3–4). If my interpretation of Genesis 34 is correct, then Simeon and Levi have just disgraced themselves in another way, shedding innocent blood and taking the sign of the covenant in vain (cf. Gen. 49.5–7). Thus, on the basis of a conventional hierarchy of genealogical status, one might infer that the burden of leadership now falls to Judah. The nature of Judah's leadership is in fact a major theme in other biblical narratives (alluded to in Gen. 49.10),[40] but in the book of Genesis the decisive leadership role is about to be passed on to Joseph. His older brothers will bow down to him in the subsequent narrative, reflecting Joseph's dream of domination which is introduced in chapter 37.

Given these proposed connections between chapters 34–37, the fleeting reference to Reuben's disgrace in 35.21–2 is not puzzling and out of place, as many commentators have supposed; it is actually a key to the overarching theme of genealogical superiority. What appears in 35.23–6 to be a genealogy carefully ordered according to principles of conventional social status turns out to be yet another case of intentional hybridity: the editors have juxtaposed material that undermines the ostensible ideologies of status. The first death mentioned in 35 is actually that of a maidservant, a person of seemingly low status. The second death notice, Rachel's, is noteworthy insofar as her elder sister Leah receives no special comment on her death (her burial site is mentioned retrospectively in Gen. 49.31). Moreover, the place of Rachel's burial is marked with a pillar, a memorial symbol that functions like the pillar marking the site of divine speech in 35.9–15. One could infer that the pillar therefore suggests a special honour for the younger sister, an honour which is not conferred on Judah's mother Leah.

The two traditions regarding Bethel, in 35.1–7 and 35.9–15, are peculiar. The chapter begins: 'And Elohim said to Jacob, "Rise, go up to Bethel and live there and make an altar to the El who appeared to you when you fled from Esau your brother."' This clearly refers to the dream episode in Genesis 28 where God is several times named 'Yahweh', not just by the narrator but by Jacob as well.[41] Yet when the patriarch sets up a pillar after the dream, he names the place Bethel – 'House of El' – a name containing no reference to Yahweh (28.18–19). In 35.7, he re-names the place 'El Bethel', and in a third naming episode he sets up another pillar and calls the place 'Bethel' yet again (35.14–15). Evidently the editors have preserved parallel traditions here, without attempting to reconcile them. But what motivates the juxtaposition of the Bethel traditions in Genesis 35?

The divine self-designation in 35.11 is 'El Shaddai', and the reiterated divine promise here says that 'an assembly of nations' and 'kings' will descend from Jacob. The closest parallel for the vocabulary in this verse is found in the Abrahamic covenant of Genesis 17, where God is similarly called El Shaddai and the scope of the divine promises has expanded to include 'nations' and 'kings' in the plural, not just the single nation promised to Abram in 12.1–3. This pluralism is given an additional eirenic emphasis in 35.11 by speaking of an 'assembly' (*qahal*) of nations. This choice of words echoes also Isaac's speech to Jacob in 28.3, just before Jacob flees to Mesopotamia: 'May El Shaddai bless you and make you fruitful and increase your numbers until you become an assembly (*qahal*) of peoples.'

It seems significant that this vision of nations and peoples is recalled in the second Bethel episode in Genesis 35, since the first Bethel episode begins with such exclusive sounding language: 'Put away the foreign gods that are in your midst, and cleanse yourselves' (35.2). This suggests a quest for purity which is actually unusual in the Genesis narrative. The possible exception would be precisely the Dinah episode in the preceding chapter: Simeon and Levi are concerned to compensate for the defilement of their sister, and the casual reader might assume that the beginning of chapter 35 takes up the same theme of purity. Yet, as we have seen, the audience in the Persian period, being familiar with Deuteronomy's laws, would have cause to question Simeon and Levi's version of purity. So, also, one would do well to question the motives behind this 'purification' story at the beginning of 35.

What exactly were 'the foreign gods they had and the rings in their ears' that Jacob buries under the oak (35.4)? There is no clear evidence with which to answer this question, although commentators often refer to the *teraphim* which Rachel brought from her father's household. A more plausible suggestion, from the perspective of the final editing, would focus attention on the plunder that was carried off after the murderous attack on the Shechemites (34.28–9). Jacob's view of the attack is clearly negative, and if part of the problem had been the abuse of the covenant symbol of circumcision it would have made sense for him to deprive his household at least of any religiously significant booty. The editors of Genesis have shrewdly suggested this possibility, precisely by making use of an orthodox idea of purity. And then they have immediately added a parallel tradition concerning Bethel which reminds the reader of the most expansive version of the covenantal divine promises. Once again, an episode that is ostensibly exclusive in tone is destabilised by its juxtaposition with a more inclusivist tradition.

This line of interpretation offers a perspective also on chapter 36, the long genealogy of Esau's descendants. We need not be concerned, for our present purposes, with the details of all the names in these lists; discussions of the names can be found in any scholarly commentary on the text. What is significant is that the lists of Edomite names and clans includes also a list of *kings* 'who reigned in Edom before any king reigned over the children of Israel' (36.31). It would be mistaken to assume that this chapter simply provides some insignificant details about a son of Isaac who is not the bearer of the covenantal promise. On the contrary, genealogical detail is extremely important to the editors of Genesis, and this chapter provides a lengthy illustration of just how the promises to Abraham were already being fulfilled. Nations and kings have descended from Abraham through Esau, even before there were kings descended from Jacob/Israel. In short, the promises to Abraham have flowed over the borders of any narrow conceptions of covenant and purity. Jacob the trickster is once again, it seems, being taught some patience by an ironic God. Just as the younger sister Rachel had to wait for the blessings of childbirth until Leah had borne all her children, so the elder brother Esau is to enjoy the blessing of kingship first.

This positive reading of the Esau material in 36 is, one could argue, linked also to the specific vocabulary of the promise to Jacob in 35.11 – 'an assembly (*qahal*) of nations will come from you'. The vocabulary of the divine promise suggests a peaceful communion of nations, yet *qahal* sometimes has exclusivist connotations in the late biblical literature where it predominately occurs. *Qahal* is a characteristic term for the community of those who returned from exile in Babylon – e.g. Ezra's reading of the law in Nehemiah is addressed to the 'assembly (*qahal*) of the exiles' (Neh. 8.2, 17; cf. Ezra 2.64 and Neh. 7.66). Most importantly, it is the '*qahal*' of the exiles (in Ezra 10.12, 14) who confess that they have wrongly married foreign women. As indicated earlier, Kenneth Hoglund (1992) has specifically drawn attention to Ezra 10.8 as evidence for his thesis that the foreign marriage question is linked to issues of land and property. This verse says that anyone failing to attend the prescribed convocation would face severe penalties: 'by the instruction of the officials and the elders, all his property is forfeited, and he is excluded from the assembly (*qahal*) of the exiles'.[42]

The audience of the Genesis narratives in the Persian period would have known all this, and we can therefore speculate that the controversies concerning marriage and property among the assembly of the exiles may well have come to mind when they heard Jacob's 'blessing' on Simeon and Levi:

> Let me not enter their council, let me not join their assembly (*qahal*), for in their anger they have killed men, and in their wantonness have hamstrung oxen.
>
> (Gen. 49.6)

The editors of Genesis seem to be implying that there is an analogy between Simeon and Levi's excessive quest for purity and a similar excess on the part of the Persian-sponsored governors. In both cases, orthodox-sounding theology has masked other motives, and in both cases the protagonists have gone beyond what the law actually demanded. Deuteronomy does not, for example, demand mass-murder as compensation for sexual humiliation, and neither does it prescribe the dissolution of all foreign marriages. Ezra 9.1 specifically prohibits marriage with Egyptian women, for example, yet Deuteronomy 23.7–8 has a much more inclusive view:

> Do not abhor an Edomite, for he is your brother. Do not abhor an Egyptian, because you lived as an alien in his land. The third generation of children born to them may enter the assembly (*qahal*) of Yahweh.

Like Simeon and Levi, Ezra 9.1 exceeds the strictures of Israelite law.

We may conclude, then, that the trickster traditions of Genesis 26–36 are full of hints that the promises of God do not entail exclusivist quests for endogamy and purity, and neither do they conflate covenantal theology with quests for genealogical dominance. Wherever the narrative's protagonists have sought to claim higher genealogical status, they have been embroiled in a complex web of trickery and counter-trickery. The God of the Genesis narratives prefers, as a matter of principle, neither the eldest sibling nor the youngest: the mysteries of divine favour are not reducible to stable principles at all. But we can reasonably conclude that the effects of God's promises extend far wider than some of the covenanted family imagine, and the careful reader should not be duped into thinking that every pious-sounding extrapolation from orthodox theology is in fact endorsed by the final editors of Genesis. As it turns out, these conclusions will also be relevant to our interpretation of the Joseph story.

4

GENESIS 37–50

Reasons of state

The beginning of the Joseph story goes straight to the heart of the genealogical tensions set up in the previous chapters. Genesis 37.2–4 suggests that Joseph was 'an assistant with the sons of Bilhah and the sons of Zilpah', yet Jacob loved Joseph more than the rest of his sons and gave him an ornamental robe as a sign of his paternal favour. The sons of the secondary wives are possessed with such resentment that they cannot speak peaceably to Joseph – literally, they cannot speak 'a word of *shalom*'. For his part, the youngest son brings evil tales about his brothers to their father. Moreover, Joseph is so thoughtlessly narcissistic that he cannot resist telling his family about two dreams within which he achieves social status not only above all his brothers, but above his parents as well. Commentators have tended to assume that the dreams are to be seen as divine revelations, since they relate to events in the subsequent narrative, but the relationship between Joseph's dreams and their 'fulfilment' is complex. The fact that the character Joseph sometimes *claims* divine knowledge is simply one of the factors that needs to shape any interpretation of the narrative (cf. Josipovici 1988: 33).

This first pair of dreams is characterized by the theme of dominance – all the sheaves bow down to Joseph's, and in the second case, all the stars (or constellations) bow down to him. But the structural features of the two dreams are by no means identical. The second case is more specific, since it includes the precise number of stars involved, as well as the sun and moon, which are taken to represent Joseph's parents. This dream is interpreted only by Jacob, who is both offended and troubled by its content: 'Will your mother and I and your brothers actually come and bow down to the ground before you?' (37.10). In his influential commentary on Genesis, Gerhard von Rad marvels at the masterful psychological treatment of the father's irritation and simply mentions in passing that 'The dreams were fulfilled in the narratives of chs 42.6 and 50.18' (1963: 347). These two verses, however, refer only to the brothers, not his mother and father, bowing down to Joseph, and hence the complexity of the father's irritation is left somewhat under-interpreted.

Another troublesome detail, however, is that Joseph's mother is already dead. Her death figured prominently in 35.16–20: unlike the other two burials mentioned in that chapter, her grave is marked with a memorial pillar. In spite of this fact, Jacob speaks of 'your mother and I' bowing down to Joseph. The problem is usually dealt with by recourse to a routine strategy of historical analysis: if Jacob assumes that Rachel is still alive, then this portion of chapter 37 must come from a literary source different from the record of her death in Genesis 35. The hypothesis makes a useful contribution to the question of sources, but it does nothing to explain why the final editors of Genesis would structure their material so that the death of Rachel is featured prominently two chapters prior to Jacob's exasperated interpretation of Joseph's dream.

In order to answer this latter question, it would be more plausible to assume that this peculiar juxtaposition is meant to suggest another layer of suspicion regarding the character of Joseph. Not only is he represented as an arrogant youth, but he also emerges as disinterested in factors which might complicate his dreams of dominance. In fact, neither his mother nor his father bow down to him in the subsequent narrative. On the contrary, Joseph bows to his father (48.12). If there ever was a version of the story with both parents bowing down to their son, the editors have removed it from the received text and thereby highlighted the incongruity. The final editing may well be designed precisely to signal caution about the nature of dreams. The first two dreams are indeed portents of what is to come, but Jacob's interpretation is simply wrong on points of detail. Joseph does nothing to clarify the dream symbolism, so his father's misinterpretation is left standing. Either Joseph is blinded by the prospect of his own grandeur, or he simply does not know what is going to happen in the future. Or perhaps both options have some truth to them. In any case, the schema of 'prediction and fulfilment' is too simplistic to deal with the interpretation of dreams in the Joseph story.

The next episode begins with two elements which bear ominous overtones. According to 37.12, the brothers had gone to graze their father's flocks near Shechem. The events concerning Dinah in chapter 34 indicate that this is a city with a history, and one would have thought that Shechem is the least desirable place in the entire land of Canaan for the sons of Jacob to graze flocks. Perhaps this implausibility indicates that the early sources of Genesis did not link the Dinah story with this part of the Joseph narrative. But the final editors have placed the mass-murder in Shechem before Joseph's journey there to find his brothers, and the dark associations of that particular city would surely have been perceptible to the audience of this text. Moreover, Jacob instructs his favoured son to enquire after the welfare of his brothers – literally, 'Go and see the *shalom* of your brothers' (37.14) – yet we have just been told in 37.4 that his brothers 'could not speak a word of *shalom* to him'. The word *shalom* can mean either 'well-being' or 'peace', and the ambiguity seems to be exploited here in order to imply that Joseph is being sent to a place where there is no peace.

When his brothers see Joseph at a distance, our anxiety is confirmed: they plot to kill him. 'Here comes that lord of dreams', they say (37.19). The ambiguous label 'lord of dreams' not only indicates that Joseph is lord in his own dreams, but it foreshadows that he is to become a master-interpreter of other people's dreams in the subsequent narrative. The brothers deliberately set out to frustrate the fulfilment of Joseph's dream of dominance (37.20), but in so doing they unwittingly initiate a chain of events that will lead precisely to Joseph's ascendance. And this is simply the first layer of irony in the story, as will become clear.

The brothers initially plot to kill Joseph, to throw his body into a cistern and to claim that he was devoured by a wild beast (37.20). Reuben intervenes, however, and takes on the role of the wise trickster, ironically assuming the leadership that one might have expected from a firstborn son. He assents to only one part of the plan – to throw Joseph into a cistern – on the pretext that the brothers would thereby save themselves from any bloodguilt (37.22). The omniscient narrator makes clear, however, that the eldest brother's secret motive is to take Joseph back to his father at some later stage. Reuben is thereby absolved of guilt for this particular incident, and his grief at the disappearance of Joseph seems genuine (37.29–30). But we know already that his character is flawed, and his genealogical status has been weakened (35.21–2; cf. 49.3–4). As with so many of the characters in Genesis, Reuben is depicted ambivalently.

Ironically, if Reuben's noble ruse had succeeded, and Joseph had been restored to his father, then the favoured son may not have ended up in Egypt where his first dream is to come to fruition. The narrative will come to the theme of family reconciliation eventually, but by a far more circuitous means. Along the way, Joseph's initiatives will save both his own family from famine and many Egyptians as well. If this last part of Genesis is in some sense a salvation story (cf. 50.20), then it is not just the covenanted family that is to be saved. The narrators of Genesis have a wider perspective, and the Joseph story may well be designed to illustrate, once again, the effectiveness of the divine promises: through Joseph, Abraham's family is becoming a 'blessing' to the nations.

The last part of 37 blends a number of traditions, and one would have to confess that the end result is not entirely perspicuous. Westermann makes the plausible suggestion that one version of the story has a group of Midianite merchants steal Joseph from the cistern (v. 27a) and then sell him to Potiphar in Egypt (v. 36). This certainly makes for an integrated story-line, especially if we also conclude that all the references to Ishmaelites belong to an alternative version of the story (i.e. vv. 25–7 and 28b). The blending of the two traditions in the final text, however, is just incoherent: v. 28b says that the Midianite merchants sold Joseph to the Ishmaelites, and one would suppose that he was therefore Ishmaelite property. Yet at the end of the chapter, it is the Midianites who sell Joseph to Potiphar (v. 36).

This problem is somewhat alleviated if one takes the view that since the Ishmaelite portions of the narrative also include the intervention of Judah (vv. 25–7), then this reflects a separate literary source which tells the story from the Judahite point of view. Accordingly, scholars have often suggested that the tradition which mentions Ishmaelites originated in the southern kingdom of Judah, rather than in the northern kingdom of Israel. Once again, such an interpretation might be helpful if one's goal is to identify sources. Yet it does nothing to explain why the final editors have introduced a logical tension into the received text. Elsewhere in Genesis where the narrative is beset by such editorial puzzles, I have suggested that there may be a gently subversive motive lying just below the surface. And this is another case in point.

Source critics have tended to assume that Judah's intervention in vv. 25–7 is essentially the same as that of Reuben in vv. 21–2, and in both cases the prestige of a tribe is enhanced by having the primary ancestor act with greater moral purpose than do the other sons of Jacob. One might assume, for example, that the tribe of Judah would be likely to preserve a tradition which depicted their ancestor Judah in a positive light. As a general hypothesis about the sociology of identity, this assumption has some plausibility, but it does not explain the details of Genesis 37.

Both Judah and Reuben point out the disadvantage of shedding Joseph's blood, but that is where the similarities end. Reuben's intervention has the effect of saving Joseph's life, whereas Judah's speech is really focused only on the question of profit: 'What gain is there if we kill our brother and cover up his blood? Come, let us sell him to the Ishmaelites' (v. 27). The fact that Judah's speech then adds a moral justification for this profitmaking serves only to heighten the impression of hypocrisy: 'For he is our brother, our own flesh' (v. 27). As Robert Alter wryly remarks, 'It is, of course, a dubious expression of brotherhood to sell someone into the ignominy and perilously uncertain future of slavery' (1996: 214). The legal traditions of Israel construed such an action as an offence punishable by death (Exod. 21.16; Deut. 24.7). Moreover, an implication of Judah's initiative would be that the sons of Jacob sold Joseph to the sons of Ishmael, i.e. that this commercial transaction took place between cousins. We are left with the impression that, from the editors' perspective, Judah's pretensions to a morality of 'brotherhood' are entirely hollow (cf. Gen. 4.9).

The negative depiction of Judah's character actually continues into chapter 38, which depicts his dealings with Tamar. In spite of the common perception that the Tamar episode is a self-contained narrative with no connection to the Joseph story, it can be shown that there are several thematic links between 38 and the subsequent chapters. But there is also a link back into chapter 37, insofar as Judah's character is called in question both by his empty discourse concerning 'brotherhood' and by his failure to live up to the *kinship* obligations laid on him by his daughter-in-law Tamar. The fact that Judah ends up pronouncing Tamar 'more righteous than I' (38.26) is highly significant given that Tamar's ethnic identity is never specified. Since she is introduced into the narrative without a tribal identity, we can safely assume that she is a foreigner.[43] In the context of the ethnic tensions in the Persian period, this story has a peculiar relevance. It provides also a kind of interpretative key for the entire Joseph story, as will be seen.

At the outset of chapter 38, we discover that Judah has married a Canaanite woman and had three sons by her – Er, Onan, and Shelah. Tamar marries Er, who, apart from his distinction as the firstborn, is noteworthy only because of his evil: 'But Er, Judah's firstborn, was wicked in Yahweh's sight; so Yahweh put him to death' (38.7). Clearly, genealogical superiority offers no protection from divine justice, but we are not given any specific details concerning the shortcomings of the firstborn. The narrator thereby opens up a gap, leaving the reader with an unanswered puzzle as to the precise reason for the divine punishment. Onan is also put to death by Yahweh, but this time the nature of the evil is specified, *coitus interruptus*: 'he would waste his seed (*zera'*) on the ground' (38.9–10). As a childless widow, Tamar had a right to her brother-in-law's semen (cf. Deut. 25.5–10), and the omniscient narrator reveals that her right is fiercely defended by

Yahweh. In leaving Er's demise unexplained, while specifying the reason for Onan's death, the narrator has drawn attention to the thematic focus of the chapter as a whole: the issue of 'seed' (*zeraʿ*).

The divine blessing of procreation is expressed in distinctive ways in Genesis, but in some contexts Abram/Abraham is specifically promised *zeraʿ* (e.g. in 15.5; 17.7–8). In Hebrew, this word is ambiguous between 'semen' and 'descendants', and while English translations often attempt to resolve the ambiguity, the translation 'seed' expresses the nuances of the language in a way that safeguards the visibility of the thematic connections. Tamar's initiatives can be read as preserving the seed of the family, as opposed to Onan who wastes it for purely selfish reasons (38.9). Judah's reluctance to give Shelah to Tamar also raises questions about Judah's judgement: he assumes that the deaths of his first two sons can be blamed on Tamar (38.11), whereas the narrator has made it perfectly clear that the responsibility lies entirely with the sons. Not only is Tamar innocent, she is arguably more in tune with the divine promises than any of the males in the story.[44] In spite of the obstacles put in her way by Onan and Judah, Tamar has an overriding concern for the continuity of the family, and in this sense she plays a significant role in the fulfilment of the divine promises regarding Abraham's seed. The audience of this story in the Persian period may well have detected this irony, since Genesis 38 conflicts so obviously with the doctrine of seminal purity promulgated by the governors of the time.

Given the thematic focus in the Tamar story, a number of analogies with the Joseph story suggest themselves (cf. Noble 1993). Both Tamar and Joseph preserve Abraham's seed against a number of obstacles. Both, as will be seen, bring about a family reconciliation through elaborate ruses. In both stories, tension is added to the plot by failures to pay for services rendered, respectively, by Tamar and by Joseph. In both cases, protagonists in the narrative unwittingly seek satisfaction of their needs from people they have wronged. Finally, the stories contain a 'reversal of primogeniture' motif, involving both Tamar's sons (Zerah and Perez) and Joseph's sons (Manasseh and Ephraim). Both these younger sons acquire a significant status within Israelite tradition, even though both are born to foreign women, i.e. Perez to Tamar (38.27–30) and Ephraim to Asenath (Joseph's Egyptian wife, 41.50–2).

The structural parallels between the stories of Tamar and Joseph are manifest, but there are also significant differences. Indeed, there is a sense in which the two characters provide alternative visions for the preservation of life. Tamar's tricksterism is exercised from a position of powerlessness, indicated most horrifyingly in her father-in-law's summary judgement that she should be burned for 'playing the whore' (38.24). She is at the mercy of Judah's authority, and only her wits save her. Joseph's tricksterism, on the other hand, exploits his powerful position as governor. When, for example, the silver cup is discovered in Benjamin's sack in Genesis 44, the brothers are completely at the mercy of Joseph's authority, even though they are guilty of no wrongdoing at this point. Tamar is guilty only of desperate measures – indeed, she is proclaimed righteous – yet the character of Joseph is rendered ambivalently. Tamar's intentions are ostensibly focused on her own family needs, yet through her son Perez (38.29) she provides a crucial link in the lineage of Judahite kings,[45] and in this sense she plays a secret part in the fulfilment of the divine promises to Abraham. Joseph's intentions are ostensibly altruistic and theological, but his character is also self-absorbed. Tamar's story provides a model of secret providence working through the marginal agency of a foreign woman. Joseph's story provides a model of providence in which life is preserved through the ambiguities of power.

Genesis 39 begins by affirming the providence of God in Joseph's life as a slave: 'Yahweh was with Joseph and he prospered, and he lived in the house of his Egyptian master. When his master saw that Yahweh was with him, and everything he did Yahweh prospered in his hand, Joseph found favour in his eyes' (39.2). Moreover, the effects of divine blessing flow outwards, just as Genesis 12.2–3 may have led us to expect: 'Yahweh blessed the Egyptian's house for Joseph's sake' (39.5). Joseph is therefore the conduit of a reciprocal blessing, and his social position rises within the household of Potiphar.

It all seems too good to be true, and indeed, Joseph's charm is more effective than he needs it to be, since he also finds a disquieting favour in the eyes of Potiphar's wife. We are told for the first time in 39.6, that he 'had a beautiful figure and was beautiful to look at', a form of words which was first used to describe Joseph's mother in 29.17.[46] Potiphar's wife is duly impressed: 'She raised her eyes to Joseph and said, "Lie with me."'

Contrary to what many commentators have assumed, this brief speech is not just about sexual desire. This is the language of power – blunt, and in the imperative mood. In the previous chapter, even when Judah is making a straightforward request for sexual services to a prostitute, there is an element of politeness in his grammar (conveyed by the Hebrew word *nah* in 38.16). The grammar of 39.7, on the other hand, reveals social inequality more explicitly; this is a woman who expects to be obeyed. Despite the extravagant description of the slave's rise to power in v. 6, not 'everything' in Potiphar's household was 'in Joseph's hands'. In v. 12, after the repeated demands for sexual services are refused, Joseph runs away leaving his garment 'in her hand'. This small narrative detail suggests that 'hand' is a metonym for power, and although everything appeared initially to be in Joseph's hand, appearances were deceptive.

For the second time in his life, his garment is used against him. On the first occasion, his brothers throw him into a cistern and use his cloak as evidence of his death. Here in chapter 39 the abandoned garment is used as evidence of his sexual impertinence, and once again he is interned, this time in a prison.

In both cases, the root of the antagonism is related to the issue of power. In Genesis 37, his brothers are angered by his dreams of dominance. In chapter 39, Potiphar's wife emphasises the impudence of one from a lower class, a Hebrew, making light of her status. This man has made light of 'us', she says in v. 14, implying that the insult is more than merely personal. Repeating the charge to her husband, she emphasises that the Hebrew slave was brought into the house at Potiphar's initiative, and he has 'made light of me' (39.17–19). She appears to succeed initially in displacing this particular threat to the social order, but the narrator informs us that Joseph quickly rose to power within the Egyptian prison system, and the language of 39.21–3 replicates 39.3–6. Once again Joseph 'finds favour in the eyes' of an authority figure (this time the prison warden), everything is placed 'in Joseph's hands', and Yahweh prospers him. The reader, however, should now be wary of extravagant claims to authority: the events in Potiphar's household have demonstrated that power is an unstable resource.

While in prison, Joseph puts himself forward as not just a dreamer himself but an interpreter of other people's dreams. He meets a cup-bearer and a baker, both of them disgraced from the royal household, who are distressed by the opacity of their night visions (40.1–8). Joseph piously informs them that interpretation belongs to Elohim, but without further qualification he immediately assumes the role of interpreter himself (40.8–18). Since his interpretations are so accurate, it is commonly assumed that this episode demonstrates, once and for all, that Joseph is a reliable character. The narrator, however, does not articulate this conclusion explicitly. The cup-bearer is indeed restored to the royal household and the baker is killed, just as predicted, yet the only point to be stressed at the end of the chapter is that the cup-bearer 'forgot Joseph' (40.23). Instead of drawing attention to the reliability of Joseph's interpretation, the editors of Genesis 40 have simply illustrated the almost arbitrary fortunes of those too close to political power: the baker is hanged, the cup-bearer is restored, and the Pharaoh's reasons for these actions remain entirely inscrutable. Joseph's fate hangs on the cup-bearer's memory, which unfortunately turns out to be unreliable.[47]

Two years later, his memory is jogged when the Pharaoh's disquieting dreams prove insoluble to the wise men of Egypt (41.8–15). The interpreter of dreams is summoned from prison, and, as was the case in 40.8, Joseph piously denies his hermeneutical skills, claiming that only God provides the answers (41.14–16). As was the case in the previous chapter, Joseph then without further qualification takes on the job, implicitly claiming divine authority.

But there are a number of significant differences between the episode in the king's court and the previous events in the prison. In the earlier case, Joseph made no promise that the interpretation would be favourable. In 40.8, he simply says to the cup-bearer and baker: 'Are not interpretations from Elohim? Please, tell me your dreams.' Only when the baker finds that the first dream has a positive meaning does he risk recounting his own (40.16). In 41.16, however, Joseph's speech to the Pharaoh seems to pre-empt the outcome by speaking of the king's well-being even before the dreams have been recounted: 'Elohim will answer for Pharaoh's *shalom*.'[48]

Joseph's interpretative strategies also seem to be different in chapter 41. In the case of the baker's dream, the birds' consumption of bread was taken negatively to imply the baker's death (40.16–19). When it comes to the Pharaoh's dreams, the two examples of consumption – by the ugly cows and by the blasted corn – are similarly taken negatively to imply famine (41.25–31). Yet, in the second case, Joseph goes on to provide unsolicited advice about how the predicted suffering can be ameliorated (41.33–6). There is no corresponding advice to the baker, who is apparently subjected to the irresistible forces of fate revealed in his dream.[49] In the royal court, Joseph emerges as not only an interpreter but a strategist. The nature of his wisdom includes not just the divination of obscure portents but actually the agency of government. Little wonder, then, that the Pharaoh concludes, 'there is no one so discerning and wise as you' (41.39).

Joseph's own rise to power is not actually inscribed on the dream symbolism, but since he knows that all the other wise men of Egypt have failed to unlock the royal visions, he could hardly be unaware that his advice implies the possibility of self-advancement: 'And now let Pharaoh look for a discerning, wise man and set him over the land of Egypt' (41.33). The basic outlines of the future have been revealed, but the opportunities for a shrewd governor are left wide open. The Pharaoh makes the obvious choice and appoints Joseph, indicating that he is quite willing to listen to Elohim.[50] The seven years of abundance come to fruition, just as predicted, as do the seven years of famine (41.47–9, 53–5). And the newly appointed governor does just what he said should be done: he collects food during the first seven years, and then he sells it during the famine. The benefits of this policy are shared widely, since we are told in 41.57 that 'all the earth' came to Egypt to buy food from Joseph. We should probably see here a partial fulfilment of the promise to Abram in Gen. 12.3 that 'all the clans of the earth' would be blessed through this chosen family.

One could wonder, however, whether the final editors of Genesis 41 want us to construe Joseph's initiatives in purely positive terms. While the partial fulfilment of a promise to Abram is implicitly evident in 41.57, it does not follow that we need to see all aspects of Joseph's agency as divinely inspired. In previous chapters, the quest for dominance has been a sub-theme of the narrative characterised by human initiatives and ironic reversals, rather than by divine promise. This should cause the reader to be wary of all quests for power, even when they are undertaken by younger sons. As already indicated, the symbolism of abundance and famine are clearly inscribed on the Pharaoh's dreams, but there is no allegory which points to Joseph's own role as governor. Joseph inserts this latter element into the action entirely on his own initiative. This raises questions about the representation of Joseph and the extent to which he should be interpreted as a undistorted mediator of divine agency.

With this reservation in mind, there is a feature of chapter 41 which is conspicuous by its absence. Earlier in the Joseph story, we find a formula which repeatedly expresses the approval of the omniscient narrator for all that Joseph does, specifically in the household of Potiphar and in prison: 'Yahweh was with Joseph' (39.2, 3, 21, 23). If this is the standard formula for expressing divine presence in the narrative, then we need to wonder why the narrator does not use the same formula in commenting on the extraordinary success story of the Pharaoh's governor. Surely, these achievements should have attracted the most glowing praise of all. How is that 'all the earth' benefited from Joseph's wise initiatives, yet the editors of Genesis 41 can apparently withhold a clear statement of their approval?

The answer to this question will arise through a reading of the subsequent chapters, but already in 41 the seeds of doubt are planted. Joseph's wise advice to the Pharaoh includes the provision that one-fifth of all the harvests during the seven years of abundance be collected and stored in the cities (41.34–5). More precisely, the appointed overseers are to 'take' this proportion of the harvest. When the famine spreads, the storehouses are opened and the food is 'sold' to the Egyptians and to foreigners who come in search of grain (41.56–7). The asymmetry of 'taking' and 'selling' guarantees the growth of economic inequities which will manifest themselves in Genesis 47, even to the extent that the Pharaoh will end up owning all the money and all the land in Egypt (cf. Watson 1994: 67–70). The extremity of these consequences is not yet revealed in 41, but an ominous note is sounded when the king establishes the scope of Joseph's authority: 'Without you, no man will raise his hand or foot in all the land of Egypt' (v. 44).[51] This vision of totalitarian power is implicitly proposed as the ideal expression of political wisdom. But before the full implications of the totalitarian model are revealed, Genesis 42–6 interposes a family drama and an alternative model of leadership.

Chapter 42 begins with Jacob sending his sons to Egypt to buy provisions. Benjamin, however, is not sent with his brothers 'lest he meet with harm' (v. 4). This reasoning is placed on the lips of Jacob, and we may presume that the brothers hear the rationale, but the decision is still fraught with ambiguity. Jacob does not explain his fear, and while he makes no accusation against his ten sons, he leaves open at least two possibilities: either he does not trust them, or he is more concerned with the welfare of Benjamin than with any other. The narrator's access to Jacob's motives is telescoped into v. 4 insofar as Benjamin is specified as 'the brother of Joseph', yet this does not resolve the questions arising. The loss of Joseph is identified as the source of Jacob's fear regarding Benjamin, and the psychological complexities of this fear are left unresolved.

When the ten brothers bow before Joseph in Egypt, he recognises them, but 'he feigned the role of stranger' and spoke harshly to them (42.6–7). The harshness of tone continues on until v. 24, where Joseph has to turn away in tears; yet when he composes himself his actions are no less aggressive. From when he first sees his brothers, he seems to be overcome with a need for vengeance, and he recapitulates the wrongs which had earlier been done to him. The brothers' failure to live up to their kinship obligations in that early episode is here met with poetic justice: Joseph's behaviour as a 'stranger' recalls Judah's vacuous appeal to 'brotherhood' in 37.27. Twice, Joseph angrily suggests that the brothers have come to see 'the nakedness of the land' (42.9, 12), a peculiar form of words which seems unsuited to the accusation of spying. The reference to nakedness, and the implication of violation, arguably reiterate the stripping off of Joseph's robe before he is thrown into the cistern (37.23–4). The inversion of the earlier brutality is then completed by having the brothers incarcerated for three days (42.17).

After the three days, Joseph adjusts his demands, but his exercise of power is still firmly within the framework of his own past experience. Initially, he had devised a test of honesty which would have had only one brother return to Canaan to fetch Benjamin (42.15–16). Now he suggests that nine of them may return, with just one brother left behind, so that the others can take food back to the starving family (vv. 18–20). Simeon remains behind, but the core demand remains the same: Benjamin must be brought to Egypt.

The narrator does not betray the motives that lie behind this demand, and it would be overly simplistic to suggest a single factor. Perhaps Joseph desires to be re-united with his own younger brother. Or perhaps he wishes to force his brothers to re-live the experience of caring for the youngest sibling, this time with their own lives absolutely dependent on their kinship obligation. Perhaps he is filled with the desire to see his early dream of dominance come to fruition, and Benjamin is the eleventh 'star' who needs to bow down before him (cf. 37.9). Of these options, only the dream is actually mentioned in the chapter (42.9), but the narrator does not explicitly suggest that this is the motive for the action.

Whatever we are to make of this ambiguity, one thing is clear: Joseph has no regard for the anguish which his demand will cause for Jacob. His power as governor allows him to orchestrate events as he chooses, his brothers playing out the sub-plots of his own devising (cf. White 1991: 259). He does not pause to consider the effect on his father, who is now being asked to relive his own painful sub-plot: the loss of his youngest son. Joseph, the man of totalitarian power and political wisdom, apparently has difficulty seeing things from another's point of view.

The narrator, on the other hand, now focuses precisely on the pain caused to Jacob, and on the different kinds of argument required in order to have the father accept, finally, that Benjamin may need to travel to Egypt. When the brothers return to Canaan, they recount everything to their father, who responds by emphasising his own view of the situation: 'Me you have bereaved: Joseph is no more, Simeon is no more, and now you want to take Benjamin' (42.36). The Hebrew syntax of this verse places emphasis on the first-person pronoun, 'me'. Jacob interprets everything as a personal attack on himself, in one sense unfairly, since he seems to place all the blame on the brothers, rather than conceding that the Egyptian governor has been cruelly manipulative. Similarly, in 43.6, the father complains: 'Why have you done this harm to *me*, telling the man you had another brother?' One might suggest that Jacob is as self-absorbed as Joseph, but at a deeper level of the narrative his accusation against the brothers has some justification: they are indeed guilty, at least in part, of initiating the cycle of revenge that now forces Jacob to recapitulate the loss of a son. The narrative does contain this deeper truth of the brothers' guilt, but one would have to recognise that it is not the whole truth. Jacob himself is partly responsible for the cycle of revenge. It was his unguarded favouring of Joseph that laid the foundations of resentment in Genesis 37. And here again, in 42, he speaks thoughtlessly: 'My son will not go down with you, for his brother is dead, and he alone is left' (v. 38). Whether or not it is to be taken as unconscious, the speech contains an implicit denial of concern for all the sons born to Leah, Bilhah and Zilpah. Only Rachel's sons, Joseph and Benjamin, are the focus of paternal concern. Hence, from the overall perspective on the story granted to the reader, it is possible to see two kinds of guilt at work behind the details of chapters 42–3: both the father and the sons have in some sense compromised their kinship obligations. Moreover, the choice of vocabulary in 43.11 hints at both layers of responsibility. Jacob, here called 'Israel', instructs his sons to 'take some of the best yield of the land in your baggage and take it down to the man as a gift (*minchah*)'. The last time this word was used was in chapter 33, where Jacob brought a 'gift' to his brother Esau in recompense for the theft of the firstborn's blessing. Even though the characters themselves are oblivious to the replay of the drama between Jacob and Esau, there is an ironic sense in which this new gift in chapter 43 functions in narrative terms as recompense to Joseph both for the sins of his brothers and for the sins of his father.

Before the gift for Joseph is assembled, however, and before Jacob agrees to part with Benjamin, there are two attempts to persuade the patriarch. The first attempt, by Reuben, has no effect at all. The firstborn tries to assume personal responsibility for his younger brother, even suggesting that if Benjamin failed to return safely, then Reuben's own two sons may be put to death in compensation. Jacob does not dignify the suggestion with a reply, although traditional Jewish commentators had no difficulty filling in the narrative gap. Rashi, for example, supplies a new speech for the father, in addition to what we find in the biblical text: 'What a fool is this oldest son of mine! He suggests that I should kill his sons. Are they his only, and not mine also?' (Silberman 1929: 212).

In the course of time, when the food has run out, another attempt is made, this time by Judah, to change Jacob's mind. Like Reuben, Judah accepts full responsibility for Benjamin's welfare, but the way this responsibility is expressed is different: 'If I do not bring him back to you, and set him before you, I will bear the sin before you for all our days' (43.9). The choice of words here is intriguing: one might have thought the religious language of 'sinning' inappropriate to a context in which Judah's agency would be limited. If, for example, the governor in Egypt chose to imprison Benjamin, the brothers would hardly be able to resist him. Yet, even given such an eventuality, Judah is willing to speak of 'bearing sin'. Many translators choose to ignore the religious overtones of the vocabulary, and refer only to 'bearing guilt'. This is, no doubt, a semantic possibility, but it only begs the question: how can someone be 'guilty' in respect of events over which he has no control?

If we retain the idea of 'sin' in translating 43.9, the problem can actually be treated within the religious framework of the Pentateuch. Both Leviticus 4 and Numbers 15 envisage a category of sins which are committed unintentionally, and even these can be dealt with by the appropriate sacrifices. In other words, these traditions can conceive of sin as something objective, regardless of intentions.[52] Judah's speech to his father, however, suggests that no sacrifice would ever remove the particular 'sin' of failing to restore Benjamin to his father. It is precisely this feature of Judah's intervention that distinguishes it from Reuben's attempt to balance Benjamin's life with offer of his two sons. In contrast, Judah's offer implies that the principle of life for life does not necessarily provide healing.[53]

The profundity of Judah's speech seems to break the deadlock, and Jacob finally agrees that Benjamin can make the second journey down to Egypt. The father, significantly, does not explicitly bind Judah to his word. On the contrary, he now seems willing to bear the suffering himself, if necessary: 'As for me, if I am bereaved, I am bereaved' (43.14). But this is the worst-case scenario. First, he assembles a lavish gift (*minchah*) for the governor in Egypt. Then, he insists that a double portion of silver be taken in payment for the food, i.e. including the silver which had mysteriously appeared in the brothers' sacks on the return journey from Egypt the first time. Then he covers the whole project with a prayer: 'May El Shaddai give you compassion before the man, so that he will let your other brother and Benjamin come back with you' (43.11–14). At least in this prayer, Jacob recognises the existence not only of Benjamin, but also of Simeon, who had been incarcerated in Egypt until the brothers could provide the evidence of Benjamin's existence. There are hints here, even before the second visit to Egypt, that the family is moving towards some kind of reconciliation.

REASONS OF STATE

The speeches in Genesis 43 frequently use the language of peace and welfare, especially the word *shalom*. When the brothers are summoned to Joseph's own house for hospitality, they initially fear the worst (43.15–18), but the steward of the household comforts them with '*shalom*' (v. 23). Joseph then inquires after the *shalom* of the whole group and 'the *shalom* of your father' (v. 27). Once again, he has to draw aside to weep privately (v. 30), and one might gain the impression that these are hopeful anticipations of reconciliation.

A closer examination of the narrative, however, reveals a somewhat less gracious representation of Joseph's actions. He weeps not because he is overcome by the presence of all his brothers, but specifically at the sight of Benjamin, the only other son of his mother Rachel (43.29–30). In one sense, this is but a marginal step forward from Joseph's private weeping in 42.21–4 which was provoked by the memory of the wrongs done to him, and not by the sight of his brothers when they first arrive (42.7). In both chapters, the reasons for the weeping are narrowly focused – evoked either by the memory of Joseph's own experience of suffering or by the presence of the brother who shares the filial relation to his mother. This narrow focus is reflected also in the description of Joseph's hospitality: an implication of 43.33–4 is that the seating plan for the meal had been determined to reflect the order of genealogical superiority, from the oldest brother to the youngest, yet the youngest is served a meal five times larger than any of the others. It is significant also that Joseph's only reference to God in chapter 43 is in the blessing addressed solely to Benjamin, and not to the other brothers (v. 29).

The other reference to God in the chapter is even more intriguing. When the steward of Joseph's household speaks of divine providence, he finds it necessary to bend the truth. In an attempt to relieve the brothers' anxiety about the money which appeared in their sacks after the first visit to Egypt, he says: 'Your Elohim and the Elohim of your father has given you treasure in your sacks; I received your silver' (43.23). It was made clear in 42.25, however, that Joseph had been responsible for the silver placed in their sacks, and while some commentators try to speak of the 'deeper' theological truth behind the steward's discourse (see e.g. Westermann 1986: 124), this ignores the fact that Joseph is about to play this same kind of trick again. In chapter 44 a silver cup is secretly placed in Benjamin's sack so that he can be falsely accused of theft, and only Judah's intervention undermines Joseph's manipulative attempt to keep his younger brother in Egypt.

As on the first journey to Egypt, the silver that should have paid for food is replaced in the brothers' bags (44.1–2), but it is only the cup that is at issue in the rest of the chapter. In returning the silver with the grain, Joseph expresses generosity for the whole family, but his desire to have Benjamin stay in Egypt still neglects the feelings of his father. When the cup is 'discovered' in Benjamin's sack, they all return to Egypt and offer themselves up as slaves (vv. 12-14). For the second time in the story, all eleven brothers prostrate themselves before Joseph (44.14; cf. 43.26), a scene evocative of the dream episode of 37.9. Joseph makes an implicit connection to his early dream in that the brothers are castigated for underestimating people who can read the portents of the future: 'Don't you know that a man like me can discover things by divination?' (44.15) Judah's reply is equally indirect, if not actually paradoxical: 'How can we prove our innocence? Elohim has found out your servants' guilt.' The brothers are actually innocent of this particular theft, and they know it, but it seems that Judah wants to confess to a much larger history of sin, and his confession is made before God and not just before the governor of Egypt.

Joseph is initially uninterested in this larger history of guilt; he simply repeats the steward's offer that only the brother who was found to have the cup would be held accountable (44.17; cf. 44.10). But Judah's speech finally brings the larger issues to light. The suffering of the father is described at great length (vv. 19-34), and the speech culminates in Judah's offer to take Benjamin's place, so that all the other brothers can return to their father (vv. 33-4). In spite of his recognition of Jacob's disproportionate love for the sons of Rachel, Judah does not allow his resentment to dominate the family any longer. He moves to break the cycle of pain by offering himself as a slave. The very brother who had once suggested that Joseph be sold as a slave now offers to put himself in the same position. The one who had spoken so vacuously of 'brotherhood' (37.27) now reveals a deeper appreciation of kinship. This decisive change in Judah's character is the catalyst that finally breaks down Joseph's defences. The floodgates are about to be opened.

Joseph clears the room of all the Egyptian attendants, and then 'he gave voice to his weeping' (45.1-2). This is the first time that he has wept in front of his brothers, and strangely, after revealing his identity, he then inquires: 'Is my father still living?' (v. 3). He already knows that Jacob is still alive, because he had asked the same question in 43.27. At least, the basic content of the question is the same, but the precise wording of 45.3 now makes explicit Joseph's own filial relationship. The question in 43.27 was framed indirectly: 'How is your aged father you told me about? Is he still living?' The question is now self-involving: 'Is *my* father still living?' This way of putting the question is doubly poignant when one compares it with 41.51 where Joseph explains the meaning of the name given to his own firstborn son, *Manasseh*: 'It is because Elohim has made me forget all my trouble and all my father's household.' Judah's intervention has transformed Joseph's memory. The elder brother may not be so well equipped as the younger in reading the future, but Judah seems to have developed a more profound capacity for dealing with the past.

In chapter 45, however, we are still left with questions about the scope of the family reconciliation. Joseph weeps (vv. 2, 14–15), and so does Benjamin (v. 14), but the other brothers do not. Initially, they are simply unable to respond, so disturbed were they (v. 3), and later we hear only that they 'talked' (v. 15). Joseph refers three times to 'my' father (vv. 3, 9, 13), but never to 'our' father. The bond with the brothers is thereby stated less strongly than it might have been. And then, as the brothers are leaving to return to Canaan, they are each given clothing, but Benjamin receives five sets of garments, as well as a huge amount of silver (v. 22). The special gift of garments curiously recapitulates the gift of an ornamental coat to Joseph in 37.3, and perhaps this analogy underlies his parting remark to his brothers in 45.24: 'Do not quarrel on the way.' The wording of v. 23 is peculiar also in that it seems to focus Joseph's attention on Jacob, rather than on the family as a whole: the gift of twenty donkeys laden with provisions is said to be 'for his father, for the journey'.

At least from the brothers' point of view, there is some residual doubt about the extent to which they have been forgiven. This is suggested indirectly by the nuances of the narrative in chapter 45, but it is later made quite explicit (cf. White 1991: 272). In 50.15–18, the brothers are thrown into a state of anxiety at the death of their father, since they fear they have been treated well only on account of Jacob. If Genesis 45 is to be read as a cathartic climax of family reconciliation, then one would also have to confess that this catharsis is limited. Joseph's concerns are focused narrowly on his father and his full brother, and the quality of the relationship with the rest of the family is still ambiguous.

The beginning of chapter 46 has the appearance of a simple travel narrative, but the details of the text evoke a host of memories. Ostensibly at least, Beersheba is the only campsite worth mentioning on the long journey to Egypt since it is the place where Jacob receives divine confirmation for the migration. The location and the wording of this divine confirmation, however, are potentially significant. Beersheba was the place where Abraham lived after the near-sacrifice of Isaac (22.19; cf. also 26.23–4), but it is first mentioned in Genesis as the place where Hagar, the Egyptian, wandered after being driven out of Abraham's household (21.14). The promise to Jacob in 46.3, moreover, speaks of his family becoming 'a great nation' in Egypt,[54] and this phrase matches the divine promise made to Hagar in Beersheba (21.18). The place therefore carries mixed memories of exile and trial, as well as of comfort and promise. Jacob's spirit has been revived with new hope (45.27–8), but the narrator in 46.1–4 is perhaps sounding an implicitly portentous note through the divine revelation in Beersheba.[55]

Genesis 46 then provides a list of Jacob's sons and grandsons (vv. 8–25). The transition to this text is curious, however, since v. 7 specifically mentions daughters and grand-daughters among 'the seed' of Jacob, yet the names in vv. 8–25 are overwhelmingly male. Only one daughter is mentioned in the list (Dinah, in v. 15), and one granddaughter (Serah, in v. 17). Moreover, unlike in the previous lists of the sons' names, there seems to be no single rationale behind the order. In 29.32–30.21, the list of Jacob's sons is structured according to the order of birth.[56] Genesis 35.23–6, on the other hand, lists the sons of the high-status wives (Leah and Rachel) before the children of the concubines (Bilhah and Zilpah). In chapter 46, the two principles of genealogical status are confused, since although the sons and grandsons are grouped according to their mother the sequence of mothers' names conforms to neither model of social status:

1   Leah (vv. 8–15)
2   Zilpah (vv. 16–18)
3   Rachel (vv. 19–22)
4   Bilhah (vv. 23–25)

In comparison with the other lists, this sequence preserves the priority only of Leah and her children.

For a cultural world in which genealogical standing was all-important, this must have provoked a puzzle among the audience of the received text. Either the editors have suddenly become indifferent to status or they are implicitly raising questions precisely about the nature of genealogical superiority. The core of the puzzle lies not with the sons' names at all, but with the *women* who are mentioned in the text.

Apart from the confusing order of Jacob's wives, it seems that there are four more women at issue in Genesis 46, although only two of them are mentioned specifically: Simeon's Canaanite wife (v. 10) and Joseph's Egyptian wife (v. 19; cf. 41.50–2). The other two women figure by implication in v. 12:

The sons of Judah: Er, Onan, Shelah, Perez and Zerah (but Er and Onan had died in the land of Canaan). The sons of Perez: Hezron and Hamul.

The reader of Genesis 38 knows that all these men were intimately related to Tamar, without her name being mentioned at all.[57] She was the wife of Er and Onan, and the mother of Perez and Zerah. While 38.27–30 does not actually mention the name of Perez and Zerah's father, we can infer that Judah finally gave Shelah to Tamar as a husband. The other piece of information that can be derived from Genesis 38 is that Judah's wife, and therefore Shelah's mother, was a Canaanite (v. 2). Thus we have a consistent picture for all four women: the wives of Simeon, Judah, Shelah and Joseph were all foreigners. This, apparently, is the key to the genealogical puzzles in Genesis 46. Having raised the question of status by mixing up the order of Jacob's wives, we discover in addition that the wives of these four characters were foreign. No other wives are either named, or even alluded to.

If the link between these four wives is that they are foreign, is there also a link between the four men? The answer to this question is less clear, but there are good reasons to think that it is the theme of leadership that unites them. As the firstborn son, Reuben has a natural claim on leadership, but he is not among the four. The most probable explanation for this is that Reuben has already lost his status by taking advantage of his father's concubine, an event reported in 35.21–2 (cf. Gen. 49.3–4). His argument with Jacob in chapter 43, moreover, is markedly ineffective in comparison with Judah's.

Simeon and Levi are next in the genealogical line, and they have disgraced themselves through the violent incident in Shechem (cf. 49.5–7). The fact that Simeon is linked with a foreign wife in 46.10 illustrates only the hypocrisy of his violence.[58] Next in the line of Leah's sons is Judah. Despite his undistinguished role in Genesis 37 and 38, Judah has in fact emerged as an insightful and self-sacrificing character whose initiative with his father, and with Joseph, has been decisive (chapters 43 and 44). His character has developed and deepened with experience, notably, the experience of being humbled by his foreign daughter-in-law. When Judah gives his son Shelah in marriage to Tamar, their son Perez marks the beginning of the genealogy which leads finally to King David, the head of the most significant dynasty in the history of Israel.[59] Finally, Joseph exemplifies another model of leadership, one founded more on charismatic gifts and strategic thinking, allied to totalitarian power.

Simeon, Judah, Shelah and Joseph all have foreign wives, and they each embody some model of authority, but what are we to infer from this observation? More specifically, why would the editors of the Persian period have structured the genealogy of Genesis 46 in order to provoke this question? The fact of having a foreign wife, taken in isolation, tells us nothing about the quality of a leader. Contrary to the view of the Persian-sponsored governors, endogamous marriage is no litmus test of piety or purity; the significant issues for leadership lie elsewhere. As is so often the case in Genesis, the most subtle literary details can be related to the wider politics of identity in this particular historical context.

Simeon stands for a defective model of genealogical superiority, and Shelah is a cipher for the distant future, so at this point in the narrative there are only two viable models of leadership: Judah and Joseph. It is fitting, then, that Genesis 46.28 has Jacob instructing Judah to travel on ahead and to raise questions with Joseph regarding the place where the family will settle. These two brothers have emerged as the strongest and most complex characters, but they also represent alternative constructions of authority. Judah's form of authority is based on hard experience and growing insight. He has recourse not to brute force but only to the power of speech. Joseph, on the other hand, has both charismatic power and access to the coercive might of the Egyptian empire.

Genesis 46.31–47.10 illustrates one intriguing facet of Joseph's authority. The district where Jacob's family are to settle is identified as Goshen several times before the Pharaoh actually gives formal permission for the settlement (Gen. 45.10; 46.28-9, 34). Joseph selects the place, informs the family, and then develops a strategy for dealing with the Egyptian monarch. The plan works like a charm, and Goshen is granted to the family in 47.6. The narrator, however, provides differing perspectives on this process. On the surface, the Pharaoh is concerned only to provide 'the best of the land' (47.6; cf. 45.18), so he grants the request for Goshen without question. Yet in a prior speech to his brothers, Joseph tells them that Goshen would be considered a favourable site for an entirely different reason: 'for all shepherds are detestable to the Egyptians' (46.34). This speech has caused some puzzlement among commentators, both because the Pharaoh clearly has his own flocks to manage (47.6) and because there is no evidence from Egyptian records that shepherding as such was a pariah profession (Westermann 1986: 168). Perhaps Joseph is rhetorically over-stating the fact that Hebrew pastoralists would be treated as social inferiors (cf. 43.32), and thus a separate territory for his shepherding family would be preferable for all concerned. But whatever one might think about this particular puzzle, the narrator has clearly indicated a significant difference between the overt rhetoric of the Pharaoh and the motives behind his land grant.

More than that, perhaps, the narrative hints at the complexity of Joseph's grasp on political power. Joseph demonstrates what can be achieved when one has access to the underlying political motives, but this model of leadership also raises the question of what happens when people lose access to that sub-text. In Joseph's hands, insider knowledge could be turned to advantage, but his political influence is based on a charismatic authority which will be short-lived. The descendants of Israel will discover the instability of this form of power in Exodus 1.8:

> Then a new king, who did not know Joseph, came to power in Egypt. And he said to his people, 'Look, the people of Israel have become too numerous and too mighty for us. Come, let us act wisely with them.'

Wisdom, in this context, means appropriating the Israelites as forced labour in order to build the store cities of Pithom and Rameses (Exod. 1.11). And it appears that the suffering of those later times is alluded to already in Genesis 47.11, where, instead of referring to Goshen, the narrator suddenly refers to 'Rameses', one of the store cities which the Israelites are yet to build. This anachronism is best understood as a subtle foreshadowing of events that lie beyond the Genesis story, and the allusion raises questions about the lasting value of Joseph's form of political wisdom. (The allusion to 'Rameses', one should note, is made by the omniscient narrator. The actors refer only to Goshen.)

Another disturbing aspect of Joseph's leadership is revealed in the remainder of Genesis 47. As already indicated in 41.56–7, the grain stored during the years of abundance is being sold. But now we hear that through these sales Joseph has collected 'all the silver that was to be found in Egypt and Canaan' (47.14). In response to pleas from the people, Joseph then acquires all the livestock in exchange for food. The following year, he takes all the land (47.16–20). Moreover, what the people offer in v. 19 is actually '*us* and our land', and this is matched by Joseph's speech in vv. 23–4: 'Now that I have taken possession of *you* and your land today for Pharaoh, here is seed for you so you can sow the land. But when the crop comes in, give a fifth of it to Pharaoh.' An implication of this is that all the people are to be seen as debt-slaves, and this is precisely what the manuscripts of the Samaritan Pentateuch and the Septuagint say: 'And Joseph reduced the people to slavery, from one end of Egypt to the other' (v. 21). The standard Hebrew manuscript (the Massoretic text) is markedly different at this point. It claims instead that 'he moved the people into the cities'. This version, however, does not grasp the logic of the surrounding verses, and it is probable, therefore, that scribes have altered the older narrative in order to protect Joseph from an unflattering portrait of his character.[60] The provision of seed for planting suggests that the people would not be living in the cities, but in the countryside.

The people's response to Joseph in 47.25 seems to be an extraordinary example of ideological incorporation: 'You have preserved our lives. May we find favour in the eyes of our lord: we will be Pharaoh's slaves.' Joseph then creates a statute demanding that the king receive one-fifth of all produce in the land, exploiting the exigencies of the famine in order to give the monarchy a permanent economic advantage. The reader is being asked to believe that the populace is joyfully entering into slavery, having lost all their money, livestock and land. Bearing in mind, however, that the narrator has foreshadowed the oppression of slavery by referring to 'Rameses' (47.11), it is unlikely that we are to take the people's speech seriously. The editors have planted a clue in v. 11 that should cause us to wonder whether v. 25 is not in fact a caricature of a willing peasantry. In effect, we are being asked to consider whether the end justifies the means: was slavery the only way to save lives?

Certainly, if one were to compare the economic values expressed elsewhere in the Hebrew Bible, Joseph's strategy would have to be seen as unacceptable. The accumulation of land was condemned by the Israelite prophets (e.g. Isa. 5.8; Mic. 2.1–5), and that families should own their own land was an ideal endorsed by prophets, historians and lawmakers (e.g. Mic. 4.4; Joshua 13–21; Leviticus 25). While the sale of land may have been seen as a necessary measure in times of poverty or famine, mechanisms were put in place to ensure that close relatives could buy property in order to keep it within the circle of the clan (e.g. Jer. 32; Ruth 4; Lev. 25.25–8). The acquisition of Naboth's vineyard by an unjust king was remembered as an attack on filial piety, undermining Naboth's attachment to his ancestral inheritance (1 Kgs. 21). All of this evidence points in the same direction: there is no Israelite justification for Joseph's totalitarian control of the land of Egypt, even if it is true that his strategic policies saved lives.

Few commentators, however, are willing to question Joseph's tactics. Gerhard von Rad suggested even that 'the expositor must resist as much as possible the question of the extent to which Joseph's measures stand the test of modern opinion' (1963: 405). What is most interesting about this comment is the unexamined assumption that only modern opinion would dare to question Joseph's actions. If this is so, why did the Massoretic scribes find it necessary to tone down the suggestion that the Egyptian populace was reduced to slavery? And would it not have occurred to the readers of the Persian period, for example, that the comprehensive dispossession of the Egyptians ran contrary to the core economic values of ancient Israel? Or was this audience so ethnocentric as to have been indifferent to the fate of all foreigners?

Even if such indifference could be attributed to the Persian-sponsored governors, I have found overwhelming evidence that the editors of Genesis were consistently opposed to such ethnocentrism. More specifically, when Ezra 9.1 suggests that Egyptian wives should be divorced, this is good evidence that they were actually part of the community at the time. Anyone married to an Egyptian could hardly have been indifferent to the story of dispossession in Genesis 47. Indeed, the spectre of dispossession hung over all foreign wives and over anyone who did not comply with Ezra's judgement. The Persian king's endorsement of Ezra's wisdom could be compared with the Pharoah's reference to Joseph's sagacity, and in both cases the governor's wisdom is used explicitly to underwrite the use of political power (Ezra 7.25–6; Gen. 41.39–40).

The analogies between Ezra and Joseph are surely too close to have passed unnoticed. Both have access to powers of state, and both have masked this power with the discourse of piety. Ezra 9, for example, suggests that Egyptians could not be part of a community faithful to Yahweh, but Deuteronomy 23.7–8 says that they could be.[61] Even the so-called 'Holiness code' of Leviticus (17–26), with its extensive collection of marriage laws, does not have a universal ban on foreign women. Leviticus 21.14 does contain a bar against exogamous marriage, but this restriction is imposed only upon priests, so the laity could inter-marry without contravening the law (cf. Joosten 1996: 85). In short, Ezra's ethnic conception of holiness is not actually based upon the laws of Moses, in spite of his rhetoric of faithfulness.

Questions can be raised also about Joseph's piety. Not all the despotic actions of the Pharaoh's governor need to be construed as divinely endorsed, even if Joseph himself lays claim to divine providence, and even if his saving of lives is a partial fulfilment of the divine promises previously made to the patriarchs. As I have already noted, his rise to power was not inscribed on the Pharaoh's dreams, and his own dream in 37.9–10 is never completely fulfilled. The rhetoric of providence has been used to justify an oppressive regime, and it is difficult to see how the reduction of all Egypt to slavery can be interpreted as a fulfilment of the promise to Abraham that his seed would be a blessing to all the earth. Moreover, a sceptical reading of Joseph's character coheres with the absence of the motif of dominance from the covenantal traditions earlier in Genesis.

The reader is reminded of these earlier traditions at the beginning of chapter 48, where Jacob recalls the divine promises made to him 'at Luz'. His recollection is actually a pastiche of phrases taken from several promises, none of which features the theme of dominance. The divine speech at Luz, as Jacob recalls it, came from El Shaddai:

> I will make you fruitful and increase your numbers. I will make you an assembly of peoples, and I will give this land to your seed as an everlasting possession.
>
> (48.4)

This wording corresponds most closely to the divine promise to Jacob at Luz in 35.11–12, on his return from Mesopotamia, but instead of mentioning an 'assembly of peoples', the promise there actually speaks of an 'assembly of nations'. The phrase 'assembly of peoples' comes from Isaac's blessing in 28.3, conferred on Jacob *before* he left for Mesopotamia. Similarly, the idea that the land would be an 'everlasting possession' is not found in 35.11–12, but rather, in the promise to Abraham in 17.8. Thus, in 48.4, Jacob has actually conflated the wording of three distinct texts – Genesis 17.8; 28.3; 35.11–12 – and it is notable that none of them entails social dominance. With regard to the audience of Genesis in the Persian period, it is striking that both 28.3 and 35.11 speak inclusively of an 'assembly' (*qahal*) of nations or peoples, envisaging precisely the sort of social intercourse that Ezra's project excludes.[62] Any implied critique of Joseph's dominance may, at the same time, be a critique of Ezra's.

As already indicated, the covenantal traditions do not contain visions of political dominance,[63] and, perhaps as a corollary of this point, they do not contain endorsements of genealogical superiority. While genealogical privilege inevitably plays a role in the dynamics of the Joseph story, it is not a determinative role. One would have thought that Joseph himself, of all the characters, would have grasped this issue. Yet Genesis 48 represents him as vainly attempting to uphold the cultural value of primogeniture on behalf of his eldest son Manasseh.

Genesis 48.5 seems to express Jacob's desire to 'adopt' Manasseh and Ephraim as his own sons, 'just as Reuben and Simeon are mine'. The reasons for this adoption are quite opaque, but Robert Alter (1996:

288) has plausibly suggested that Jacob's desire may have been to compensate for the sons that Rachel, because of her untimely death, was unable to bear. This explanation would account for the puzzling reference to her death in v. 7. Whatever the reasoning, the ironies of the narrative are manifest: Joseph's older sons are linked with Jacob's older sons and ritually blessed (v. 9) by the very patriarch who stole his elder brother's blessing. When Joseph attempts to ensure that the firstborn's blessing falls on Manasseh, he is rebuked by his father, who favours the younger son Ephraim (48.17–19). The governor of all Egypt is powerless against his father's will, and this impotence is reinforced thematically by having Joseph bow before his father (v. 12), even though the dream of dominance back in 37.9–10 suggested that it was Jacob who would bow to Joseph. In short, the covenantal blessings introduced at the beginning of Genesis 48 are transferred to Jacob's grandsons without regard to the cultural rationale of primogeniture.

Genesis 49 then contains a testament for each of Jacob's sons, and the displacement of primogeniture is further reflected in the fact that the speeches addressed to Jacob's first three sons are actually curses, rather than blessings. In spite of his rank Reuben 'will be pre-eminent no more' because he profaned his father's bed (49.3–4; cf. 35.22). The significance of his impropriety with Bilhah is unclear, but it may be that the firstborn, by sleeping with his father's concubine, has made an importunate claim on the status of the head of the family.[64] Simeon and Levi will be dispersed in Israel because of their violence (49.5–7), and this can only be a reference to their actions against Shechem in Genesis 34.

Leadership is then passed to Judah in 49.8–12, a blessing that reiterates a motif from the wider context of the Joseph story: 'Judah, your brothers will praise you; your hand will be on the neck of your enemies; your father's sons will bow down to you' (v. 8). A key feature of Joseph's dream is taken up here, but the father's final testament envisages the other brothers bowing down to Judah rather than to Joseph. If this poetry is to be taken as political allegory, then it perhaps reflects the political reality that only King David succeeded in unifying all the tribes into a single state. The northern kingdom, where the tribes of Joseph settled, had no stable dynasty, and it succumbed to external military aggression more than a century before the southern kingdom fell.

In the literary context of Genesis, the mention of Judah's enemies in 49.8 is one of the few allusions to military success in the whole book,[65] and, as already indicated, this verse should probably be taken as allusion to the achievements of David and his dynasty. Much more puzzling is the significance of Jacob's gift of land to Joseph in 48.22, land that Jacob claims to have taken from Amorites 'with my sword and bow'. There is no such conquest tradition in Genesis, and the content of the gift is obscure: 'one shoulder' is a literal rendering of the Hebrew, although this is most often taken as a metaphor for 'mountain slope' or 'ridge' (even though there is no evidence for this meaning elsewhere in the Hebrew Bible). The word at issue, however, is *shechem*, and the city of that name was indeed located in the territory later occupied by the tribes of Joseph. Moreover, according to Joshua 24.32, Joseph's bones were buried in Shechem. In his commentary on Genesis, Claus Westermann is willing to see a word-play in Genesis 48.22, so he translates *shechem* as 'ridge' but discerns an allusion to the city as well. On the other hand, he claims that this verse has nothing to do with Simeon and Levi's violence against Shechem in Genesis 34 (1986: 192–3).

It seems to me that the problems of 49.8 are best accounted for by the hypothesis that the editors are here being deliberately ironic. There is only one tradition of violent conquest of Shechem, and this is precisely the tradition in Genesis 34. Jacob's attitude to that violence is indicated in his final testament in the indictment against Simeon and Levi. The 'gift' of Shechem reflects the historical fact that this was indeed the territory of Joseph, but the idea that the city was taken by Jacob's violent conquest simply draws attention to the oddity of the notion within the otherwise eirenic context of Genesis. While the Hebrew of 48.22 is difficult, it seems to be saying that this is a gift that befits Joseph's pre-eminent role in the Genesis narrative. But the allusion to a violent conquest of Shechem gives Joseph's leadership a negative connotation which coheres with his displacement in the testament of Genesis 49. The irony implicit in the gift of Shechem is suggested only obliquely – by the puzzling juxtaposition of traditions, rather than by an explicit didacticism. But the subtlety of the editor's communicative strategy is similar to what we have found elsewhere in Genesis.

The other sons of Jacob are treated only briefly in the final testament, but the conclusion to the chapter is significant. Jacob's dying request is that he be buried 'in the cave in the field of Ephron the Hittite, the cave in the field of Machpelah, near Mamre in the land of Canaan, which Abraham bought from Ephron the Hittite as a burial holding' (49.29–30). Jacob indicates that this is the holding where Abraham, Sarah, Isaac, Rebekah and Leah are buried. But then he emphasises, for the third time, that 'the field and the cave in it were bought from the

Hittites' (49.32; cf. 50.13). Without a hint of the conquest ideology that frames Deuteronomy and Joshua, Jacob emphasises that this possession was legally acquired from the local inhabitants. The family's connection to the land of promise is thereby established without aggression, i.e. without the use of 'sword and bow'.

The account of Jacob's burial at the beginning of Genesis 50 is understandably devoid of any references to the covenantal land promises. The embalming and the length of mourning correspond more to Egyptian practices than to Israelite ones. When Joseph makes his request to the Pharaoh to bury his father in Canaan, he refers not to the cave of Machpelah but to a tomb which Jacob himself has dug (50.5). There is no need to offend the Pharaoh's sensibilities, and the conformity to Egyptian practice is so complete that the funeral entourage is understood by Canaanite witnesses to be fully Egyptian (50.11).

With Jacob now buried, the brothers' anxieties surface once again (50.15–18). And one would have to admit that Joseph's actions have been ambiguous, both because he has consistently favoured his full brother, Benjamin, and because his wider family loyalties have been mediated primarily through his father.[66] The brothers send a message to Joseph claiming knowledge of a special testament from Jacob requesting that the brothers be forgiven all the crimes they have committed. The indirectness of their appeal is striking: they present themselves not as brothers but as 'the servants of the Elohim of your father' (50.17). The assumption of this rhetoric is that the discourse of brotherhood will be ineffective, and it is therefore necessary to ground Joseph's sense of responsibility directly in God. When they present themselves to their brother, they say: 'We are your servants' (v. 18).[67]

Joseph's response is intriguing. When he first hears the message, he weeps. Presumably it does not matter whether or not the special testament is a fabrication: he is distressed by the brothers' fear. He begins by saying, 'Do not be afraid. For am I in the place of Elohim?' (50.19). This is a more ambiguous speech than commentators have tended to assume. The brothers have presented themselves both as the servants of Elohim and as Joseph's servants. They see no tension in their language, but perhaps Joseph is suggesting a contradiction: the brothers cannot be both kinds of servant, and so he refuses to take the place of Elohim.[68] In effect, they will be not his servants but his brothers. This would be the most charitable way to interpret the speech, and at the same time it would indicate that he has renounced the dream of having them bow down to him.

On the other hand, he does not explicitly deny the brothers' self-description as servants, and he does not actually address them as 'brothers'. It is still possible to read Joseph's speech in 50.19 as false humility. As was the case in 40.8 and 41.15–16, he initially appears to deny any knowledge of the divine mind, but then he immediately goes on to speak confidently of God's intentions: 'You meant evil towards me, but Elohim intended it for good, in order to accomplish what is now being done, the saving of many lives' (50.20). This statement of providence recapitulates the content of Joseph's speech in 45.5–7, but this time he 'spoke to their hearts' (50.21), and we can presume that the brothers were finally pacified.

No matter how charitably we read Joseph's speech at this point, there are some things which remain unspoken. As George Coats has argued (1973: 296), Joseph's actions towards his brothers in the past have been governed 'not by wisdom and discretion, not by justice for his brothers under the authority of his office, but by capricious use of power, by deception, by false accusation as severe as the accusation against Joseph in ch. 39'. His brothers have asked for forgiveness, but Joseph has not. He speaks only the language of providence. The narrative ends with a residual ambiguity about the nature of this reconciliation: will Joseph continue to cloak his dream of dominance with divine authority, or will he discover the breadth of true kinship?

The conclusion of the Genesis narrative, one may infer, has subtly formed an analogous question for the governors of the Persian period: will they continue to mask the imperial project of social control under the guise of ethnic holiness, or will they discover the complexity of kinship? Are the purposes of God advanced through the marginal agency of foreign women, like Tamar, or should theological and material privileges be reserved only for those with the strongest claims on genealogical status? However these questions are to be answered, the editors of Genesis appear to have shaped their traditions around a subversive suggestion: the manner of God's acting in the world often eludes the grasp of a story's central characters, even when the character at issue is a pious-sounding imperial governor.

5

WHOSE GENESIS?
WHICH ORTHODOXY?

> If I do not answer for myself, who will answer for me?
> But if I answer only for myself, am I still myself?
> (Babylonian Talmud: *Aboth* 6a)

The final editing of Genesis is the product of an 'intentional hybridity'.[69] The text reveals a complex inter-subjectivity incorporating diverse cultural elements both from within Israelite tradition and from outside it. Older literary sources may well have been used without any knowledge of their origins, but if those sources were ancient and reliable, then this would have made the implied arguments all the more convincing to an audience conditioned to respect tradition.[70] Whether or not the sources were ancient, the editors were directly engaged with the issues of their *own* day and, in particular, with controversies over the nature of authentic community. Against the ideology of the 'holy seed' in Ezra 9.1–2, marriage within the covenant community is not seen as a holy ideal that ensures divine favour; on the contrary, divine blessing flows extravagantly over the covenant's borders. The endogamous marriages of Abram, Isaac and Jacob are all called in question by the details of the Genesis narratives, and the conventional privilege attaching to the firstborn son is relentlessly undermined. The stories concerned with Hagar, Dinah and Tamar are indicative of the editors' theology, in that they subtly subvert any version of genealogical exclusivism or moral superiority. This perspective on Israel's beginnings is conveyed artfully but indirectly, in view of the fact that the editors were contesting the ideology of the Persian-sponsored governors. As postcolonial theory has suggested, resistance is often an exercise of the art of indirectness.

These are the major hypotheses that have shaped this reading of Genesis. In his influential philosophy of objective knowledge, Karl Popper (1972) argued that all observations are guided by hypotheses, some of which may be shaped by unconscious prejudice. Many modern commentaries on Genesis are organised so atomistically that one gains the impression that the authors have assumed what Popper calls 'the bucket theory of knowledge' – throw only atomic facts into a bucket, and when it is full you can perhaps risk an overall theory. Against this view, Popper argued that science progresses on the basis of conjectures which can never be proven, but which can be subjected to rigorous testing and refutation. It matters very little, therefore, how a hypothesis is produced, and the peculiar configuration of cultural prejudices that lie behind this book, for example, are therefore quite separable from the task of assessing its arguments. The hypotheses presented can only ever be an invitation to further conversation.

Popper's epistemology was in some senses revolutionary for its time, and it was certainly critical of an older, more atomistic, understanding of inductive research. Yet it continued the modernist tradition of representing the business of scientific knowledge as relatively detachable from the particular circumstances of investigators. In more recent theoretical discussions, however, both the making and the testing of hypotheses have been located more historically within the discourses and practices of the researcher, and this is particularly true in the human sciences. Without needing to subscribe to any particular epistemological theory, it is appropriate in this final chapter to reflect on my own circumstances as a reader and on the implications arising from the account of Genesis offered in the preceding chapters.

A simplistic version of postmodernism might suggest that when interpreters look at a text they see only the reflections of their own faces – in this case, of a white, male, Protestant, Australian. But a more subtle version of postmodernism recognises that an individual's identity is always constituted by innumerable traces of other identities (see e.g. Furrow 1995: 192). This subtler version is the more persuasive when one considers that although the interpretations of Genesis offered in the preceding chapters have a measure of novelty about them, they stand on the shoulders of innumerable commentators. If I have emphasised, for example, that the moral character of Abraham is questionable, and that there is no justification for the divine favour shown to him, the reader might want to put this down to Protestant prejudice. On the other hand, the same opinion has been expressed by the distinguished Jewish scholar, Jon D. Levenson:

> Unlike later rabbinic exegesis, the Torah itself offers no grounds for the selection of Abram for this awesome assignment. It makes no claim that he had earned it or that

he was endowed with some innate predisposition that made his selection rational.

(1996: 151–2)

In short, my reading of Abraham is not entirely the product of an individual subjectivity, since it intersects with perceptions of Genesis that derive from very different social locations.

To mention just one more example, the significance attached to Hagar and Ishmael in the preceding chapters arguably has more in common with Islamic traditions of interpretation than it does with Paul's account in Galatians 3–4. For example, Muslim scholars came to understand the test of Abraham in Genesis 22 as a demand to sacrifice Ishmael, not Isaac, partly because Islam traces its connection to Abraham through Ishmael (cf. Firestone 1990; Kuschel 1995). While my reading stays with the received Hebrew text, I have shown how the displacement of Ishmael is not entirely successful: since God identifies Ishmael as the seed of Abraham in 21.13, it makes little sense to have the divine voice speak of Abraham's 'only son' in 22.2.[71] Similarly, the reference to Beersheba in 22.19 calls to mind the promise made to Hagar at that same site in 21.18: Ishmael will become a 'great nation' (just as Abram was promised in 12.2). In other words, the narrative of Genesis provides no justification for Paul's argument that God's promise is associated only with Isaac (Gal. 4.21–31).[72] The editors have juxtaposed the traditions in Genesis 21–2 in a way that undermines an exclusive covenant – a point which applies equally to the circumcision of Ishmael in 17.23–7. In this respect, my reading overlaps with Islamic tradition.

One might suggest, nevertheless, that there is a Christian prejudice at work in the overall thesis – that the book of Genesis has been edited in order to undermine the ethnocentrism of Ezra and Nehemiah. It may be that I have drawn selectively on the diversity of interpretative options in order to highlight the legitimacy of the 'gentiles' rather than the 'Jews' in Genesis. In this sense, perhaps, the heterogeneous voices of other commentators have been carefully orchestrated. If this is true, then there might be a fundamental agreement with the apostle Paul, not so much in the details of his reading of the Genesis narratives but in his theological claim: 'There is neither Jew nor Greek, slave nor free, male nor female, for you are all one in Christ Jesus' (Gal. 3.28). The divisive discourses of race, class and gender are called in question by Paul's argument, and some might see an analogy between this feature of Christian spirituality and the tone of the preceding interpretation of Genesis.

There are several reasons, however, why such a suggestion would need to be qualified. Building on recent historical studies of the Persian period, I have attempted to show how the editing of Genesis seeks to undermine an excessively narrow understanding of Israelite identity. But as several other traditions in the Hebrew Bible have roughly the same purpose, what is at issue is a set of tensions within the Israelite traditions themselves. The notion of the 'holy seed' in Ezra 9 was apparently designed to narrow the membership of the covenant community, while the undermining of genealogical superiority by the editors of Genesis has the opposite effect of opening it up. The strongest contemporary analogies with this controversy can probably be found in recent Israeli history than in any comparisons between Judaism and Christianity (Eskenazi and Judd 1994).[73]

A more tenaciously suspicious critic might suggest, however, that this qualification simply masks an underlying Christian prejudice which privileges the liberal side of Judaism over any of its ethnocentric tendencies. Paul's theological claim in Galations 3.28 supposedly makes ethnicity a redundant feature of Christian identity, and one could assume that Galatians establishes a framework for all Christian readings of Genesis. On this view, my identity as a reader would constrain me to look for 'universalist' tendencies in the Hebrew Bible and to play down anything that could underwrite Jewish particularism.

Such an argument would contain at least two mistaken assumptions. First, Christians have conventionally domesticated the exclusivist tendencies within the Hebrew Bible by relegating them to an 'old covenant' which is seen as simply the preface to the more universalistic 'new covenant'.[74] This line of argument would suggest that Christian interests are best served by seeing the Hebrew Bible in terms only of Jewish particularism, and within that framework, therefore, there would be little motivation for my reading of Genesis. The uniqueness of the new covenant would be eroded if it were discovered that 'the old covenant' were more inclusive than previously thought.

Second, even if my reading of Genesis could be justifiably accused of imposing some version of universalism on the text, this may not be the result of peculiarly Christian prejudice. There are philosophical and political versions of 'universalisability' which were sometimes forged precisely in opposition to traditional forms of Christianity. Enlightenment philosophers argued, for example, that unless a norm can be advocated universally, it is not a properly ethical norm. Hence, Immanuel Kant could suggest that 'Pure moral religion is the euthanasia of Judaism' (Weischedel 1964: 321), i.e. insofar as religion has any rational philosophical justification, Jewish particularism should be superseded (cf. Rose 1990). Kant's philosophy was, however, directed against any form of religion that based its authority on tradition, and, indeed, I argue presently that this rational principle of 'universalisability' is only tangentally related to contemporary Christian theology.

Similarly, modern versions of civic nationalism adopted the concept of universal citizenship in order to override any form of social identity which might inhibit the unity of a nation state (Greenfeld 1992). This has often been perceived as a liberating idea, notably during the French Revolution, and one would need to recognise that the egalitarian impulse was directed not only against the nobility but also against the traditional authority of the Church. Once again, this version of universalism is only tangentally related to Christian theology, but ironically there has in fact been an alliance between the two of a highly problematic kind.

Historically, civic nationalism has produced numerous examples of 'internal colonization' (McPhee 1980), and, in this tradition, civic administrations in Australia, for example, have often sought to undermine the distinctiveness of the Aboriginal people. The principle of universal citizenship has been used to deny the uniqueness of indigenous people, and the social policy of assimilation has been characteristically advocated on the ground that it was politically enlightened. But assimilationism has had its counterpart in the practices of certain Christian missions which attempted to dismantle Aboriginal culture (Swain and Rose 1988).

The oppression of indigenous people is not a uniquely Australian experience, and it has been shaped by many sources, modern and ancient, but it would not be unreasonable to suggest that the letters of the apostle Paul are implicated in the ideology of assimilation as it has been practised by Christian missionaries. This thesis has been argued with particular force by the Jewish scholar Daniel Boyarin in his 1994 work *A Radical Jew: Paul and the Politics of Identity*. The idea of a non-differentiated humanity in Galatians 3.28 has historically often been co-opted by colonialism, Boyarin suggests, and his critique of Paul applies equally well to Aboriginal missions in Australia:

> In terms of ethnicity, [Paul's] system required that all human cultural specificities – first and foremost, that of the Jews – be eradicated, whether or not the people in question were willing. Moreover, since of course there is no such thing as cultural unspecificity, merging of all people into one common culture means ultimately (as it has meant in the history of

European cultural imperialism) merging all people into the dominant culture.[75]

(1994: 8)

This kind of argument leads Boyarin to assert that, under certain conditions, ethnocentrism is a legitimate strategy of cultural resistance, especially when adopted by minority groups (cf. Smith 1989).[76] Such resistance is quite different from the imposition of ethnocentric policies by the machinery of a state, and the ethical difference can be as clear as the difference between aggression and defence. Boyarin puts this view forward as a Jewish argument, but some recent Christian theologies have been equally concerned to recover the dignity of people groups which have suffered under the cultural imperialism of mission movements in the past (e.g. Trompf 1987). The fact that these theological projects have appeared under the heading of 'local' or 'contextual' theologies reveals the extent to which the older ideals of universal mission have been called in question. The attempt to formulate an 'Afrocentric' theology in North America is driven by the same kind of impetus (Saunders 1995).

This discussion relates directly to my reading of the Genesis traditions. If the inclusivism of the final editors is to be read, as I have suggested, as a reaction against policies promulgated by the Persian-sponsored governors, then this is a case of resistance to state-imposed ethnocentrism. On the other hand, when the Genesis stories were revised in *Jubilees*, in the second century BCE,[77] they were rewritten in such a way that foreign marriages were categorically prohibited, and the foreign women in the earlier tradition are given a more legitimate identity (see e.g. *Jub.* 20.4; 22.20; 30.7–23; cf. Werman 1997). This rewritten version of Genesis, however, was apparently produced in a context of extreme persecution of the Jews, when Hellenising policies were designed to eradicate distinctive Jewish practices. Given Boyarin's reasoning, it would be pointless to say that *Jubilees* has 'misunderstood' the dynamics of Genesis; the historical contexts were dramatically different, and the forms of ethnocentrism in the two periods are therefore not comparable.

Following on from the argument that ethnocentrism is malign only when it is enforced by the machinery of state, Boyarin suggests (1994: 252–8) that Jewish faith needs to be disassociated from claims to sovereignty. Although Judaism has revolved around the tension between ideas of 'genealogy' and ideas of 'territory' (both articulated in Genesis), genealogy should be given priority over territory, and ethnicity should be separated from all forms of political dominance.

WHICH ORTHODOXY?

Boyarin's view therefore combines a renunciation of sovereignty with a tenacious hold on cultural identity, i.e. a complete separation of religion and state such as permits a diversity of ethnic difference (1994: 257–60).

This line of argument supplies the background for Boyarin's critique of Galatians. Paul's gospel, he suggests, is shaped too much by his Hellenistic background:

> Paul was motivated by a Hellenistic desire for the One, which among other things produced an ideal of a universal human essence beyond difference and hierarchy. This universal humanity, however, was predicated (and still is) on the dualism of the flesh and the spirit, such that while the body is particular, marked through practice as Jew or Greek, and through anatomy as male or female, the spirit is universal.
>
> (1994: 7)

The new community of the spirit, Boyarin suggests, attempted to supplant the fleshly genealogy of Abraham, the literal Torah, the literal land of promise, but Jews refused 'to be allegorized into a spiritual disembodiment' (1994: 230–1).

This aspect of Boyarin's argument is less compelling than are his comments on colonialism. Within the context of Galatians, Paul emphasises new patterns of communal life, embodied in concrete social practices rather than in spiritual withdrawal (Gal. 5.13–6.10; Barclay 1996). The distinction between flesh and spirit does not have the implications suggested for the body, and it is precisely this issue that lies at the centre of later Christian debates about 'incarnation'. Orthodox Christianity reacted against any attempt to disembody the historical Jesus, and in claiming paradoxically that Christ was both human and divine the Church decisively rejected any dualism of spirit and body.[78] Indeed, in response to Boyarin's account of Paul, the Croation theologian Miroslav Volf emphasises that the principle of unity in Christianity is constituted by the particularity of a suffering body:

> The body of Christ lives as a complex interplay of differentiated bodies – Jewish and gentile, female and male, slave and free – of those who have partaken of Christ's self-sacrifice. The Pauline move is not from the particularity of the body to the universality of the spirit, but from separated bodies to the community of interrelated bodies.
>
> (1996: 47–8)

Precisely for this reason (and in partial agreement with Boyarin), Volf rejects any model of reconciliation based on neglect of cultural differences. He suggests that a responsible theology will seek a 'non-final reconciliation', forged in a perpetual struggle against oppression but not seduced by universalist projects of liberation (Volf 1996: 108–10; cf. Lyotard 1984). The drive towards 'local' Christian theology has its counterpart in Volf's advocacy of local forms of reconciliation.

Interestingly, there is one aspect of Boyarin's work that has its own spiritualising tendency. In his renunciation of political self-determination, he recommends that the possession of the promised land be seen as deferred and that Diaspora identity replace national self-determination (1994: 249). He suggests at one point that Rabbinic Judaism rightly renounced the land until the final redemption, and in this respect his ethical stance is in agreement with the example of the orthodox *Natorei Karta* who refuse to visit the Western Wall in Jerusalem without Arab 'visas', because the Wall was taken by violence (Boyarin 1994: 252–8).

As it happens, Boyarin's advocacy of the separation of religion and state coincides with my own church's tradition, which forged this doctrine over against the homogenising power of the Church of England (Hill 1988). In a context where religious freedom was being denied by a state church this doctrine made good sense, but in the contemporary Australian context, it needs some rethinking. For example, land is not such a negotiable item in the repertoire of Aboriginal religion, while the question of indigenous land rights is a matter for the state.[79] This poses a peculiar problem for indigenous Christians, even if they have no strong claim to make regarding their own sovereignty. The issue points up the limits of abstract notions of citizenship, since there are some indigenous communities for which land rights are a constitutive feature of their identity in a much stronger sense than they are for non-indigenous Australians. Analogies to this kind of 'politics of difference' can be found in any country with indigenous populations, but there are other ethnic groups which, for different reasons, refuse to be subsumed under homogenising visions of national culture (Taylor 1992). The complete separation of religion and state is no longer workable where the rights of these groups are a matter for the state. And, ironically, this applies precisely in contexts where governments are concerned to defend multicultural pluralism.

Some Australian Aboriginal theologians have begun to reclaim the sacred sites bequeathed to them by their tribal law, drawing analogies between their own culture and the significance of sites like Bethel and

WHICH ORTHODOXY?

Sinai for the construction of Jewish identity. For example, Djiniyini Gondarra (1986) has compared the traditional laws of his Aboriginal Dreaming with the laws of Israel, and he sees no incompatibility between these and his Christian faith. In implicit agreement with Miroslav Volf (1996), Gondarra's argument implies that the spirit of Christ should be seen not in terms of a 'final reconciliation' in which either Aboriginal or Jewish identity is erased but rather as the foundation for multicultural communities (cf. Barclay 1996: 209–14; Volf 1996: 43). And perhaps even more strongly than Boyarin's, this argument retains the particularity of law, ritual and sacred topography as part of the exercise of authentic Aboriginal faith.

Aboriginal theologians like Gondarra occupy a precarious position between the more conventional constructions of identity. He is both complicit with the dominant Christian culture and opposed to it – precisely that hybrid form of cultural resistance which has been a focus in postcolonial studies (see e.g. Bhaba 1994: 171–97). Gondarra's position has been criticised from both sides, either for being inauthentic Christianity or for being inauthentic Aboriginality.[80] Such criticisms are examples of what has been called the 'myth of authenticity', one which creates a hierarchy of voices from the 'purer' exponents of an identity, at the top, to the hybrid voices at the bottom (Griffiths 1994).

But all cultures and ethnicities are in some respect hybrid, whether or not this is consciously acknowledged (Said 1993: 317; Brett 1996). Indeed, the book of Genesis itself offers a clear illustration of Homi Bhabha's point that 'Hybridity is never simply a question of the admixture of pre-given identities or essences' (Bhabha 1990: 314).[81] The complexity of the received text is indicative of a long history of cultural interaction and contestation. Miroslav Volf has provided a theological framework for this aspects of postcolonial theory, arguing that the spirit of Christ affirms hybridity, making space for the other without projecting a final reconciliation (Volf 1996: 51–2; 109–10).

If there is a Christian prejudice in my reading of Genesis, it is a prejudice refracted through theologians like Gondarra. He holds both to his Aboriginality and to those aspects of his identity which have been shaped by the intersecting relationships of Christianity. Within Aboriginal culture, the details of genealogy and topography are still constitutive of social identity, and the analogies with the world of Genesis are strong. There is not a great distance between Gondarra's hybrid identity and the representation of social interrelatedness which places the seed of Abraham within a comprehensive picture of all humanity.

In a discussion of the genealogies of Genesis, Frank Crüsemann is able to conclude that 'all of humanity and the kinships of Israel are grasped in one single system; between them there exists an abundance of intermediate stages and a continuous, sliding scale of linkages' (1996: 65–6). There is no clear distinction between the divinely elected family and other nations, but rather, a complex and hybrid set of relationships. I have shown that this argument regarding the genealogies holds also for the narratives of Genesis, and the final editors have produced precisely the kind of sociality for which Boyarin has appealed, 'one that will allow for stubborn hanging on to ethnic, cultural specificity but in a context of deeply felt and enacted human solidarity' (1994: 257). The world created by Genesis holds together both types of moral concern – universal solidarity and the particularities of identity.

NOTES

1 See Brett (1991a: 123–43) for a discussion of the notion of epistemological 'horizons' reflected variously in the work of Karl Popper, Hans-Georg Gadamer and Hans-Robert Jauss.
2 Here Albertz cites the innovative work of Blum (1990), but for at least a century now it has been common to suggest that the literary sources of Genesis were combined and edited only after the exile in Babylon (587–538 BCE). Even Israel Knohl, who dates the literary sources much earlier than most biblical scholars, is willing to concede that the final editing of the Pentateuch took place during the Persian period, when many of the Israelite 'exiles' returned from Babylon to Judah (1995: 100–3, 201).
3 Cf. also Eskenazi (1992: 35–6); Douglas (1993: 216–47); Eskenazi and Judd (1994).
4 'The defilement system described in Leviticus and Numbers protects the sanctuary; it does not organize social categories. Admittedly, it separates priests from laity, but only in respect of access to the sanctuary' (Douglas 1993: 155). Cf. Joosten (1996: 85) who concludes that in view of the extensive marriage laws in Leviticus 17–26, it is significant that there is no prohibition against marrying non-Israelite women. Lev. 21.14 is the 'exception that proves the rule': it is binding only on priests.
5 Knohl draws a distinction between the earliest layer of the Priestly tradition, which he calls the Priestly Torah, and a later Holiness School, to whom he ascribes the ethical concern with aliens (1995: 21, 53, 93). This diachronic distinction does not affect Douglas's thesis, since Knohl asserts that the Holiness School influenced Priestly tradition even before the exile in Babylon.
6 In a detailed reconstruction of Priestly tradition, Grünwaldt (1992: 27–70) suggests that this verse – as well as any reference to covenant obligation in Genesis 17 – was an addition to the first layer of *P* (the Priestly tradition). The first layer contained, indeed, the circumcision of Ishmael (17.24–6) but no statement of his exclusion from the covenant. Since, however, Grünwaldt argues that the supplement was

NOTES

added in the Persian period, his thesis could be construed as support for my overall argument concerning the final editing.

7 On the implications of primogeniture in Israel, i.e. granting the firstborn son inheritance privileges, see especially Rogerson (1986: 22–4) and Stager (1985: 25–8).

8 The exception here would be Harold Bloom's *The Book of J* (1990), which focuses on a reconstructed literary source, but see the severe critique of this book in Alter (1992: 153–69).

9 A more detailed analysis would suggest that while narratological studies characteristically deal with the surface of the text they also deal with inexplicit considerations (e.g. the primogeniture implied by Genesis 27). There is still a difference, however, between implications drawn from the linguistic context and implications drawn from the non-linguistic context of utterance.

10 I have argued elsewhere (Brett 1995b) that Hirsch's Kantian ethic can be turned against the principle of respect for authors: if all persons – not just authors – are to be respected as ends in themselves, then it would be important to discover whether ancient authors have suppressed or distorted the views of others, regardless of whether that distortion was conscious or unconscious. Critics of authorial ideology could therefore be motivated by the very same ethic as is Hirsch.

11 A notable exception can be found in Hermann Gunkel's *Schöpfung und Chaos in Urzeit und Endzeit* (1895) which argued, against the source criticism of the day, that the author of Genesis 1 had preserved traditions at odds with his own intention. In some ways, this argument anticipates the claims of deconstructive criticism (Brett 1991b: 1–4).

12 The term is borrowed from Mikhail Bakhtin *The Dialogic Imagination* (1981: 358–61), and it has shaped some of the key theoretical work of Homi Bhabha in *The Location of Culture* (1994) and Henry Louis Gates' *The Signifying Monkey* (1988). In each case, the deliberate juxtaposition of different voices is seen as potentially subversive of dominant ideologies. See, further, Young's *Colonial Desire: Hybridity in Theory, Culture and Race* (1995), and Werbner and Modood's *Debating Cultural Hybridity* (1997).

13 I have translated the rhyming phrase *tohu wabohu* as 'welter and waste', following Robert Alter's elegant rendering (1996: 3).

14 Deut. 32.10–11 uses the same verb (*rhp*) of an eagle hovering over its young, comparing the image to Yahweh who found the children of Israel in a wasteland (*tohu*), and cared for them. Ironically, in Deut. 32.11, and in Exod. 19.4, God is being compared to a ritually unclean bird (Deut. 14.12).

15 Septuagint and Samaritan manuscripts apparently try to eliminate the problem by making the verb 'judge' singular.

16 See, e.g., 1 Kgs. 22.19–22; Isa. 6.8; Jer. 23.22; Job 1.6–12; Ps. 82.

17 The verb *qnh* used here is ambiguous in classical Hebrew between 'making' and 'possessing'. Umberto Cassuto (1961: 198–201) convincingly

NOTES

argued that this text makes best sense if *qnh* is taken in the sense of 'making', as do the uses in Gen. 14.22, Deut. 32.6 and Ps. 139.13.

18 It is worth noting that the Sabbath law in Deut. 5.14 also envisages a rest for animals, not just humans. Keeping the Sabbath is a specifically Yahwist practice and not part of the religion of Genesis, but even the exclusivist theology of Deuteronomy allows that the wider created order can participate.

19 *Adam* is a generic term throughout Gen. 3, but it has a specific referent indicated by the definite article '*the* human' – the character in the story. Strictly speaking, *adam* is semantically vague in the same way as the word 'animal' is vague in English: 'animal', for example, does not distinguish between 'cats' and 'dogs', and *adam* does not distinguish semantically between male and female, as indicated by its use in Gen. 1.27. But just as, in context, the word 'animal' can refer to a particular cat or dog, so *adam* can refer to a particular man, as it does in Gen. 2.23. One wonders, however, whether gender is meaningful before the creation of woman.

20 The politics of naming is crucial for postcolonial theory and is illustrated by the change from 'Rhodesia' to 'Zimbabwe'. In Australia, the capacity to recognise local tribal names marks a transition from the generalising label 'aboriginal'. Keith Whitelam (1996) advocates a similar postcolonial logic in his argument for 'Palestinians', rather than ancient 'Israelites'. Cf. my 1997 response.

21 The *robets* used here is normally used of animals, and hence there is a thematic connection between 4.7 and 1.26, 28. The first vocation was to rule over animals, but now Cain is exhorted to rule over sin.

22 Paradoxically, the favour Abel receives makes a similar point, since it is only in 4.26 that people 'begin to call on the name Yahweh'; Abel did not know this particular divine name. References to Yahweh in Gen. 4 are spoken exclusively in the narrator's voice, not Cain's or Abel's. Cf. also Exod. 6.2–3 which even denies that the name Yahweh was known in this period.

23 It is just as clear that the final editors of Genesis have used more than one literary source in their own narrative: in 6.19–20, Elohim speaks of only two kinds of each animal to be brought into the ark, while 7.2–3 has Yahweh speaking of seven pairs of clean animals and two pairs of unclean animals.

24 A relentlessly deconstructive reader might point out the irony that the word *chat* occurs only once more in the Hebrew Bible, when Job 41.33 describes the mighty creature of the sea who has no fear at all.

25 Scholars are unanimous in recognising that the ancient city of Ur could not have been known as 'Ur of the Chaldeans' until the rise of the neo-Babylonian empire, i.e. the sixth century BCE (see Westermann 1985: 139–40). This example indicates that the final text is far removed from the events being narrated, as do the anachronistic references to camels (e.g. in Genesis 24), which were probably not domesticated until the

NOTES

eleventh century BCE. However, at several points, the narrator betrays this historical distance quite explicitly: see e.g. 12.6; 13.7; 19.37–8.

26 One might want to argue that the very definition of 'clan' implies an exogamous group, and since Abraham could not be recommending an incestuous marriage, *moledet* refers simply to a kinship group larger than his clan. However, not all anthropologists consider exogamy a defining characteristic of clans, and in any case a social template derived from comparative anthropology cannot simply be imposed upon the Israelite *mishpachah* without further discussion. It is clear, for example, that a *mishpachah* was routinely endogamous (see further Lemche 1985: 231–44). In short, the term *moledet* was not used in 24.4 in order to avoid the possible implication of incest, and this observation is supported by the fact that *mishpachah* is used instead of *moledet* in 24.38, 40–1.

27 Cf. Abraham's questions to God in his defence of Sodom, in 18.23–5.

28 This text can be considered comparable to Gen. 4.1, where, as I have noted, Eve's naming of Cain implicitly contests the way the world is constructed in Adam's eyes (Pardes 1993).

29 This command can hardly be reconciled with Joshua 5.1–9 which associates circumcision with entry into the promised land; that narrative implies that the men born during the wilderness wanderings were not yet circumcised. The early Joshua tradition could not have known this version of the Abrahamic covenant, since Gen. 17.12 stipulates that circumcision should take place eight days after a child's birth.

30 There is clearly a patriarchal assumption at this point: the narrative occludes the possibility that Sodom has ten righteous women among its population.

31 Abraham's question is arguably related to the logic of 18.19, where Yahweh says of Abraham that 'he will charge his children and his household after him to keep the way of Yahweh by doing righteousness and justice'. If Abraham is to keep the 'way of Yahweh', then divine justice must in some sense be understandable in human categories.

32 It might be thought that the theme of foreignness could not be taken up in Jud. 19, as the characters in the story are all Israelites. However, the Ephraimite host is considered a resident alien among the Benjaminites of Gibeah, since they come from different tribes. Jud. 19.16 uses the same verb (*gur*: 'to live as an alien') in reference to the Ephraimite as does Gen. 19.9 in reference to Lot. The social status of the resident alien (*ger*), however, was different from the non-resident foreigner (see e.g. Exod. 12.43–9), and the visitors in Gen. 19 and Jud. 19 fall into this latter non-resident category.

33 Intriguingly, Gen. 19.30–8 sees the Ammonites and Moabites as beginning peacefully in an uninhabited area, whereas Deut. 2.9–22 represents their origins in terms of conquests legitimated by Yahweh (Van Seters 1992: 238). This observation coheres with our earlier suggestion that, unlike Deuteronomy, Genesis has no ideology of dispossession (cf. Habel 1995: 115–33).

NOTES

34 2 Sam. 5.6 identifies the inhabitants of Jerusalem as Jebusites.
35 See above, note 12.
36 On the concept of indirect communication, see above pp. 12–13.
37 This translation comes from Alter (1996: 155). Cf. also Midrash Tanhuma, in Leibowitz (1980: 323).
38 See above, p. 16.
39 Some commentators have suggested that the translation 'lay with' implies too much mutuality, since the Hebrew vowels indicate simply the definite object, not the preposition 'with'. But this grammatical argument is dubious, especially when one considers the additional problems posed by variations in the ancient manuscripts of Genesis. One needs to recognise first that the vowels were not actually present in the ancient Hebrew texts; they were added on the basis of later editorial decisions. The Septuagint, Syriac, Vulgate and Targum Jonathan all read the text as containing the preposition 'with'. Thus, it is not clear whether the editors of the Persian period intended to use the preposition or the mark of the definite object. More importantly, Deut. 22.25 clearly envisages a case where a man lies 'with' a woman having overpowered her. In short, the presence or absence of a preposition is not decisive in deciding whether violence is involved. See further Bechtel (1994: 23).
40 King David, who founded the longest dynasty in Israelite history, came from the tribe of Judah. And, as Genesis might lead us to expect, he was a younger son (1 Sam. 16).
41 Yahweh is named from multiple points of view in Genesis 28 – by the narrator in v. 13; by the divine self-description in v. 13; and by Jacob himself in vv. 16 and 21.
42 See above, p. 60.
43 The ambiguity in Tamar's identity was unacceptable to the later authors of *Jubilees*, who retold this story in the second century BCE. They represented her as Aramean (*Jub.* 41.1), reflecting a tendency to grant Aramean women honorary 'Jewishness' (Werman 1997). See further, Menn (1997).
44 Judah's pre-emptive judgement against a foreigner may be compared with Abraham's mistaken assumption that 'there is no fear of Elohim in this place' (20.11).
45 In the genealogy in Ruth 4.18–22, Perez stands at the head of the lineage of King David. Tamar therefore shares with Ruth, the Moabitess, the distinction of being a foreign woman in the Davidic lineage. David was a younger brother, and this fact is perhaps also relevant to the Tamar narrative: although Perez was born before his brother Zerah, the narrative of Gen. 38.27–30 suggests that since Zerah's hand emerged first, he was displaced by Perez.
46 Men can be described as 'beautiful' (*yapheh*) in biblical Hebrew, and as having a 'beautiful figure', even though this language is more often used to represent women. Cf. the description of Absalom in 2 Sam.

NOTES

14.25, and of the male beloved in the Song of Songs 1.16. The Genesis narrator describes physical beauty in androgynous terms, but one should note that the same words are used to describe cows that are in good form (41.2, 18)!

47 The instability of power is also reflected in Exod. 1.8–10, although in this latter case the reasons of state are made clear: 'Then a new king, who did not know Joseph, came to power in Egypt. And he said to his people, "Look, the people of Israel have become too numerous and too mighty for us. Come, let us act wisely with them."' In Joseph's hands, political wisdom could be turned to advantage, but when he is forgotten the politics turn sour.

48 The same kind of observation applies to the Septuagint and Samaritan renderings of this verse, although they have slightly different formulations: 'Without God an answer of prosperity [or 'salvation'] will not be given to Pharaoh.'

49 This difference is all the more striking given that the doubling of the Pharaoh's dreams is taken to mean that the future is securely determined (41.32). The baker has only one dream, so one could infer that the baker's fate is somewhat less determined.

50 In this respect, the characterisation of the Pharaoh in 41.38–9 is comparable with that of Abimelech in Gen. 20.3–11.

51 The excessiveness of this rhetoric is ironically revealed by the Hebrew midwives in Exod. 1.15–20 who defy the Pharaoh's decree to kill all newly born males. Some hands are eventually raised in resistance, in spite of royal power.

52 Intention can, however, be a mitigating factor, for example in Num. 15 and 35.

53 If this is indeed an implication of Judah's speech, then it puts a question mark against the principle of 'blood for blood' in Gen. 9.6.

54 Semantic studies of *goy* (commonly translated as 'nation') indicate that the term normally carries connotations of territory and sovereignty. The uses of *goy* in Gen. 21.18 and 46.3 are therefore unusual in that these texts envisage Israel as a 'nation' while still in Egypt, i.e. without Israel having its own territory or sovereignty. See further Weisman (1985), and Brett (1995a).

55 The mixed memories associated with the site may also bring to mind Gen. 15.12–16 which predicts 400 years of harsh treatment in a strange land. The audience of Genesis in the Persian period would have known that this text in chapter 15 is alluding to Egypt, and in this respect Joseph's role in saving his family from famine is just the beginning of the story. The later exodus narrative is also alluded to in Gen. 47.11 which anachronistically speaks of 'Rameses' (cf. Exod. 1.11). Prior to this verse, the region where Joseph's family is to reside is called 'Goshen' (Gen. 45.10; 46.28–9, 34; 47.1, 4, 6).

56 Leah, for example, had to be mentioned in different sections, 29.32–5 and 30.18–21. See above (p. 90).

NOTES

57 In view of the fact that women are normally excluded from patriarchal genealogies, a feminist reader might question the argument that Gen. 46.12 constitutes an allusion to Tamar. But this is an abnormal case: first, because every male in this verse is closely related to Tamar, and a whole chapter of Genesis has been devoted to explaining how; second, Genesis 46 actually names only two wives – and both are foreign; third, when Chronicles recapitulates the genealogy from Judah to King David, the only two wives who are thought worthy of mention are Tamar and Bathshua, the Canaanite wife of Judah (1 Chron. 2.3–15). The withholding of Tamar's name from Gen. 46.12 could possibly be a subtle way of enhancing her presence.

58 See above, p. 102.

59 See the genealogies in Ruth 4.18–22 and 1 Chron. 2.3–15.

60 There are numerous variations among the ancient manuscripts, but most differences are minor and have little bearing on my argument. In this case, however, the Samaritan and the Septuagint texts preserve an older form of the narrative which captures the darker side of Joseph more explicitly. There is no manuscript of Genesis dating back to the Persian period, but in general we can presume that the Massoretic text is a largely reliable witness.

61 Deut. 23.8 has a temporary exclusion on Egyptians: they could enter 'the assembly of Yahweh' three generations after the exodus events. This restriction had expired long before the Persian period.

62 See above, pp. 105–7.

63 Gen. 22.16–18 is a peculiar exception, framed within an exclusivist ideology. For a discussion of this text within the wider context of Genesis 21–3, see above pp. 74–9.

64 This seems to be the force of the incident in 2 Sam. 16.21–2, where Absalom sleeps with his father's concubines.

65 The ironies implicit in Gen. 14 and 22.16–18 have been discussed at length above, pp. 53–5, 75–9.

66 See above, pp. 124–5.

67 The word for 'servant' (*'ebed*) is the same in both v. 17 and v. 18; it may also be translated 'slave'.

68 This possibility is latent in Gen. 50.19, but the idea comes to explicit expression in a divine speech in Lev. 25.42: 'Because they are my servants, whom I brought out from the land of Egypt, they must not be sold as servants.'

69 See note 12 above.

70 Cf. Žižek 1994, and above, p. 21.

71 See above, pp. 72–4.

72 Paul's interpretation of Hagar is a polemical allegory, not a reading of Genesis for its own sake (Fowl 1998: 128–60).

73 Tamara Eskenazi and Eleanore Judd (1994) have suggested that there is an analogy between Israel under Persian administration and Palestine under the British Mandate. They indicate that tensions between ethnic

NOTES

groups in the 1930s and 1940s led to a struggle for control over marriage and divorce laws, with the Chief Rabbinate enjoying British patronage. Eastern European orthodox rabbis occasionally contested the Chief Rabbinate's rulings and denied Jewish identity to non-orthodox Jews. Any such analogy will entail differences, but Israel under the Persian administration may well have been shaped by similar controversies.

74 This tired opposition has been thoroughly deconstructed by Jon Levenson (1996).

75 Boyarin (1994: 262) rightly dismisses any anachronistic suggestion that the apostle Paul was himself 'anti-Semitic'; he was a Jew, conducting a liberal argument about the nature of gentile faith, but still within the terms of a living Jewish tradition. Anti-Semitism is a much later, and unintended, application of Paul's letters. The separation of Judaism and Christianity took place in historical contexts within which both religious groups were minorities. Neither wielded significant political power, and it was only when Christianity took on the institutional forms of Christendom that anti-Jewish rhetoric could be combined with political power to form systematic anti-Semitic violence.

76 Note, however, Jon Levenson's cautionary remarks: 'At its worst, the absolutization of Jewish survival leads to the denial of ethical constraints on Jewry in danger. And since Jewry is usually in danger, this grants the Jew a moral *carte blanche* – quite the reverse of the biblical intent' (1996: 169).

77 See above, note 43.

78 One could argue that recent liberation theology constitutes a radical reclaiming of incarnational doctrine (cf. Löwy 1996).

79 This is only one example of the complex relationship between identity politics and public life. See further Calhoun (1995: 231–82).

80 Cf. the controversy surrounding the nineteenth-century Pequot Methodist William Apess in Donaldson (1999). For an introduction to native American versions of Christianity, see Jace Weaver (1996).

81 A recent history of Israelite religion concludes that the hybrid religion of Genesis

> is to be defined not as a preliminary stage but as a substratum of Yahweh religion. This stratum of family religion is a preliminary stage only to the degree that it shows an amazing similarity to other Near Eastern religions, going as far back as Sumero-Babylonian religion at the beginning of the second millenium.
> (Albertz 1994: 29)

BIBLIOGRAPHY

Albertz, R. (1994) *A History of Israelite Religion in the Old Testament Period*, vol. 1, London: SCM; trans. of *Religionsgeschichte in alttestamentlicher Zeit*, Göttingen: Vandenhoeck & Ruprecht, 1992.

Alter, R. (1981) *The Art of Biblical Narrative*, New York: Basic Books.

—— (1990) *The Pleasures of Reading in an Ideological Age*, Berkeley: University of California Press.

—— (1992) *The World of Biblical Literature*, London: SPCK.

—— (1996) *Genesis: Translation and Commentary*, New York: W. W. Norton.

Alter, R. and F. Kermode (eds) (1987) *The Literary Guide to the Bible*, London: Fontana.

Anderson, B. W. (1994) *From Creation to New Creation*, Minneapolis, MN: Fortress.

Ardener, E. (1972) 'Belief and the Problem of Women', in J. S. La Fontaine (ed.) *The Interpretation of Ritual*, London: Tavistock.

Bakhtin, M. (1981) *The Dialogic Imagination: Four Essays*, trans. C. Emerson and M. Holquist, Austin: University of Texas Press.

Barclay, J. (1996) '"Neither Jew nor Greek": Multiculturalism and the New Perspective on Paul', in M. G. Brett (ed.) *Ethnicity and the Bible*, Leiden: E. J. Brill.

Barthes, R. (1977) 'The Struggle with the Angel', in *Image, Music, Text*, trans. S. Heath, London: Fontana Collins.

Bechtel, L. (1994) 'What if Dinah Is Not Raped? (Genesis 34)', *Journal for the Study of the Old Testament* 62: 19–36

Bhabha, H. (1990) *Nation and Narration*, London: Routledge.

—— (1994) *The Location of Culture*, London: Routledge.

Bird, P. (1997) *Missing Persons and Mistaken Identities: Women and Gender in Ancient Israel*, Minneapolis, MN: Fortress.

Bledstein, A. J. (1993) 'Binder, Trickster, Heel and Hairy-Man: Re-reading Genesis 27 as a Trickster Tale Told by a Woman', in A. Brenner (ed.) *A Feminist Companion to Genesis*, Sheffield: Sheffield Academic Press.

BIBLIOGRAPHY

Bloom, H. (1990) *The Book of J*, New York: Grove Weidenfeld.

Blum, E. (1990) *Studien zur Komposition des Pentateuch*, Berlin: W. de Gruyter.

Boyarin, D. (1994) *A Radical Jew: Paul and the Politics of Identity*, Berkeley: University of California Press.

Brenner, A. (ed.) (1993) *A Feminist Companion to Genesis*, Sheffield: Sheffield Academic Press.

Brett, M. G. (1991a) *Biblical Criticism in Crisis?*, Cambridge: Cambridge University Press.

—— (1991b) 'Motives and Intentions in Genesis 1', *Journal of Theological Studies* 42: 1–16.

—— (1993) 'The Future of Reader Criticisms?', in F. Watson (ed.) *The Open Text*, London: SCM.

—— (1995a) 'Nationalism and the Hebrew Bible', in J. W. Rogerson, M. Davies and M. D. Carroll R. (eds) *The Bible in Ethics*, Sheffield: JSOT Press.

—— (1995b) 'The Political Ethics of Postmodern Allegory', in M. D. Carroll R., D. J. A. Clives and P. Davies (eds) *The Bible in Human Society*, Sheffield: JSOT Press.

—— (1996) 'Interpreting Ethnicity: Method, Hermeneutics, Ethics', in M. G. Brett (ed.) *Ethnicity and the Bible*, Leiden: E. J. Brill.

—— (1997) 'The Implied Ethics of Postcolonialism', *Jian Dao* 8: 1–13.

Calhoun, C. (1995) *Critical Social Theory*, Oxford: Blackwell.

Carr, D. (1996) *Reading the Fractures of Genesis*, Louisville, KY: Westminster–John Knox.

Cassuto, U. (1961) *A Commentary on the Book of Genesis*, Jerusalem: Magnes.

Coats, G. (1973) 'The Joseph Story and Ancient Wisdom: A Reappraisal', *Catholic Biblical Quarterly* 35: 285–97.

Crüsemann, F. (1996) 'Human Solidarity and Ethnic Identity: Israel's Self-Definition in the Geneaological System of Genesis', in M. G. Brett (ed.) *Ethnicity and the Bible*, Leiden: E. J. Brill.

Derrida, J. (1995) *The Gift of Death*, Chicago, IL: Chicago University Press.

Donaldson, L. (1999) 'Son of the Forest, Child of God: William Apess and the Scene of Postcolonial Nativity', in R. King (ed.) *Postcolonialism and American Literature*, Urbana: University of Illinois Press.

Donaldson, M. E. (1981) 'Kinship Theory in the Patriarchal Narratives', *Journal of the American Academy of Religion* 49: 77–87.

Douglas, M. (1993) *In the Wilderness: The Doctrine of Defilement in the Book of Numbers*, Sheffield: JSOT Press.

Eagleton, T. (1991) *Ideology: An Introduction*, London: Verso.

Emerton, J. (1988) 'The Priestly Writer in Genesis', *Journal of Theological Studies* 39: 381–400.

BIBLIOGRAPHY

Eskenazi, T. C. (1992) 'Out from the Shadows: Biblical Women in the Postexilic Era', *Journal for the Study of the Old Testament* 54: 25–43.
Eskenazi T. C. and E. P. Judd (1994) 'Marriage to a Stranger in Ezra 9–10', in T. C. Eskenazi and K. H. Richards (eds) *Second Temple Studies*, Sheffield: JSOT Press.
Fewell, D. and D. Gunn (1991) 'Tipping the Balance: Sternberg's Reader and the Rape of Dinah', *Journal of Biblical Literature* 110: 193–212.
Firestone, R. (1990) *Journeys in Holy Lands: The Evolution of the Abraham–Ishmael Legends in Islamic Exegesis*, Albany: State University of New York Press.
Firth, R. (1964) *Essays in Social Organization and Values*, London: Athlone.
Fish, S. (1980) *Is There a Text in This Class?*, Cambridge, MA: Harvard University Press.
—— (1989) *Doing What Comes Naturally*, Oxford: Clarendon.
Foucault, M. (1972) *The Archaeology of Knowledge and the Discourse on Language*, New York: Harper & Row.
Fowl, S. (1998) *Engaging Scripture*, Oxford: Blackwell.
Furrow, D. (1995) *Against Theory: Continental and Analytic Challenges in Moral Philosophy*, New York: Routledge.
Gardner, A. (1990) 'Gen. 2.4b–3: A Mythological Paradigm of Sexual Equality or of the Religious History of Pre-Exilic Israel?', *Scottish Journal of Theology* 43: 1–18.
Gates, H. L. (1988) *The Signifying Monkey: A Theory of African American Literary Criticism*, New York: Oxford University Press.
Giddens, A. (1984) *The Constitution of Society*, Oxford: Polity.
—— (1987) *Social Theory and Modern Sociology*, Oxford: Polity.
Goldberg, D. T. (1994) *Multiculturalism: A Critical Reader*, Oxford: Blackwell.
Gondarra, D. (1986) *Series of Reflections on Aboriginal Religion*, Darwin: Bethel Presbytery, Uniting Church in Australia.
Gowan, D. E. (1986) *Eschatology in the Old Testament*, Edinburgh: T. & T. Clark.
Greenblatt, S. and G. Gunn (eds) (1992) *Redrawing the Boundaries: The Transformation of English and American Literary Studies*, New York: Modern Language Association.
Greenfeld, L. (1992) *Nationalism: Five Roads to Modernity*, Cambridge, MA: Harvard University Press.
Griffiths, G. (1994) 'The Myth of Authenticity', in C. Tiffin and A. Lawson (eds) *De-Scribing Empire*, London: Routledge.
Grünwaldt, K. (1992) *Exil und Identität: Beschneidung, Passa und Shabbat in der Priesterschrift*, Frankfurt: Anton Hain.
Guha, R. (1983) 'The Prose of Counter-Insurgency', in R. Guha (ed.) *Subaltern Studies*, vol. 2, New Delhi: Oxford University Press.

BIBLIOGRAPHY

Gumperz, J. J. (1977) 'Sociocultural Knowledge in Conversational Inference', in M. Saville-Troike (ed.) *Linguistics and Anthropology*, Washington, DC: Georgetown University Press.

Gunkel, H. (1895) *Schöpfung und Chaos in Urzeit und Endzeit*, Göttingen: Vandenhoeck & Ruprecht.

—— (1910) *Genesis*, Göttingen: Vandenhoeck & Ruprecht.

Habel, N. C. (1995) *The Land Is Mine: Six Biblical Land Ideologies*, Minneapolis, MN: Fortress.

Handel, W. H. (1993) *Contemporary Sociological Theory*, Englewood Cliffs, NJ: Prentice-Hall.

Haynes, S. R. (1991) *Prospects for Post-Holocaust Theology*, Atlanta, GA: Scholars Press.

Hill, C. (1988) *A Turbulent, Seditious, and Factious People: John Bunyan and His Church*, Oxford: Oxford University Press.

Hirsch, E. D. (1967) *Validity in Interpretation*, New Haven, CT: Yale University Press.

—— (1976) *Aims of Interpretation*, Chicago, IL: Chicago University Press.

Hoglund, K. (1992) *Achaemenid Imperial Administration in Syria–Palestine and the Missions of Ezra and Nehemiah*, Atlanta, GA: Scholars Press.

Hudson, R. (1981) 'Some Issues on which Linguists Can Agree', *Journal of Linguistics* 7: 333–43.

Janzen, G. (1994) 'On the Moral Nature of God's Power: Yahweh and the Sea in Job and Deutero-Isaiah', *Catholic Biblical Quarterly* 56: 458–78.

Joosten, J. (1996) *People and Land in the Holiness Code*, Leiden: E. J. Brill.

Josipovici, G. (1988) *The Book of God: A Response to the Bible*, New Haven, CT: Yale University Press.

Kapelrud, A. S. (1974) 'The Mythological Features in Genesis Chapter 1 and the Author's Intentions', *Vetus Testamentum* 24: 17–86.

Keesing, R. M. (1987) 'Anthropology as Interpretative Quest', *Current Anthropology* 28: 161–75.

Kitzberger, I. R. (1998) *The Personal Voice in Biblical Studies*, London: Routledge.

Knohl, I. (1995) *The Sanctuary of Silence: The Priestly Torah and the Holiness School*, Minneapolis, MN: Fortress.

Kuschel, K.-J. (1995) *Abraham: A Symbol of Hope for Jews, Christians and Muslims*, London: SCM.

Leach, G. N. (1983) *Principles of Pragmatics*, London: Longman.

Leibowitz, N. (1980) *Studies in Bereshit (Genesis)*, Jerusalem: World Zionist Organization.

Lemche, N. P. (1985) *Early Israel: Anthropological and Historical Studies on the Israelite Society before the Monarchy*, Leiden: E. J. Brill.

BIBLIOGRAPHY

Levenson, J. D. (1987) *Creation and the Persistence of Evil: The Jewish Drama of Divine Omnipotence*, New York: Harper & Row.

—— (1993a) *The Hebrew Bible, the Old Testament, and Historical Criticism: Jews and Christians in Biblical Studies*, Louisville, KT: Westminster–John Knox Press.

—— (1993b) *The Death and Resurrection of the Beloved Son: The Transformation of Child Sacrifice in Judaism and Christianity*, New Haven, CT: Yale University Press.

—— (1996) 'The Universal Horizon of Biblical Particularism', in M. G. Brett (ed.) *Ethnicity and the Bible*, Leiden: E. J. Brill.

Levenson, S. C. (1983) *Pragmatics*, Cambridge: Cambridge University Press.

Lévi-Strauss, C. (1963) *Structural Anthropology*, London: Basic Books.

Löwy, M. (1996) *The War of Gods: Religion and Politics in Latin America*, London: Verso.

Lyotard, J.-F. (1984) *The Postmodern Condition*, Minneapolis, MN: University of Minnesota Press.

McPhee, P. (1980) 'A Case-Study of Internal Colonization: the *Francisation* of Northern Catalonia', *Review: A Journal of the Fernand Braudel Center* 3: 399–428.

Martin, W. (1986) *Recent Theories of Narrative*, Ithaca, NY: Cornell University Press.

Mayes, A. D. H. (1989) *The Old Testament in Sociological Perspective*, London: Marshall Pickering.

Mendenhall, G. (1974) 'The Shady Side of Wisdom: The Date and Purpose of Genesis 3', in H. Bream (ed.) *A Light Unto My Path*, Philadelphia, PA: Temple University Press.

Menn, E. M. (1997) *Judah and Tamar (Genesis 38) in Ancient Jewish Exegesis*, Leiden: E. J. Brill.

Miles, M. (1988) *The Image and Practice of Holiness*, London: SCM.

Miller, J. H. (1987) 'Presidential Address 1986: The Triumph of Theory, the Resistance to Reading, and the Question of Material Base', *Publications of the Modern Language Association* 102: 281–91.

Moberly, R. W. L. (1992) *The Old Testament of the Old Testament: Patriarchal Narratives and Mosaic Yahwism*, Minneapolis, MN: Fortress.

Mullen, E. T. (1997) *Ethnic Myths and Pentateuchal Foundations*, Atlanta, GA: Scholars Press.

Niditch, S. (1987) *Underdogs and Tricksters: A Prelude to Biblical Folklore*, San Francisco, CA: Harper & Row.

Noble, P. (1993) 'Synchronic and Diachronic Approaches to Biblical Interpretation', *Journal of Literature and Theology* 7: 130–48.

Norris, C. (1990) *What's Wrong with Postmodernism: Critical Theory and the Ends of Postmodernism*, New York: Harvester Wheatsheaf.

BIBLIOGRAPHY

Obed, B. (1986) 'The Table of Nations (Genesis 10): A Socio-Cultural Approach', *Zeitschrift für die alttestamentliche Wissenschaft* 98: 14–31.

Oden, R. A. (1987) *The Bible Without Theology*, San Francisco, CA: Harper & Row.

Pardes, I. (1993) 'Beyond Genesis 3: The Politics of Maternal Naming', in A. Brenner (ed.) *A Feminist Companion to Genesis*, Sheffield: Sheffield Academic Press.

Patterson, A. (1990) 'Intention', in F. Lentricchia and F. McLaughlin (eds) *Critical Terms for Literary Study*, Chicago, IL: University of Chicago Press.

Pike, K. (1964) 'Towards a Theory of the Structure of Human Behaviour', in D. Hymes (ed.) *Language in Culture and Society*, New York: Harper & Row.

Popper, K. (1972) *Objective Knowledge*, Oxford: Oxford University Press.

Prewitt, T. J. (1990) *The Elusive Covenant: A Structural–Semiotic Reading of Genesis*, Bloomington, IN: Indiana University Press.

Rad, G. von (1963) *Genesis*, London: SCM, 2nd edn; trans. of *Das erste Buch Mose, Genesis*, Göttingen: Vandenhoeck & Ruprecht, 1956.

Rendtorff, R. (1996) 'The *Ger* in the Priestly Laws of the Pentateuch', in M. G. Brett (ed.) *Ethnicity and the Bible*, Leiden: E. J. Brill.

Rogerson, J. W. (1978) *Anthropology and the Old Testament*, Oxford: Blackwell.

—— (1985) 'The Use of Sociology in Old Testament Studies', *Supplements to Vetus Testamentum* 36: 245–56

—— (1986) 'Was Early Israel a Segmentary Society?', *Journal for the Study of the Old Testament* 36: 17–26

Rorty, R. (1992) 'The Pragmatist's Progress', in S. Collini (ed.) *Interpretation and Overinterpretation*, Cambridge: Cambridge University Press.

Rose, P. L. (1990) *Revolutionary Antisemitism in Germany from Kant to Wagner*, Princeton, NJ: Princeton University Press.

Runciman, W. G. (1983) *A Treatise on Social Theory*, vol. 1: *The Methodology of Social Theory*, Cambridge: Cambridge University Press.

Said, E. (1993) *Cultural Imperialism*, New York: Alfred Knopf.

Sarna, N. (1966) *Understanding Genesis*, New York: Schocken.

Saunders, C. (ed.) (1995) *Living the Intersections: Womanism and Afrocentrism in Theology*, Minneapolis, MN: Fortress.

Saussure, F. de (1916) *Cours de linguistique générale*, Paris: Payot.

Scott, J. (1990) *Domination and the Arts of Resistance: Hidden Transcripts*, New Haven, CT: Yale University Press.

Silbermann, A. M. (ed.) (1929) *Pentateuch with Rashi's Commentary: Bereshit*, London: Shapiro, Vallentine & Co.

Smith, D. L. (1989) *The Religion of the Landless*, Bloomington, IN: Meyer–Stone.

BIBLIOGRAPHY

Smith, M. S. (1990) *The Early History of God*, London: Harper & Row.
Sperber, D. and D. Wilson (1986) *Relevance: Communication and Cognition*, Oxford: Blackwell.
Spina, F. (1992) 'The "Ground" for Cain's Rejection', *Zeitschrift für die alttestamentliche Wissenschaft* 104: 319–32.
Stager, L. (1985) 'The Archaeology of the Family in Ancient Israel', *Bulletin of the American School of Oriental Research* 260: 1–35.
Steinberg, N. (1993) *Kinship and Marriage in Genesis: A Household Economics Perspective*, Minneapolis, MN: Fortress.
Sternberg, M. (1985) *The Poetics of Biblical Narrative*, Bloomington: Indiana University Press.
—— (1992) 'Biblical Poetics and Sexual Politics', *Journal of Biblical Literature* 111: 463–88.
Stone, K. (1995) 'Gender and Homosexuality in Judges 19: Subject-Honour, Object-Shame?', *Journal for the Study of the Old Testament* 67: 87–107.
Stout, J. (1981) *The Flight from Authority: Religion, Morality and the Quest for Autonomy*, Notre Dame: University of Notre Dame Press.
Swain, T. and D. B. Rose (eds) (1988) *Aboriginal Australians and Christian Missions*, Adelaide: Australian Association for the Study of Religions.
Taylor, C. (1985) 'Understanding and Ethnocentrism', in Taylor, *Philosophy and the Human Sciences*, Cambridge: Cambridge University Press.
—— (1992) 'The Politics of Recognition', in A. Gutman (ed.) *Multiculturalism and 'The Politics of Recognition'*, Princeton, NJ: Princeton University Press.
Terrien, S. (1985) *Till the Heart Sings: A Biblical Theology of Manhood and Womanhood*, Philadelphia: Fortress.
Thiselton, A. C. (1992) *New Horizons in Hermeneutics*, London: HarperCollins.
Trompf, G. (ed.) (1987) *The Gospel Is Not Western: Black Theologies from the Southwest Pacific*, Maryknoll, NJ: Orbis.
Turner, B. S. (1994) *Orientalism, Postmodernism and Globalism*, London: Routledge.
Van Seters, J. (1992) *Prologue to History: The Yahwist as Historian in Genesis*, Louisville, KT: Westminster–John Knox.
Veeser, H. A. (ed.) (1996) *Confessions of the Critics*, London: Routledge.
Volf, M. (1996) *Exclusion and Embrace: A Theological Exploration of Identity, Otherness, and Reconciliation*, Nashville, TN: Abingdon.
Wallace, H. N. (1985) *The Eden Narrative*, Atlanta, GA: Scholars Press.
Watson, F. (1994) *Text, Church and World: Biblical Interpretation in Theological Perspective*, Edinburgh: T. & T. Clark.
Weaver, J. (1996) 'From I-Hermeneutics to We-Hermeneutics: Native Americans and the Post-Colonial', *Semeia* 75: 153–76.

Weischedel, W. (ed.) (1964) *Werke Bd. 6: Der Streit der Fakultäten*, Frankfurt: Insel.

Weisman, Z. (1985) 'National Consciousness in the Patriarchal Promises', *Journal for the Study of the Old Testament* 31: 55–73.

Werbner, P. and T. Modood (eds) (1997) *Debating Cultural Hybridity*, London: Zed Books.

Werman, C. (1997) 'Jubilees 30: Building a Paradigm for the Ban on Intermarriage', *Harvard Theological Review* 90: 1–22.

Westermann, C. (1984) *Genesis 1–11*, Minneapolis, MN: Augsburg.

—— (1985) *Genesis 12–36*, Minneapolis, MN: Augsburg.

—— (1986) *Genesis 37–50*, Minneapolis, MN: Augsburg.

White, H. C. (1991) *Narration and Discourse in the Book of Genesis*, Cambridge: Cambridge University Press.

Whitelam, K. (1996) *The Invention of Ancient Israel: The Silencing of Palestinian History*, London: Routledge.

Whybray, N. (1987) *The Making of the Pentateuch*, Sheffield: JSOT Press.

Wildavsky, A. (1994) 'Survival Must Not Be Gained Through Sin: The Moral of the Joseph Stories Prefigured Through Judah and Tamar', *Journal for the Study of the Old Testament* 62: 37–48.

Wimsatt, W. K. and M. C. Beardsley (1972 [1946]) 'The Intentional Fallacy', in D. Lodge (ed.) *20th Century Literary Criticism*, London: Longman.

Young, R. (1995) *Colonial Desire: Hybridity in Theory, Culture and Race*, London: Routledge.

Žižek, S. (1994) 'The Spectre of Ideology', in Žižek (ed.) *Mapping Ideology*, London: Verso.

GENERAL INDEX

aboriginality 3, 141, 144–5
agency 17–18, 20, 23, 89, 101, 115, 118
Albertz, R. 4, 147, 154
Alter, R. 8–9, 113, 132–3, 148, 151
Anderson, B. 47
Atrahasis Epic 40–1
authorial intention 11–14, 22–3, 28, see also intentional hybridity
autobiographical criticism 2

Bakhtin, M. 32, 148
Barclay, J. 143, 145
Barthes, R. 17
Bechtel, L. 101–2, 151
Bhabha, H. 8, 23, 57–8, 145, 148
Bird, P. 28
Bloom, H. 148
Blum, E. 147
Boyarin, D. 141–4, 146, 154
Brett, M. G. 8, 12, 13, 145, 147, 148, 152

Calhoun, C. 154
Carr, D. 11
Cassuto, U. 148–9
'clan' 50, 81, 150
Coats, G. 136
Crüsemann, F. 146
cultural hybridity 1, 45, 145 see also intentional hybridity
'curse of Ham' 45, 83–4

deconstruction 23
Derrida, J. 72

Donaldson, L. 154
Donaldson, M. 15
Douglas, M. 6–7, 147

Eagleton, T. 23
Emerton, J. 10
emic 19
endogamy 16–18, 50–1, 76–7, 80–1, 84–5, 91–3, 95, 97, 107–8
Enlightenment 1, 4
Enuma Elish 25
Eskenazi, T. 140, 147
ethnocentrism 10, 69, 88–9, 102–3, 131, 142
etic 19
exogamy 50–1, 76–7, 88

Fewell, D. 9
Firestone, R. 139
Firth, R. 17
Fish, S. 2, 13
foreigners 7, 52, 54, 61, 63, 67, 79, 92–3, 131, 136
Foucault, M. 18
Furrow, D. 138

Gadamer, H.-G. 147
Gardner, A. 33
Gates, H. L. 148
gerim 6, 67
Giddens, A. 18
Gilgamesh Epic 41
Gondarra, D. 145
Gowan, D. 29
Greenblatt, S. 5

GENERAL INDEX

Greenfeld, L. 141
Grünwaldt, K. 63, 147
Guha, R. 57
Gumperz, J. 12
Gunkel, H. 10, 148
Gunn, D. 9
Gunn, G. 5

Habel, N. 57, 150
Hill, C. 144
Hirsch, E. D. 14, 148
historicism 10–11, 21, 46, 63, 71, 76, 92
Hoglund, K. 5–6, 61, 107
'holy seed' 5, 31, 35, 45, 47, 51, 64, 68, 76, 80, 136, 137, 140
'horizon of expectation' 2

ideology 21
'image of God' 27–9, 32–4, 41–2
indirect communication 12–13, 89
intentional hybridity 22, 46, 87–8, 91, 104, 137
interpretative communities 2

Janzen, J. G. 25
Jauss, H.-R. 147
Joosten, J. 131, 147
Josipovici, G. 109
Judd, E. 140, 147

Kant, I. 140, 148
Kapelrud, A. 26
Keesing, R. M. 19
Kermode, F. 9
Kitzberger, I. 2
Knohl, I. 147
Kuschel, A. 139

land tenure 6
Leech, G. 12
Leibowitz, N. 151
Lemche, N. 150
Levenson, J. D. 25, 72, 138–9, 154
Levinson, S. 12
Lévi-Strauss, C. 15–16, 18
Löwy, M. 1, 154
Lyotard, J.-F. 144

McPhee, P. 141
Mayes, A. 17
Mendenhall, G. 33
Menn, E. 151
Miller, J. H. 4
Moberly, R. W. L. 27, 57
Mullen, E. 18, 26

New Criticism 13–14
New Historicism 2
Niditch, S. 92
Noble, P. 114
Norris, C. 23

Obed, B. 46
Oden, R. 15

Pardes, I. 30, 150
patriarchy 10, 34, 101,
Patterson, A. 13
Pike, K. 19
pluralism 9, 12, 14, 19, 144
'point of view' 8, 59, 80, 88
Popper, K. 137, 147
postcolonial studies 2, 57–8, 137, 141–2, 145, 149
postmodernism 23, 138
poststructuralism 13, 15, 20, 22
Prewitt, T. 15
Priestly tradition (P) 6–7, 10
primogeniture 10, 37–8, 45, 83, 84–5, 89–92, 132, 137, 148
Protestantism 3–4

Rad, G. von 68, 109–10, 130
reconciliation 3, 100, 114, 144, 145
Rendtorff, R. 6–7
resistance 23
Rogerson, J. 15, 18, 148
Rorty, R. 2
Rose, D. 141
Rose, P. 141
Runciman, W. G. 18–19

Said, E. 145
Sarna, N. 42, 89
Saunders, C. 142
Saussure, F. de 15, 20
Scott, J. 8, 17

GENERAL INDEX

Silbermann, A. 73, 121
Smith, D. 142
Smith, M. 55
Sperber, D. 12
Spina, F. 38
Stager, L. 148
Steinberg, N. 16–18
Sternberg, M. 8–9, 14–15, 102
Stone, K. 67
Stout, J. 1
structuralism 13, 15
Swain, T. 141
synchronic 20–1

Taylor, C. 19, 144
Terrien, S. 31
Thiselton, A. 3, 18
Trompf, G. 142
Turner, B. 1

Van Seters, J. 150
Veeser, H. A. 2
Volf, M. 143–5

Wallace, H. 33
Watson, F. 119
Weaver, J. 154
Weisman, Z. 152
Werman, C. 142, 151
Westermann, C. 23, 54, 100, 112, 123, 128, 134, 149
White, H. 120, 125
Whitelam, K. 149
Whybray, R. N. 22
Wilson, D. 12

Young, R. 148

Žižek, S. 21

SCRIPTURE INDEX

Genesis
1.1–2.3   24
1.1–2   24
1.3–5   26
1.7   26
1.9   32
1.10   26
1.11   26–7
1.12   26
1.14   26
1.18   26
1.21   26
1.22   27, 44
1.24   26–7
1.25   26
1.26–8   27–8, 30, 33–4, 149
1.27   39, 149
1.28   33
1.29–30   29

2.2–3   27, 35
2.4–3.24   24
2.4   30–1, 35, 83
2.5–6   32
2.7   30–1
2.8   32
2.9   32, 34
2.10–14   33, 40
2.13   35
2.15   30
2.17   34, 36, 43
2.18–21   31
2.19   30
2.22–3   30–3
2.23   149

2.24   31, 34

3.5   33
3.14   29
3.15   34, 35
3.16   34–7, 39
3.17–19   35, 38
3.17   38–9
3.19   30
3.21   43
3.22   24–5, 32–3, 36
3.23   35–6

4   91
4.1   27, 30, 150
4.2   38
4.3   35–6
4.6–7   36–7
4.7   38, 42, 149
4.9   38, 113
4.10–12   38, 43
4.11   45
4.16   38
4.17–18   39
4.17   38
4.20   38
4.23–4   39, 43
4.25   37
4.25–6   39, 149

5.1–32   39, 47
5.2   39
5.3–26   37, 83
5.3–8   39
5.18–19   37
5.24   40

SCRIPTURE INDEX

5.29 38
5.32 47

6.1–9.27 40
6.1–4 41, 49
6.4 47, 49
6.5 39
6.6 39
6.9 38, 40, 52, 62, 83, 93
6.11 39
6.19–20 149

7.2–3 149

8.21–2 42–3
8.21 93

9.1 44
9.2 43–4
9.3–5 43–4
9.6 43–4, 152
9.7 43
9.8–17 27, 44, 61
9.9 44
9.10–17 44
9.11 42
9.15–16 42
9.20–7 45, 83
9.20–4 45
9.20 38
9.25–7 45
9.28–9 40

10.1 83
10.2–4 45
10.5 46
10.6–20 46
10.10 46
10.20 46
10.21–31 45
10.31 45

11.1 46
11.2 46
11.4 46–7, 49
11.6–8 47, 53
11.7 24, 25
11.10–26 37, 40, 44, 83
11.10 83
11.26 47

11.29–31 50
11.31 47

12.1–3 49–51, 105
12.1 18, 47, 50, 81, 91, 94
12.2–3 55, 63, 70, 72, 115, 139
12.3 50, 118
12.4–5 50
12.4 47
12.6–7 51, 53, 100
12.6 65, 150
12.8–9 51, 58
12.10–20 52, 58, 87
12.12–14 52
12.12–13 43, 53
12.16 52, 58

13.2 52
13.3–4 51, 53, 58
13.5–7 53
13.7 65, 150
13.10 53–4
13.13 55, 56, 66
13.14–17 53–4, 56
13.16 63
13.18 51, 53

14 54
14.2–4 54
14.7 54
14.13 53–4, 82
14.14 54, 79
14.18–22 32, 55–6, 61
14.18–20 79
14.21–4 55
14.22 100, 149
14.24 54, 56, 79, 82

15.1 56
15.2–3 56, 62
15.4 56, 58
15.5 63, 114
15.6 43, 56, 62
15.8 56, 62
15.9–21 56–7
15.12–16 152
15.13 58
15.14 52
15.16 57
15.18 57, 61

SCRIPTURE INDEX

15.19–21   57, 79

16.1–6   59
16.1–2   58
16.5   58
16.6   58–9, 66
16.8–9   59
16.10   58
16.11–14   82
16.11   58, 60, 75
16.12   70, 82
16.13   31, 58, 61–2, 75
16.14   59, 75
16.15   59

17.1   61–2, 70
17.5   63–4, 105
17.7–8   114, 132
17.9–14   63–4
17.12   7, 64, 150
17.15–22   63
17.15–16   63
17.17–18   56, 60, 62, 73
17.18–22   72, 75
17.19–21   7, 63–4, 71
17.20   64, 83
17.23–7   7, 63–4, 71, 76, 139
17.24–6   147

18   55
18.1–8   66
18.1   65
18.2   65
18.3   65
18.12–15   60
18.13   65
18.16   65
18.17   65
18.19   62, 150
18.20   65
18.21   66
18.22   65
18.23–5   150
18.25   65
18.26   65
18.27   65
18.30–3   65

19.1–3   66
19.1   65

19.2   65
19.3   66
19.4   65
19.6   67
19.8   66
19.9   67, 150
19.10–12   65
19.16   65–6
19.18   65
19.29   66
19.30–8   150
19.30–5   68
19.31–2   68
19.37–8   65, 150

20   52, 67
20.1–18   71
20.3–11   152
20.4   52
20.5–6   52, 70
20.11–12   52, 63, 69, 80, 151

21.1–21   71
21.3   60
21.6–7   60
21.8–9   60, 86
21.9–10   60–1, 83, 86
21.10–11   73, 83
21.11   60, 74
21.12–13   69
21.12   77
21.13   73, 76, 139
21.14–18   86
21.14   71, 76, 126
21.16–17   74
21.18   70, 126, 139, 152
21.20–1   64
21.22–34   70–71
21.22   86
21.27   71, 86
21.30–1   71, 86
21.32   71

22   84
22.1   72, 75
22.2   73–4, 139
22.6   74
22.10   74
22.14   75
22.16–18   75, 78, 87, 153

168

SCRIPTURE INDEX

22.17 78
22.19–24 76, 81
22.19 125, 139

23.4 79
23.6 79
23.7 78
23.11 79
23.19–20 79

24 150
24.4 50, 81, 150
24.6–8 80
24.7 81
24.12–14 80
24.26–7 80
24.29 81
24.30 81
24.34–48 80
24.35–41 81
24.35 81
24.38 150
24.40–1 150
24.50–1 80–1

25.1–4 82–3
25.5 82–3
25.6 82–3
25.9 82
25.11 82
25.12–18 82
25.12 83
25.13–16 83
25.19 83
25.23 83, 91
25.28 89
25.31 83

26.1–12 52
26.2–6 86–7, 91, 93, 98
26.5 87–8
26.7 86
26.23–4 125
26.26 86
26.28 86
26.33 86
26.34–5 10, 88
26.35 89

27.1–45 10

27.11–17 89
27.29 91, 98
27.34–7 89
27.38 89
27.42–5 10, 89
27.46–28.5 10
27.46 9–11, 88–9

28.1–2 89
28.3 105, 131
28.6–9 88
28.10–22 95
28.11–12 93
28.13–15 91, 93, 97–8, 100
28.16–19 93
28.16 97
28.18–29 105
28.19 97
28.20–2 97
28.21 97

29 89
29.16 89
29.17 115
29.26 81, 89, 93
29.31 90
29.32–30.21 90, 103–4, 126
29.32–5 152

30 93
30.2 90
30.18–21 152
30.22 90
30.25 93–4
30.26 93
30.32 95
30.34–6 94
30.34 94
30.37–43 94

31.3 94, 95, 100
31.5–13 95
31.7 95
31.13 95
31.14–16 95
31.19 96
31.24 96
31.29 96
31.30 96
31.35 96

SCRIPTURE INDEX

31.42 96
31.43 96
31.52 96
31.53 25, 96
31.54 96

32 97
32.2 97, 98
32.4–5 98
32.7 98
32.8 98
32.9 97
32.10 98
32.13–21 98–9
32.18–20 98
32.20 98–9
32.24–7 98
32.28 99
32.30 97, 99, 100

33 99, 121
33.5 100
33.8 100
33.9 100
33.10 99–100
33.11 98
33.13–15 100
33.14 100
33.27 124

34 66, 100, 110, 134
34.1 100–2
34.2–3 101
34.2 101
34.8–10 102
34.12 101
34.13–14 101
34.28–9 106
34.30 102

35.1–7 103, 105
35.2 105
35.4 106
35.7 105
35.8 103
35.9–15 103, 105
35.9–10 98–9
35.11–12 132
35.11 105–6
35.14–15 105

35.16–20 103, 110
35.21–2 83, 103, 104, 111, 127, 133
35.23–6 103–4, 126
35.27–9 103

36.1–43 103, 106
36.31 106

37 113
37.2–4 109
37.3 125
37.9–10 131, 133
37.9 120, 124
37.10 109
37.12 110
37.14 111
37.19 111
37.20 111
37.22 111
37.23–4 120
37.25–7 112
37.27 112–13, 119, 124
37.28 112
37.29–30 111
37.36 112

38 69, 113
38.2 127
38.7 113
38.9–10 113–14
38.11 114
38.16 115
38.24 115
38.26 69, 113
38.27–30 114, 127, 151
38.29 115

39.2 115, 118
39.3–6 116
39.3 118
39.5 115
39.6 115–16
39.7 115
39.12 116
39.14 116
39.17–19 116
39.21–3 116, 118

40.1–8 116

SCRIPTURE INDEX

40.8–18 116
40.8 117, 136
40.16–19 117
40.16 117
40.23 116

41.2 132
41.8–15 117
41.8 7
41.14–16 117, 136
41.16 117
41.18 152
41.25–31 117
41.32 152
41.33–6 117
41.34–5 119
41.38–9 152
41.39–40 131
41.39 7, 117
41.44 119
41.47–9 118
41.50–2 114, 126
41.51 125
41.53–5 118
41.56–7 119, 129
41.57 118

42.4 119
42.6–7 119, 123
42.6 110
42.9 119–20
42.12 119
42.15–16 120
42.17 120
42.18–20 120
42.21–4 123
42.24 119
42.25 123
42.36 120
42.38 121

43.6 120
43.9 122
43.11 121–2
43.14 122
43.15–18 123
43.23 123
43.26 123
43.27 123–4
43.29–30 123

43.32 128
43.33–4 123
43.33 83

44 115, 123
44.1–2 123
44.10 124
44.12–14 123–4
44.15 124
44.17 124
44.19–34 124

45.1–2 124
45.3 124–5
45.5–7 136
45.9 125
45.10 128, 152
45.13 125
45.14–15 125
45.18 128
45.22 125
45.23–4 125
45.27–8 126

46 125
46.1–4 126
46.3 126, 152
46.7 126
46.8–25 126
46.10 102, 126–7
46.12 126, 153
46.15 126
46.17 126
46.19 126
46.28–9 128, 152
46.31–47.10 128
46.34 128, 152

47.1 152
47.4 152
47.6 128, 152
47.11 129–30, 152
47.14 129
47.16–20 129
47.21 129–30
47.23–4 129
47.25 130

48.4 132
48.5 132

171

SCRIPTURE INDEX

48.7   133
48.9   133
48.12   110, 133
48.17–19   133
48.22   134

49.3–4   83, 91, 104, 111, 127, 133
49.3   37
49.5–7   102, 104, 127, 133
49.6   107
49.8–12   133
49.8   133–4
49.10   104
49.29–30   134
49.31   104
49.32   135

50.5   135
50.11   135
50.13   135
50.15–18   125, 135
50.17–18   153
50.18   110
50.19   135–6, 153
50.20   7, 111, 136
50.21   136

Exodus

1.8–10   152
1.8   129
1.11   129, 152
1.15–20   152
3.7   58
6.2–3   62, 149
9.30   32
12.36   52
12.38   52
12.43–9   150
12.48–9   101
19.4   148
21.16   113
24.7   113
33.17–23   59
33.20   99

Leviticus

4   122
15.19–20   96
18.9   52, 69
18.11   52, 69
18.18   91
20.17   52, 69
21.14   131, 147
25   130
25.25–8   130
25.39–46   64
25.42   153

Numbers

15.22–31   6, 122, 152
19.10   6
35   152

Deuteronomy

2.9–22   150
5.14   149
7.1   78–9
9.4   57
11.23–5   44
12.12–15   64
14.12   148
15.12–15   64
16.21   51
20.17   78–9
21.15–17   82–3
22.25   151
22.28–9   101
23.3   6
23.7–8   107, 131
23.8   153
24.7   113
25.5–10   113
27.22   53, 69, 80
28   62, 77
28.1–14   78
32.6   149
32.10–11   148
33.10   102

SCRIPTURE INDEX

Joshua
5.1–9 150
8.7 44
10.19 44
13–21 130
24.8 44
24.32 134

Judges
3.28 44
6.22–3 99
7.15 44
8.3 44
13.22 99
18.10 44
19 150
19.16 150
19.22–4 67
19.23 67
19.25–7 67

Ruth 6
4 130
4.18–22 151, 153

1 Samuel
16 151

2 Samuel
5.6 151
14.17 34
14.20 34
14.25 152
16.21–2 153

1 Kings
1.33 35
1.38 35
3.9 34
4.21 57
21 130
22.19–22 148

1 Chronicles
2.3–15 153
5.1–2 83, 91

2 Chronicles
32.30 35

Ezra
2.64 107
7.25–6 6, 7, 35, 131
9.1–2 5, 7, 10, 61, 64–5, 76–7, 80, 107, 131, 137
10.3 35
10.8 6, 35, 105
10.12 107
10.14 107

Nehemiah
2.8 5
7.2 5
7.66 107
8.2 107
8.17 107

Job
1.6–12 148
1.9 77
6.7 28
41.33 149
41.34 28

Psalms
33.20 31
72 28
74.13–14 25
76.2 55
82 148
89.7–11 25
115.9–10 31
139.13 149

Proverbs

12.16 33
12.23 33
13.16 33
14.8 33
14.15–16 33
16.23 33
21.11 33
21.20 33
22.3 33
27.12 33

Ecclesiastes

1.14 37

Song of Songs

1.16 152

Isaiah

1.10 68
3.9 68
5.8 130
6.8 148
51.9 25
56.6–7 27
65.25 29

Jeremiah

9.25–6 64–5, 69
23.14 68
23.22 148
32 130

Ezekiel

16.49 68
28.2 34
28.12 34
28.13 34
28.16–18 34

Hosea

2.18 29
4.3 29
4.13 51

Amos

5.19 29

Micah

2.1–5 130
4.4 130